*By the same author*


HUMAN DEBRIS:
The Injured Worker in America
*(by Lawrence White)*

# MERCHANTS OF DEATH

## THE AMERICAN TOBACCO INDUSTRY

*Larry C. White*

BTB
BEECH TREE BOOKS
WILLIAM MORROW
*New York*

Library of Congress Cataloging-in-Publication Data

White, Larry C.
    Merchants of death : the American tobacco industry / Larry C. White.
        p.  cm.
    Includes index.
    ISBN 0-688-06706-9
    1. Tobacco industry—United States.   2. Advertising—Cigarettes—United States.   3. Tobacco—Physiological effect.   I. Title.
    HD9135.W47 1988
    338.1'7371'0973—dc19                                              87-33762
                                                                       CIP

Printed in the United States of America

First Edition

1 2 3 4 5 6 7 8 9 10

BOOK DESIGN BY RICHARD ORIOLO

BﬧB

The word "book" is said to derive from *boka,* or beech.
The beech tree has been the patron tree of writers since ancient times and represents the flowering of literature and knowledge.

*For Mark D. Greenberg*

# ACKNOWLEDGMENTS

I was given much help and encouragement in writing this book by Dr. Elizabeth Whelan, whose unfailing generosity made my job much easier. The Fund for Investigative Journalism gave me a grant that enabled me to learn firsthand the situation and the views of tobacco growers, and also to watch the drama of the Marsee trial against U.S. Tobacco. I would like to thank the many others who have given me their thoughts about my work in progress. My thanks also to my agent, Diane Cleaver, who helped keep me on the right track, and to my wife, Jane, without whose support this book could not have been written.

# CONTENTS

| | | |
|---|---|---|
| | Foreword | 9 |
| 1 | The Big Lie | 13 |
| 2 | The Fifties: An Implacable Unity | 25 |
| 3 | Dissent in Tobaccoland | 45 |
| 4 | Lawsuits—a Potent Curse | 72 |
| 5 | Tobacco on Trial | 88 |
| 6 | Advertising Addiction | 116 |
| 7 | Banning Cigarette Advertising —the Magic Bullet? | 143 |
| 8 | Hiding Behind the First Amendment | 169 |
| 9 | Diversification—the Cancer Spreads | 186 |
| 10 | The Corrupting Touch | 214 |
| | Index | 233 |

# FOREWORD

During my time as surgeon general, I've been given many complex assignments—the "Baby Doe" issue, organ transplants, care for the aged, and now . . . AIDS. But one issue was waiting for me when I arrived in this position, and it's been part of my daily agenda for the past seven years. That issue is smoking. During all this time, I've been in the forefront of the campaign to educate all Americans about the dangers of using tobacco.

At first, I had the assignment because it belonged to my office. But now, after being immersed in the data for a number of years, and after closely observing just how the tobacco industry works, I feel a personal responsibility to continue working on this issue.

In addition to my own annual reports on smoking and health, I announced the goal of making the United States a smoke-free society by the year 2000. The foundation for the smoke-free campaign is the accumulation of more than thirty years' worth of research on the hazards of smoking. Biomedical researchers, physicians, and public health personnel in more than eighty countries have generated more than fifty thousand studies on smoking and health. About two thousand more are added each year. The overwhelming majority of these studies conclude that cigarette smoking is either a contributing or primary cause of illness and death.

Those are facts that have been documented since 1964 by five surgeons general—Luther Terry, William Stewart, Jesse Steinfeld, Julius Richmond, and myself—and published in eighteen official reports. I regard the scientific case against cigarettes as being airtight. And I am joined in that opinion by the vast majority of the men and women in medicine and public health today.

As you may have gathered, the case thus far has dealt mainly with the health risks of *people who smoke,* the so-called *mainstream* smokers who inhale smoke directly from the cigarette. However, behind the cloud of mainstream smoke is no silver lining but another cloud . . . and it's known as *sidestream* smoke, the cigarette smoke that *non*smokers inhale involuntarily from the ambient air. Research in sidestream smoke has evolved slowly but steadily over the past ten years, so that by now we have a pretty good idea of its effects. And we published these data and our conclusions in the eighteenth Surgeon General's Report, which we released on December 16, 1986.

The children of parents who smoke have a much higher upper-respiratory infection rate, compared to children whose parents do not smoke. And the nonsmoking wife of a smoker runs a higher risk of lung cancer than does the nonsmoking wife of a *non*smoker.

Also, sidestream "smokers" exposed to other people's heavy smoking in the same office space or workroom absorb as much smoke as if they themselves were mainstream-smoking two or three cigarettes per day.

Our problems do not stop with mainstream and sidestream smoke, however. Smokeless tobacco presents additional, significant health risks. Use of smokeless tobacco has been heavily promoted and, as a result, we're seeing it become fairly popular among susceptible male adolescents, who use it daily. And daily usage can lead to nicotine addiction and dependence.

That's the bad news. Is there any good news? Yes, there is. We can take some comfort in the fact that cigarette consumption is going down. Per capita consumption is at its lowest point in about forty years. The trend lines are heading down . . . but the fact remains that approximately fifty-three million Americans still smoke. And the burden they place upon society is enormous. So while we can take comfort from some of the trend lines, we are far from the day when we can feel smug about how well we've done. There's still a very big job left to do.

I assure you that the U.S. Public Health Service and its surgeon general—I and whoever comes after me—will do whatever we can to make the dream of a smoke-free society come true. I intend to leave for my successor not just the impressive collection of smoking and health reports that I found, but the eight additional reports that will be my contribution to this country's lifesaving campaign against cigarettes. I will also leave a note inviting that person to continue the tradition.

We need an informed public that understands the political, social, and economic dimensions of this twentieth-century plague. Comprehensive reviews and analysis of the total problem are necessary for us to create this smoke-free society by the year 2000. This book is a major contribution toward that goal. *Merchants of Death*, because it tells the truth, is likely to be dangerous to the health of the tobacco industry.

—C. Everett Koop, M.D., Sc.D.
Surgeon General

# 1

# THE BIG LIE

Smoking cigarettes was an important part of my growing up. It was a rite of passage into the mysterious realm of men and women. At the same time, smoking was completely familiar. My father smoked cigars mainly, although he would not look askance at a cigarette from time to time. My mother smoked Chesterfields when I was very young, but switched later to Pall Mall, the tall red pack with the motto *In Hoc Signo Vinces*—"Under This Sign Be Victorious."

The great broadcaster Edward R. Murrow was one of my heroes. Even in the middle fifties, when I was not yet a teenager, I was aware that his voice was inextricably linked with World War II. The war, as it was still called without need for further qualification, had an irresistible glamour for me. The documentaries I loved to watch (especially *Victory at Sea*, with music by Richard Rodgers) showed flyers wearing fleece-lined caps bombing the daylights out of the Nazis, and vast armadas of ships steaming toward the invasion of North Africa.

Murrow had two television shows, the serious *See It Now* and a lighter one called *Person to Person* where he interviewed famous people by remote. He would sit in the studio smoking cigarette after cigarette and chatting casually in his calm deep voice. Sometimes the smoke would rise up and curl around him protectively. It all seemed so sophisticated. One of the best shows was broadcast in 1954, when he interviewed Humphrey Bogart and Lauren Bacall. Both Murrow and Bogey had cigarettes between their fingers. I was still too young to smoke, but I didn't doubt that I would. Edward R. Murrow produced a *See It Now* episode that same year on the studies showing the connection between smoking and lung cancer, but I missed it.

I started smoking a few years later when I was about sixteen. My friend Mark was the first of our group to smoke and he was my role model. He insisted that we all smoke unfiltered cigarettes and drink our coffee black. I think he imagined that the agents who parachuted into occupied France at night or the brave Russians at Stalingrad had disdained filters and anyone who smoked them.

When I started college in 1960, it seemed that everyone smoked. We'd joke about how you couldn't see across a room when three or four of us had been together for a few hours. The smoke was thick and blue. In my first apartment away from home I had a huge ashtray that someone had given me; it could hold the ashes and butts of maybe fifty cigarettes. It was so convenient, you didn't have to empty it more than once or twice a day.

The following year I spent in Europe and Israel and got acquainted with foreign cigarettes. The French said their "black tobacco" was much more healthful than American tobacco. This was definitely sour grapes, and in any case I had never heard that there was anything unhealthful about our own cigarettes. I did get addicted to a British brand called Senior Service, which had an almost sweet taste; Virginia tobacco was what the English called it. These cigarettes came in a flat hard pack that pictured a ship, probably outbound to India, in sunny seas.

In Israel, which was still dominated by pioneers at that time, I stayed on a kibbutz where cigarettes were given out free. They contained dried vegetable matter that had a vague resemblance to tobacco and fell out if you held them upright. But they cost me nothing, which was an important consideration. When I returned to the States, it seemed a great luxury to be able to smoke American cigarettes as much as I wanted. Mark had gone to California and I didn't have to smoke Camels. I switched to filters—Winstons, I think.

In 1963 I started dating a woman who didn't smoke. This struck me as rather eccentric, like the Chinese silk housecoat she often wore in her basement apartment. Peggy was bothered by too much cigarette smoke; she'd quietly leave a gathering just to get away from it. It seemed peculiar behavior.

Three years later I met a woman in San Francisco who afterward became my wife. Jane hated the smell of smoke. She would tell me that my clothes, and her clothes, smelled of cigarette smoke, that my hair smelled, that even the curtains of my room smelled. I thought that she was hypersensitive and making some of it up as well. She was determined to get me to stop, and was not above using guerrilla tactics. Smoking became a real battle when she began blowing out my match as I tried to light up.

By now there was no romance at all in cigarettes. Murrow and Bogart were both dead of lung cancer. I didn't think that I would be one of the victims of smoking, but I wasn't sure that I even enjoyed it anymore. The first cigarette of the day really bothered me. I never allowed myself to smoke before breakfast and had always sort of looked down on people who reached for a cigarette before they opened their eyes in the morning. I was never as hooked as those people whose craving wakes them up in the middle of the night just for a smoke.

Despite a regular cough and congestion in my chest in the morning, I usually felt pretty good—until right after breakfast, when I lit up. The smoke tasted filthy and I would start to feel rotten—like I was poisoning myself.

But when I thought of quitting, it seemed just about impossible. Cigarettes were a necessary accompaniment to everything I did. In fact, everything else had become an accompaniment to smoking. When the phone rang I had to light a cigarette; when I met someone I had to smoke. Eating had become something I did so I could get to the cigarette at the end. The tobacco companies call smoking a "pleasure," but smokers know that only a few cigarettes a day feel good. Mostly you smoke because that's how you satisfy the craving to smoke. It's a little like an itch, a poison ivy itch that drives you crazy if you don't scratch it.

Also, I was still in college and was afraid that I wouldn't be able to study. At the time I thought that smoking aided concentration. Now I think that quitters have a hard time concentrating because they are continually distracted by the unsatisfied craving for cigarettes. I tried several times to quit by tapering down, but within a few days I would be smoking my usual pack a day. I thought often about smoking and wondered what possible good it did me. One day I realized that there was only one beneficiary of my smoking—the tobacco companies that profited from my addiction.

Finally my friend Penny told me how she had quit, and her method worked. First of all, it was "cold turkey." I was not to smoke another cigarette, not one, for the rest of my life. Also, I had to avoid things that stimulated the craving. Coffee dropped out of my diet for a few weeks. Alcohol was particularly hard to deal with at first, because it not only brought on the craving to smoke, but also undercut inhibitions. It was best to quit when other things were changing in my life. I became a nonsmoker the day I graduated from college in 1969.

My smoking history is fairly typical. I'm one of the 34 million Americans who quit. I knew that smoking was not a very healthy thing to do, but I had no idea of the real risks. As for lung cancer, I had heard that many kinds of cancer were now curable and I thought maybe it was one of those. I didn't know that lung cancer is usually lethal; 90 percent of all cases result in death within five years. I did not know that smoking is the leading cause of cardiovascular disease and I had never heard that there is a disease that is only rarely contracted by nonsmokers, called emphysema. I certainly did not know that smoking has killed more Americans than have died in all the wars against our enemies from the British to the Vietnamese. At least 350,000 Americans were killed by cigarettes in 1986 alone (293,000 died in World War II).

There's no way that I could have known when I started smoking in 1958 that I was under virtual attack by a killer industry that had not the slightest qualm about sacrificing me for its profits. The epidemiological studies indicating that cigarettes killed people had been completed by that time, but the medical journals that published them in 1953 and subsequent years were not on my teenage reading list.

If the cigarette companies had been sensible and enlightened, their response to the studies would have been to place a voluntary warning on cigarette packs and then carefully assess the evidence. Instead, the companies simply denied the validity of the studies and conspired to develop a range of strategies whose purpose was to allow the continued sale of cigarettes no matter what the consequences to human life.

The tactics of the tobacco companies have changed over the years in response to changing times, but the same basic approach has been maintained. Everything depends on a technique perfected by the Nazis: the Big Lie. The industry has formed all its defenses around the single great lie that the link between smoking and disease has not been scientifically proven.

While there were some legitimate scientists who were not yet convinced in 1953, the same cannot be said today. Surgeon General C. Everett Koop will no longer debate the industry about the issue of smoking and health. Dr. Koop told me, "The only scientists in the world who take a position opposing the fifty-thousand published articles on the dangers of smoking are those in the employ of the tobacco industry. It would be ridiculous for me to lower myself to discuss that kind of 'science.' " Dr. Koop says that smoking is the number one public health problem of our time.

Few health issues have ever met with such a unanimity of opinion. Even tobacco farmers and many of their representatives in Congress admit that smoking is unhealthful. Opposition to smoking has become one of the few genuinely nonpartisan issues. Right-wing Republicans such as Utah Senator Orrin Hatch and liberal Democrats like Congressman Henry Waxman agree readily on the menace of smoking, even if they don't always agree on how to deal with the problem.

But the manufacturers, and only the manufacturers, cynically continue to assert that there is a "controversy" about smoking and health. William Kloepfer, vice president of the Tobacco Institute, a trade organization of the manufacturers, said to me, "Smoking may cause illness; it may not. We don't know and we don't think anybody knows."

Only the money and power of the industry permits it to get away with this. If the Flat Earth Society could pay fat salaries, there's no doubt that it could find people with Ph.D.'s who would claim that the assertion that the earth is a sphere is only one side of a continuing "controversy."

Ironically, the bad news about cigarettes has had the effect of keeping out competitors and allowing six established manufacturers to dominate the American cigarette market totally, thus virtually ensuring their profitability. The American cigarette industry is a classic case of oligopoly. Five of the manufacturers have been making cigarettes for almost one hundred years. Philip Morris Companies Inc., which now has the largest share of the market, is a relative newcomer, having begun marketing in the United States in 1902. It shot to the top in the past fifteen years because of the popularity of Marlboro, the largest-selling cigarette in the United States and worldwide. Everyone loves cowboys. PM also was hugely successful with its women's brand, Virginia Slims.

R. J. Reynolds Tobacco Company (RJR), now part of RJR/Nabisco, manufactures Winston and Salem, among others. RJR dominated the cigarette market for many years, falling behind Philip Morris only in 1983. Between them, the two companies make more than 70 percent of all the cigarettes consumed in the United States. RJR's tobacco sales in the United States and abroad in 1986 were close to $6 billion; Philip Morris sold $12.5 billion worth of tobacco products in that year.

Both the tobacco giants are now diversified companies that nevertheless make most of their profits from cigarettes. Some of the smaller manufacturers are now owned by conglomerates. Lorillard, manufacturer of Kent, Newport, and True, is part of the Loews Corporation, whose major stockholder, Laurence Tisch, is now the CEO and chief stockholder of CBS.

Brown and Williamson Industries, manufacturer of Kool, Viceroy, and Richland, is a subsidiary of BATUS, which is the American division of the British American Tobacco Company, the largest tobacco company in the world. This company's other U.S. subsidiaries include Saks Fifth Avenue, Marshall Field's, and Appleton Papers.

American Tobacco, which makes the Pall Malls my mother smoked (as well as Lucky Strike and Carlton), has made itself into the financial centerpiece of a diversified corporation now called American Brands, headquartered in Stamford, Connecticut. Liggett and Myers, now part of the Liggett Group, maker of Chesterfield, Eve, and generic cigarettes, is the only American cigarette company that has not been a spectacular financial success in the last two decades. It is now owned by the New York investors.

Americans spend about $30 *billion* per year on tobacco products. Almost 94 percent of this amount is for cigarettes.

Because of grower and manufacturer clout in Congress over the past century, tobacco products enjoy a virtual immunity from government regulation that makes them unique among consumer products. Tobacco products cannot be regulated for wholesomeness by the Food and Drug Administration or for safety by the Consumer Product Safety Commission. This immunity extends to additives. (Cigarettes contain substances intended to add flavor and to make them burn longer. Over two thousand of these have been used in making cigarettes.) In 1985, Congress for the first time required the cigarette companies to disclose to the government, confidentially, what additives they put in cigarettes. The government still does not have the power to order them to cease using any additives, no matter how carcinogenic or toxic.

The cigarette companies have worked together through their joint lobbying organization, the Tobacco Institute, to keep the bad news away from the public, fighting every warning-label proposal in Congress. There have been three federal warning-label bills and in each case the industry has lobbied hard to weaken the warning. The first one was passed in 1965, seven years after I started smoking. By that time, the evidence that smoking caused lung cancer had been around for at least twelve years and had become almost universally accepted in the medical community. The pitifully watered-down warning that got through Congress said that smoking "may be hazardous" to health.

In 1970, after I had quit, the warning was upgraded to declare that smoking "is dangerous." Even now, with warnings about specific diseases on four rotating labels mandated by the 1985 law, the industry has managed to keep the most critical news from the public. Because of violent industry protests, two words do not appear on cigarette pack and advertising warning labels. They are: *death* and *addiction*.

The demographics of smoking have changed profoundly in the past twenty years. In 1965, some 52.4 percent of white men smoked, while 59.6 percent of black men did so. In the same year 34.1 percent of white women smoked, as did 32.7 percent of black women. By 1986 the percentage of smokers was down to 29.5 percent among white men and 32.5 among black men. In that year, 23.7 percent of white women and 25.1 percent of black women smoked.

These statistics correlate with lung cancer rates. Lung cancer among white males started decreasing in the mid-1980's for the first time in the century. This has been heartening news. Said Dr. Vincent DeVita, director of the National Cancer Institute, "This proves that people can successfully reduce their cancer risk by quitting smoking or not taking up smoking."

But the news is still bad for women and minorities. The cancer institute does not expect to see any significant decline in lung cancer among women for another fifteen to twenty years. The decline in smoking among women is just too slight to produce a change in the number of lung cancer cases. In some states, including California, lung cancer has surpassed breast cancer as the number one cancer killer of women. There are 140,000 new cases of lung cancer and 130,000 deaths from it each year in the United States. Lung cancer is the major cause of cancer deaths in the United States, accounting for 27 percent of all such deaths. "No other cancer site comes close to that," said Dr. Edward Sondik of the National Cancer Institute.

The health care costs to society of smoking-related illnesses (including heart disease, emphysema, and several different types of cancer) are huge. Five health economists, led by Dr. Dorothy P. Rice of the University of California at San Francisco, published a study in 1986 that found that cigarettes cost the nation $53.7 *billion* each year in health care costs and income lost by sick smokers and those who die. Direct medical care costs for smokers were found to be $23.3 billion more than for nonsmokers. This includes hospital and nursing home outlays, doctors' bills, and drugs. Salary losses attributable to smoking by people who were sick with smoking-related diseases totaled about $9.3 billion. Lifetime earnings losses of people who died of smoking-related diseases were estimated at $21.1 billion in 1984.

The authors of the study said, "A total of 270,269 deaths in 1980 were due to smoking, resulting in 3.9 million person years lost." They went on to say, "Our estimates are conservative for several reasons. We have not taken into account the adverse effects of passive smoking, risks of abortions, stillbirths and neonatal deaths, or deaths under age 20 that might be associated with smoking."

Other estimates of the costs are even higher, up to $65 billion in lost productivity and health expenditures each year. This would mean that every pack of cigarettes sold in the United States costs the economy $2.17.

The response of the cigarette companies to the havoc they have wrought is simple. As Joseph Cullman III of Philip Morris said to the Tobacco Merchants Association in 1983, "We have to stand firm on the health issue."

But the Big Lie doesn't work anymore in Washington. Cigarette companies can no longer oppose health warnings on the basis that cigarettes have not been proven to be dangerous, because no one, not even their congressional allies, believes this. So they say that warning labels are not needed because everyone is already aware of the "claim" that smoking is harmful.

Arguments based on this weird premise tend to get very convoluted. Curtis Judge, former president of Lorillard (thus Laurence Tisch's subordinate), testified before a Senate committee against the 1985 cigarette-labeling act. In referring to a 1981 Federal Trade Commission report showing that a large number of people do not understand the real risk of smoking, Judge said, "In that report, the staff erroneously concluded that anyone who does not believe the official line on smoking and health must be unaware of the alleged risks."

Using language that sounded borrowed from George Orwell's *1984*, he went on to say, "The distinction between belief and awareness is as crucial as it is overlooked. The fact is that a poll of people's beliefs about smoking and health says nothing about their awareness of claims that smoking is harmful. And the fact that people do not believe these claims does not mean that they are unaware of them, but rather that they are not prepared to conform to Government views on smoking and health. That result may frustrate those who want to prevent people from smoking, but it surely provides no support for the claim that people need to know more about the Government's position on this issue.''

Perhaps, like all practitioners of the Big Lie, Judge is in the habit of ascribing to others his own mental state. The split between "belief" and "awareness" for cigarette company executives must be an acute dilemma. As fiscally responsible corporate executives, they have to be aware of all the damning evidence against cigarettes, but as would-be members of the legitimate business community, they must make themselves believe that the products they sell are not killing people (while at the same time knowing they do kill).

Orwell's definition of *doublethink* fits the tobacco company executives very well: "to know and not to know, to be conscious of complete truthfulness while telling carefully constructed lies, to hold simultaneously two opinions which cancelled out, knowing them to be contradictory and believing in both of them, to use logic against logic . . .''

The industry would, of course, like the public to know as little as possible about the dangers of smoking. And since cigarettes are the most advertised product in the United States, with an annual ad budget close to $2 billion, the merchants of death have a large club to hold over the heads of the media. It's not too surprising that the news of the link between smoking and a host of diseases is one of the most underreported health stories of the century.

The reason women's magazines do not report that smoking has been found to cause cervical cancer or low-birth-weight babies, the reason magazines of general circulation have not told us what the tobacco industry is doing to defend itself, is as simple as dollars and cents. Tobacco advertising is an important source of revenue, and editors do not doubt that stories about the dangers of smoking would make their advertisers angry and probably lead to withdrawal of their ads.

In 1985, thirty-two years after smoking had been shown to cause cancer, the American Medical Association called for a complete ban on the advertising and promotion of cigarettes. This had been discussed by health advocates before, but the AMA's endorsement gave the whole movement a new head of steam. The tobacco industry, which had done everything it could to restrict information that could mean life or death to consumers, now discovered the First Amendment.

R. J. Reynolds, which had commissioned a series of ads that looked like editorials, defended them against Federal Trade Commission action by claiming the right of free speech; Philip Morris sponsored an essay competition, the subject of which was how the First Amendment ensured the right to advertise cigarettes. It was quite a spectacle, two giant multinational corporations covering themselves with principles that were meant to protect dissenters, the weakest of society. A classic case of wolves in sheep's clothing.

I did not become one of the tobacco industry's victims. It's been eighteen years since I was a smoker and the studies indicate that my risk of lung cancer, heart disease, and emphysema is virtually the same as that of someone who never smoked. New evidence of the probable dangers of breathing other people's smoke concerns me, but I don't have to work near smokers and I rarely encounter smoking in other people's houses.

Attitudes about smoking and cigarettes have changed profoundly. There's no one quite as good as Edward R. Murrow on television, but the Ted Koppels and Bill Moyerses either don't smoke or wouldn't dare be seen with a cigarette. Their credibility would suffer. I've watched almost all of my friends give up smoking and I've seen the United States become far healthier and fitter than anyone in the fifties would have imagined. More than twenty-two thousand people run in the New York Marathon, and millions work out regularly.

Since I took my first cigarette, the environmental movement began and Lake Erie, once thought to be irretrievably polluted, came alive with fish. The federal government established the Consumer Product Safety Commission. Traces of substances suspected of causing cancer are immediately banned from the marketplace. The growth in product liability law has resulted in extreme safety-consciousness among most manufacturers.

Bizarre arguments before congressional committees and corporations' attempts to wrap themselves in the First Amendment are signs of an industry on the defensive. Fewer and fewer Americans smoke and the image of cigarettes continues to deteriorate. These should be deservedly dark days for the people who make cigarettes, but they are not. The tobacco industry is not only surviving, it is actually becoming richer and more powerful than ever. The six cigarette companies that operate in the United States have had years to plan for a hostile environment, since before I started smoking in those long-ago days of the fifties, and they haven't wasted their time. Philip Morris, R. J. Reynolds, Liggett and Myers, American Tobacco, Lorillard, and Brown and Williamson are determined to survive and prosper—whatever the cost in disease and death.

As in the war, the tobacco axis is fighting on many fronts at the same time. There are battles in the realm of images; in courtrooms dealing with product-liability suits; in legislative chambers over warning labels, excise taxes, and no-smoking laws; and even in the tobacco fields, where onetime allies are rapidly becoming disaffected.

The strategies and tactics the industry has chosen to defend itself are based on its need to be perceived as a business just like any other business in the complex mosaic of capitalist America. But this is a unique industry; it is selling death. Cigarettes are the only products on the market (aside from weapons) that kill and injure when used as they are intended to be used. The stakes are high, $30 billion in sales in 1985, and the industry will fight to its last dying gasp to continue to reap profits, even as it reaps death for its customers.

# 2

## THE FIFTIES:
## AN IMPLACABLE
## UNITY

Most people now think that cigarettes were first popularly known to be dangerous on January 11, 1964. That's when U.S. Surgeon General Luther Terry issued his famous report linking smoking with lung cancer. Actually, this report was a review and summary of evidence that had been accumulated by scientists since the beginning of the previous decade. The link between smoking and lung cancer was starkly revealed by epidemiological studies published in the early 1950's.

The cigarette industry faced the biggest threat to its existence in this century in 1952 and 1953. For about a year and a half the industry was in disarray and the future of smoking was in serious doubt. But by 1955 there had been a major shift. The cigarette makers had managed to beat down their enemies and emerge from the crisis stronger than ever.

I smoked my first cigarette soon after my sixteenth birthday, in 1958. Nobody had ever told me that smoking was unhealthful or addictive. It was said that smoking stunted growth, but I didn't believe that old wives' tale and anyway I was already almost six feet tall. Most of my friends were beginning to smoke and it seemed like the natural thing to do.

Of course, I didn't know that only five years earlier there had been a number of stories in newspapers across the country about studies that showed the link between smoking and lung cancer as well as heart disease. By 1958 all that had been forgotten by the media, which profited so handsomely from cigarette advertising. The industry had organized a debunking program that was highly effective. It's not that the cigarette makers were able to find any evidence exonerating smoking. All the new studies showed that smoking was dangerous. The scientific evidence built upon itself until there was a substantial edifice of proof. But after 1954 the industry had carefully organized itself to undermine the notion that smoking was harmful. Its reassurances were received gratefully by a public that wanted to continue to smoke and wanted to believe that it was OK.

The fifties already seem like another age. It was a time of cars that grew bigger and bigger and finally sprouted fins, and of the mass production of vast suburban tracts. After a depression and a world war, people could finally indulge themselves. Things were in. Health and fitness were not. It was a primitive time. Skiers slid up hillsides clutching rope tows and pointed their long skis down slopes almost empty of people. No one knew what caused cancer.

My father and mother smoked, like most fathers and a growing number of mothers. Smoking was the norm in the 1950's. By 1953 there were 63 million smokers in a population of 160 million (in 1986 there would be 50 million smokers out of a population of 230 million). Before the health scare of 1952, when the 1950 studies indicating a link between smoking and lung cancer began to sink into the public's consciousness, the cigarette makers' biggest problem had been how to extract more profits from a stable sales base. Since everyone smoked who could be reasonably expected to smoke, expansion would have to wait for the coming of age of the war babies—my friends and me.

Naturally I had no idea, when I choked over my first Camel, that I was faithfully following the marketing strategy of cigarette executives in Winston-Salem.

From the first introduction of tobacco to Europeans, there had been opposition to the habit and claims that it was harmful. Until the late nineteenth century these were based on little more than common sense. But starting in the 1890's scientists began to apply the scientific method to the study of the relationship between tobacco use and disease, especially cancer. The results of these early studies were inconclusive.

But the practice of inhaling the smoke of a burning cigarette, a mass phenomenon only in the twentieth century, led to vastly increased numbers of what we know now were smoking-related diseases and deaths. In 1938 Professor Raymond Pearl of Johns Hopkins University reported to the New York Academy of Medicine on a major study he had directed that showed that "smoking is associated with a definite impairment of longevity." This should have been major news at the time, but it was buried in the back pages of *The New York Times* near an article headlined "More Slam Hands in Five-Suit Bridge." *Time* magazine did note the importance of the study, which it said was "enough to scare the life out of the tobacco manufacturers and make tobacco users' flesh creep."

World War II preempted all other threats to public health and gave a big boost to the cigarette companies. War and cigarettes go together and the country achieved victory more addicted to tobacco than ever. The war helped the industry reach one of its fundamental goals—to get women to smoke in numbers approximating men.

With the war over, much scientific attention turned to the alarming increase in lung cancer and its possible connection with cigarette smoking (before large numbers of people smoked cigarettes, lung cancer had been extremely rare). In May of 1950, Dr. Evarts A. Graham, former president of the American College of Surgeons, and an assistant named Ernst L. Wynder published an article in the prestigious *Journal of the American Medical Association* (*JAMA*) entitled "Tobacco Smoking as a Possible Etiologic Factor in Bronchogenic Carcinoma."

The article reported their study, which had found that of 605 men with lung cancer, 96.5 percent were smokers. In the control group, men without lung cancer, only 73.7 percent were smokers. The authors' conclusion was: "Excessive and prolonged use of tobacco . . . especially cigarettes, seems to be an important factor in the induction of bronchogenic carcinoma." Dr. Graham, who had been a heavy smoker, gave it up when the results of the study were in. Unfortunately, it was already too late for him. He died of lung cancer in 1957.

Other studies confirmed these results. In Great Britain, Drs. Richard Doll and A. Bradford Hill reported in the *British Medical Journal* in September of 1950 that between 1922 and 1947 the annual number of deaths from lung cancer had increased about fifteen times. Doll and Hill had examined the smoking rates of lung cancer patients admitted to twenty London hospitals and obtained data that closely resembled the Graham and Wynder study.

In late 1953, Drs. Wynder and Graham reported the results of a study in which they had painted the backs of mice with cigarette tars. Some of the animals developed skin cancer.

Bad news for cigarettes piled upon bad news. On December 8, 1953, participants at the Greater New York Dental Meeting heard about four studies that linked cigarette smoking with lung cancer. And there was no equivocation. The researchers, some of the most eminent scientists in the nation, concluded that it was not air pollution or any other factor in the environment that was causing the epidemic of lung cancer. Cigarettes were the cause.

The most striking statement came from Dr. Alton Ochsner, chairman of the Department of Surgery of the Tulane University School of Medicine. Dr. Ochsner was "extremely concerned about the possibility that the male population of the United States will be decimated by cancer of the lung in another fifty years if cigarette smoking increases as it has in the past unless some steps are taken to remove the cancer producing factor in tobacco."

Dr. Wynder reported that more than five thousand lung cancer patients had been studied in England, Germany, Switzerland, Denmark, Czechoslovakia, and the United States. While there were some variations in the independent studies, all of them had the same conclusion: "The prolonged and heavy use of cigarettes increases the risk of developing cancer of the lung." (Later it was shown that even moderate or light smoking can cause disease.)

Cigarettes caused cardiovascular disease as well as lung cancer, it was reported at this 1953 meeting. Participants heard about a study done by Dr. Irving S. Wright of the Cornell University Medical College. His conclusion was not hard to understand. The use of tobacco may mean the difference between life and death for persons with diseases of the circulation.

When the American College of Surgeons met in Chicago in October of 1953, there was much discussion of the cigarette–lung cancer link. Speaking for the prestigious group, Dr. I. S. Ravdin, professor of surgery at the University of Pennsylvania, said, "Within the past five years there has been an increasing amount of evidence that there is a certain factor in cigarette smoking that helps cause lung cancer. There are many specialists who believe that cancer of the lungs is the leading cancer problem."

But there were still many unknowns about smoking. Was there something *in* cigarettes that caused cancer, and could it be removed? Would it make any difference if smokers quit, or was the damage irreversible? Did the risk of lung cancer have any correlation with the number of cigarettes smoked? Also, did cigarettes cause diseases other than lung cancer?* These questions needed to be answered, and Dr. Ravdin thought the cigarette companies ought to fund the research. The tobacco industry had a moral obligation, he said, to pay for the research. "Who else should be more interested?" Unfortunately, the learned doctor apparently did not know the old adage "He who pays the piper calls the tune."

The initial reaction of the cigarette companies to the bad news was strictly defensive. After months of silence, Paul Hahn, president of the American Tobacco Company, finally issued a statement on

---

*By 1987 it was known that the main carcinogen in cigarettes is tobacco itself; no way has ever been found to make tobacco noncarcinogenic. In addition, some additives used in making cigarettes are known carcinogens. Quitting was found to be extremely worthwhile in lowering chances for both heart disease and cancer; lung damage leading to emphysema, however, is irreversible. There is a strong correlation between the number of cigarettes smoked and lung cancer. Cigarettes have been found to cause a number of other types of cancer, including cancer of the cervix in women.

November 26, 1953. There was no connection between cigarettes and lung cancer, he said; not a single case had been proven to be caused by smoking. Hahn went on to denounce the "loose talk on the subject as reported in the press during recent months." E. A. Darr, president of R. J. Reynolds, agreed with Hahn and went on to try to slur the doctors who had attacked his product: "One of the best ways of getting publicity is for a doctor to make some startling claim relative to people's health regardless of whether such statement is based on fact or theory."

Immediately after the dentists' meeting, the research director of Lorillard, Harris B. Parmele, said that his company was convinced that "the majority of smokers smoke cigarettes for pleasure and are unalarmed by unproven rumors relating to their general health." Even so, he said, "there is a cautious minority who place potential health considerations ahead of everything else." For the benefit of these people, Lorillard was contributing "thousands of dollars each year" for grants to study health questions.

But it was evident to the cigarette executives that mere denial would not work. The day after the dentists' meeting, cigarette stocks dropped four points. They soon rebounded, but much more significant were the sales figures for 1953. For nineteen consecutive years, sales of cigarettes had set a new record each year. But in 1953 sales actually declined. By November of that year the projections were for a sales decrease of 1 percent. Most commentators felt that the decrease was directly attributable to the lung cancer scare.

The industry responded to the health news in several different areas. First, there was product innovation. Until the fifties, most American cigarettes were "standards" (the one remaining best-seller of this type is Camel). Longer, king-size cigarettes became popular in the early fifties. American Tobacco's Pall Malls seemed for a few years to be the wave of the future. But the real news was filter-tipped cigarettes. In 1950 they were a negligible segment of the market, but by the end of the decade more than 50 percent of all cigarettes sold in the United States were filters. By the 1980's filter cigarettes were to make up more than 90 percent of all cigarettes sold in the United States.

Along with new products came new advertising strategies. The theme of health, implying health benefits for a particular brand above other brands, had been a staple of cigarette advertising for many years. In the thirties Camel had advertised, "More doctors smoke Camels than any other cigarette" (this was at a time when Camels were the number one brand; more everybody smoked Camels than any other cigarette).

But mentioning health had the potential for bringing up nasty thoughts of lung cancer. Yet some filter brands could not compete without claiming a health advantage. The dilemma agonized the cigarette world throughout the fifties, but finally got resolved with a happy ending appropriate to a fifties Hollywood movie. Cigarette advertising became strictly positive, and even more vacuous than before. Just when health became a real concern, health was eliminated as an advertising theme. The new words were *flavor* and *enjoyment*. Amazingly, the industry manipulated the federal government into enforcing this strategy.

The six major cigarette companies fought each other vigorously for market share, but they had always tended to cooperate when threatened from the outside. Up to the end of 1953 there seemed a possibility that the companies might try to turn the health scare to competitive advantage. But this was clearly self-defeating and in early 1954 the leaders of the American cigarette companies met in a secret conclave in New York with the public relations firm of Hill and Knowlton. Out of this came the Tobacco Industry Research Committee (TIRC) and, later, the Tobacco Institute.

Some sort of significant move had been anticipated by observers of the industry. *Chemical Week,* the chemical manufacturers' trade magazine, reported on January 16, 1954, "Jarred to the marrow by an apparition marked 'cancer,' the cigarette industry last week rallied to offset the threat to its continued well-being. First move of the counter-offensive was a broadside of full-page newspaper ads heralding the formation of the Tobacco Industry Research Committee by 14 prominent tobacco firms, growers' associations, and warehouse groups. . . . Hatched in an aura of careful deliberation, the new cooperative venture has rekindled memories of 1911 and the breakup of American Tobacco by the Trust Busters." This article didn't mince words about its readers' concerns: "Not the least interested of sideline spectators awaiting the next development are the manufacturers who satisfy the cigarette industry's ravenous appetite for chemicals."

The year 1954 marked the beginning of the cigarette Big Lie. It was in this year that the cigarette companies got together to plot the strategies that would keep them viable far into the future, strategies that still guide their response to the fact that their products kill 10 percent of their customers.

Speaking frankly to investors in June of 1954, O. Parker McComas, then president of Philip Morris, said that the health problem must be taken seriously—that is, "carefully evaluated for its effect on industry public relations, as well as its effect on the consumer market." Therefore, he said, Philip Morris had joined with "practically all elements of industry" to form the Tobacco Industry Research Committee. There were great expectations for the TIRC: "We hope that the work of TIRC will open new vistas not only in research, but in liaison between industry and the scientific world." As for the nature of the TIRC, McComas said that it was similar to other industries' organizations such as the American Meat Institute, the American Petroleum Institute, and so on.

This was not for consumption by the general public, of course. An ad was run in newspapers across the country on January 4, 1954, that announced the formation of the TIRC and touted the committee's objectivity. "In charge of the research activities of the Committee will be a scientist of unimpeachable integrity and national repute. In addition, there will be an Advisory Board of scientists disinterested in the cigarette industry. A group of distinguished men from medicine, science, and education will be invited to serve on this Board. These scientists will advise the Committee on its research activities."

The TIRC was formed just in the nick of time. A few weeks earlier Governor Thomas Dewey had announced plans to ask the New York legislature for money to fund research on smoking and lung cancer. Genuinely independent government-funded research was a distinct threat to the industry.

Of course, there were doubters right from the first. The Protestant magazine *Christian Century* commented on January 20, 1954, "It is impossible for any research which they [the cigarette industry] set up and ultimately control, whatever the eminence of its staff and advisory committee, to convince the public that it is telling the truth, the whole truth, and nothing but the truth.''

The writer of this article could be excused for not understanding the fine points of the cigarette industry's public relations strategy. There would be no procigarette studies funded by the committee—fakes would be too easily discredited. Instead, research would be done around the periphery—keeping scientists busy on incidental issues, diverting attention from the main point: the link between cigarettes and disease. For example, one of the committee's first priorities was funding of studies on why people smoke. Another favored area for research was whether some people have a genetic predisposition to cancer. This could keep scientists busy indefinitely.

Still, it was obvious that independent scientists would continue to investigate the health effects of smoking. There was much more bad news to come (as of 1987, there were about fifty thousand studies that demonstrated that smoking was harmful) and the industry had to be able to formulate arguments that had some minimal credibility. The basic public relations strategy was to emphasize the few studies that did not prove that smoking caused disease. What could never be mentioned was that a study that does not prove a relationship between smoking and disease cannot logically prove the opposite—that no relationship exists.

But the industry was not interested in logic, or in the truth about smoking. With the advent of the TIRC, the cigarette companies could say that no one spent more on research on smoking and health than they did. Most important, the TIRC would serve the function of *creating a controversy*. The current name of the committee is the Council for Tobacco Research and it still serves the function of making it seem like there is a valid difference of opinion among scientists about whether smoking is dangerous.

The value of the Tobacco Industry Research Committee to the industry was revealed only a few months after its creation. At a meeting in Atlantic City, New Jersey, in early June of 1954, the American Cancer Society announced that a majority of cancer researchers, chest surgeons, and pathologists believed that smoking might lead to lung cancer. This news was carried on the front page of *The New York Times* on June 7, 1954. But, unlike pre-1954 articles that had allowed the news to stand alone, this article included in its third paragraph a denunciation of the statement.

Timothy V. Hartnett, chairman of the Tobacco Industry Research Committee, called the poll of doctors "biased, unscientific and filled with shortcomings." In an irony apparent to 1980's observers, Hartnett's statement in the *Times* article was immediately followed by a report that Lewis L. Strauss, the chairman of the Atomic Energy Commission, charged that it was "irresponsible" to suggest that the atmosphere was being poisoned by radiation from atomic tests. "No one knows the long range effects of radiation," he claimed.

The word *credibility* was not in general circulation in the fifties. It wasn't yet needed; we were still a credulous nation.

Of course, it took more than the TIRC to save the cigarette industry. The lung cancer scare of the early fifties had forced cigarette companies to innovate. At first it seemed that king-size cigarettes (eighty-five millimeters long, compared to seventy-millimeters standards) would be the wave of the future. American Tobacco's Pall Malls, aided by my mother's pack-a-day purchases, took off. The idea was that the extra tobacco would somehow make the cigarette safer. Tobacco is its own best filter, was the claim.

In 1950, filter cigarettes had only about 1 percent of the market. That was the same year that the *Reader's Digest* came out with an article brilliantly titled "Cancer by the Carton." Filters had historically been exotic, foreign products, Turkish or Russian brands with stiff paper mouthpieces. Viceroys, filter cigarettes made by Brown and Williamson with U.S.-grown tobacco, were introduced in 1936, but did not make a splash until many years later. After World War II, a small elite cigarette company called Benson and Hedges (later bought out by Philip Morris) marketed two brands that contained tobacco blended to American tastes with a European filter mouthpiece. These were called Parliament and Virginia Rounds (this brand became successful when "Rounds" was changed to "Slims"). The filters were made of cardboard with a small wad of cotton. These brands were not advertised or widely marketed and they had a tiny share of the market, less than 0.1 percent.

But in 1948, sales increased dramatically. Benson and Hedges had its offices and shop on Manhattan's Fifth Avenue and it was patronized by New York's elite. By the late 1940's, some eminent New York doctors were telling their moneyed patients to switch to filter cigarettes for health reasons. Robert Sobel wrote in his history of the tobacco industry, *They Satisfy*, "On the basis of an increasing number of scientific papers, unavailable to and unknown by the general public, they had concluded that smoking was harmful to the health. They urged their patients to stop smoking, but most were unable to do so. For these, the doctors recommended a filtered smoke, which they assumed passed less tar and nicotine to the lungs." Benson and Hedges was deluged with orders from retailers as well as smokers themselves.

In 1950 there was only one major brand of filter-tipped cigarettes, Brown and Williamson's Viceroy. This heretofore lackluster brand suddenly began to take off. In 1951 it made the biggest sales gain of any brand in the top fifteen, a jump of over 50 percent. The next company to come out with a filter cigarette, in 1952, was P. Lorillard, which introduced a brand called Kent, named after the company's president, Herbert A. Kent.

The promotion for Kents clearly implied a strong health concern—it focused almost entirely on the filter. Without specifying exactly what it was made of, Lorillard said that the filter material had originally been developed for gas masks during the war and was currently being used to remove radioactive materials from the air at atomic plants. The ad copy was so oriented toward health concerns that it made industry observers nervous. *Business Week* noted on March 22, 1952, "One interesting thing about the advertising claims: Lorillard is willing to push them at the risk of damning, by inference, its non-filtered cigarettes. Lorillard's willingness to go out on a limb shows how strong a groundswell is developing against the smoking habit."

Just four weeks later, *Business Week* reiterated, "The last few years have seen the beginnings of what seems to be a nationwide revolt against cigarettes." As a result of health fears, sales of Kents were taking off right from the beginning. Kent's initial success was un-precedented. Customers flocked to cigar stores on the very first day Kents were introduced. Dealers in New York, Chicago, Los Angeles, were placing repeat orders the same day they got their first shipments. Responding to pleas from West Coast dealers, Lorillard shipped repeat orders to California by air express. It was noted with puzzlement at the time that the strongest demand for the new filters was on the West Coast. This was surely one of the early manifestations of California's role as avant-garde in health consciousness.

Philip Morris responded to the news that cigarettes were causing cancer with its own extensive research effort in 1955. It was decided that the cedar-colored pack of the Philip Morris brand was not up to the challenges of the fifties. So the Color Research Institute of Chicago was called in to conduct extensive physiological and psychological tests on the effects of bright colors on potential customers. A great deal of corporate effort and thought was put into developing a new white, red, and gold pack for the old brand. Philip Morris's next contribution to humanity was the flip-top box.

Filters were clearly the wave of the future. In 1953, R. J. Reynolds introduced Winston, and the next year Philip Morris brought out Marl-boro. When the cigarette makers finally accepted the fact that they would have to make filter cigarettes, they found that filters could be even more profitable than standards. The filter material was cheaper than tobacco and filter cigarettes used less tobacco than standards. Also, filters could get by with poorer-quality tobacco.

But in the fifties it was not yet clear whether the filters were actually meant to attempt to protect smokers' health or merely give smokers the illusion of protection. After a spectacular initial sales surge, the original Kents went into a serious slump. The filter was too effective—too little smoke got through and nicotine addicts were not able to get enough to satisfy their craving. In 1956, Lorillard changed the filter to allow more smoke through, as well as more tar and nicotine. Of course, consumers were not told about the change. With the new filter promising health but the actual cigarette delivering a real tar and nicotine kick, Kents climbed by 1958 to become the fifth-largest brand in the nation, with annual sales of over 36 billion cigarettes.

There's some evidence that the new Kent micronite filter contained asbestos, according to Dr. Allan Blum, former editor of the New York State Journal of Medicine. This would be a very serious matter, since asbestos and smoking act synergistically to promote lung cancer. People exposed to both are about ten times more likely to develop the disease than people who smoke but are not exposed to asbestos. Smokers who are not exposed already have a risk of lung cancer eight to ten times higher than nonsmokers.

It is possible that documents uncovered in product liability litigation but kept from the public by gag orders prove that the filter contained asbestos. There is very suggestive circumstantial evidence. In a *Reader's Digest* article about the Kent Micronite filter, it was reported that the new filter contained "tiny natural fibers (so small to the naked eye, the stuff looks like fine powder)." This could be a description of asbestos.

By the late 1950's it was clear that the future of the industry lay in filter-tipped cigarettes. But there was no evidence that even the few brands that actually delivered less tar and nicotine offered any significant protection from the diseases of smoking. And, in any case, many filter cigarettes delivered as much tar and nicotine as standards, if not more. But then filters were designed not to protect smokers, but to protect cigarette industry profits.

Cigarette advertising was the industry's artillery in the battle against the health menace. Philip Morris initially tried to address the health concerns with Barnum-and-Bailey-type hype. A 1953 ad said that the Philip Morris brand was "the cigarette that takes the FEAR out of smoking." It wasn't filters that did the trick, PM claimed, it was an ingredient called "Di-Gl," diethylene glycol. This magic ingredient, PM said, ensures that Philip Morris "does not produce irritating vapors present in every other cigarette." The Federal Trade Commission acted against this ad, not on the grounds that consumers would be fooled into believing that the cigarette was actually safe, but because the ad was unfairly disparaging other companies' cigarettes.

This ad was not a departure. In fact, it was the culmination of the main theme of cigarette advertising since the early 1930's. The manufacturers had found health claims very effective in promoting cigarettes. "Chesterfields are milder"; "Not a cough in a carload"; "They steady your nerves." Kent had television commercials that showed how cigarette smoke stains filter paper.

Why were the cigarette makers hooked on this negative advertising theme? *Business Week* explained on December 19, 1953:

> The reason is contained in a piece of motivation research recently made public by the *Chicago Tribune,* which discovered that consumers think that "Cigarettes are considered morally and physically wrong, but their use is justified by the psychological satisfactions they provide."
>
> The cigarette companies knew this years ago. They sensed that the majority of adult Americans have always been uneasy smokers, thanks to an inherited puritanical feeling about cigarettes and conviction from the state of their own bronchial tubes that cigarettes just aren't good for you. In their own way the cigarette people tried to reassure the smoker that everything was all right just as long as he smoked X brand, which, of course, is milder, easier on the throat and so on.

But now, in 1953, that there was real evidence that smoking was harmful, health-oriented advertising was a real danger to the industry. However, it could not yet be given up. It had worked very well in the past, and no company wanted to be the first to put its guns on the table.

What should the poor cigarette manufacturers of 1953 do? *Business Week* said that the cigarette makers were listening to psychologist Ernest Dichter, who had counseled them on motivational research in the past. Dichter thought that no matter what happened, people would probably go on smoking. "He reasons they will think something like this: If I give up this there are a lot of other things I do—drink, overeat, strive for success—that I ought to cut out too." However, Dichter thought, many smokers were "going through the process of 're-examining' their addiction."

So Dichter advised the cigarette advertisers to help in this process and "prove that they are on the side of the smoker."

To readers of *The Philip Morris Magazine,* first published in 1986, or the R. J. Reynolds controversy ads, published in 1983, this approach will sound eerily familiar.

Until the summer of 1955, the cigarette makers fought phantom tar and nicotine battles. While denying that there was anything harmful in cigarettes, they competed by claiming lower tar and nicotine content for their brands. But some of the new filter brands were never advertised for their alleged health benefits. R. J. Reynolds's Winstons were sold with the slogan "Tastes good like a cigarette should." While much attention was devoted to the grammar, or lack of it, of the slogan, no one outside of the trade noticed the incongruity: People were changing brands to buy Winstons because of health concerns, but the advertising ignored health and stressed flavor. The Winston ad campaign, which was highly successful, showed an order of psychological sophistication much higher than the fear ads.

In September of 1955, the Federal Trade Commission finally laid down some rules that cigarette advertising was required to obey. Among the seven "guides" were: a ban on assertions that smoking had favorable effects on the respiratory, digestive, or nervous system; a ban on claims of medical approval of smoking, or of a particular brand; and a ban on any unproven claim of nicotine content.

But by the time the FTC acted, the companies were already abandoning much of the health-oriented advertising. The reaction of the industry to the new guides was a collective shrug of the shoulders. It had begun to find that ads based on claims of good taste and enjoyment, selling the new filter brands, were working.

There had been a miraculous turnaround in 1955. By the end of the year it was obvious that the industry had stopped the decline in sales and resumed its upward climb. Sales of standards continued to stagnate, but filters were hot. Overall, sales increased 3 percent from the previous year. The companies' strategy was working. Many of the 1.5 million Americans who had given up smoking during the health scare were reassured by the propaganda of the industry and lured back to cigarettes by filters, which they thought, incorrectly, would offer some protection.

In February of 1956, Dr. Evarts A. Graham reported on another study in which he had painted mice with tobacco tars. He had been criticized for his earlier study of this kind because he had used only one type of mouse. In this new study he used other strains and also painted rabbits' ears with the tars. Again, he induced cancer.

This time the industry was ready for him—thanks to the Tobacco Industry Research Committee. When newspapers reported Dr. Graham's study they also reported the response of the TIRC: "Doctors and scientists have often stressed the many pitfalls present in all attempts to apply flatly to humans any findings resulting from animal experiments." To a scientist, the response was worthless, but it was enough to cast doubt in the public's mind. Most important for the industry, the TIRC provided smokers with some ammunition, some arguments that justified their not quitting.

The late fifties were as good to the cigarette makers as the early fifties had been bad. At the beginning of the decade the companies had had to fight the bad news about smoking and they also had a very small generation coming of age. The so-called hollow generation born before the war provided little opportunity for growth. But coming along was the huge generation of which I was an early member, the baby boomers. The future of cigarette company growth and profits was keyed to this generation. *Barron's* reported on September 3, 1956, "The industry is making a conscious effort to key advertising to the younger age group. And it is this bracket of the population, the 'war babies,' which cigarette economists are awaiting eagerly. Some 28 million of them will begin advancing on the market in another year or two."

Since the war-baby generation started in 1942, this means that the cigarette advertising was aimed at fifteen- and sixteen-year-olds. Indeed, a few years later (April 23, 1960), *Chemical Week,* exulting in the booming cigarette business, prophesied ever larger numbers of smokers because of "the swelling ranks of persons over 15." I don't remember any cigarette advertising when I was a teenager, but it was in fact aimed at me and my friends. And almost all of us smoked.

Despite the FTC's 1955 "guides," health crept back into cigarette advertising. After all, the main selling point of some filter brands, those that actually delivered less tar and nicotine, was health. And in a time when companies were forced to innovate, there was no way a new highly filtered brand could be marketed without an emphasis on health.

The *Reader's Digest*, the most widely read magazine in America at the time (also the quintessential fifties publication, the very expression of the fifties zeitgeist), had published anticigarette stories for years. It had been instrumental in breaking the lung cancer story in 1950. In 1957, the *Digest* ran an article about a test of filter cigarettes. The results were surprising. Some filters delivered more tar and nicotine than some nonfilters. Among these filter brands were Winston and Marlboro. Old Gold filters actually had more tar and nicotine than Old Gold standards.

But there was one cigarette that had a much more effective filter than the others: Kent. Although the article said that an even better filter than Kent's could be made, it was seen as the *Reader's Digest* endorsement of Lorillard's brand. Sales of Kents skyrocketed from 3.4 billion to over 15 billion cigarettes in one year.

The brilliant new success of Kents tempted other companies to join the highly filtered club. Liggett and Myers produced a brand that was actually lower in tar and nicotine than Kent. They called it Duke of Durham. Brown and Williamson made a cigarette called Life and coined the unsubtle slogan "The secret of Life is in the filter."

In 1959, the *Reader's Digest* ran another article rating filter cigarettes. There was a significant difference between the genuinely "low-tar brands" and other filters. Dukes were the lowest, with 7.2 milligrams of tar in the smoke of each cigarette, compared to Winston's 20.4 milligrams. Duke had 0.4 milligrams of nicotine, compared to Winston's 1.6. Nevertheless, there had been a change since the 1957 article. Before being exposed, Winston had had a whopping 32.6 milligrams of tar.

Dukes, like Kents, appealed to smokers who were becoming health conscious and wanted to protect themselves as much as they could while continuing to smoke (this is often a step toward real protection—quitting smoking). The advertising strategy for these brands had to emphasize health—that was their claim to fame.

Although it was not clear that filter cigarettes offered any protection, health-oriented advertising served an important function. It helped make the smoking public aware that smoking was dangerous. Implicit in the claims of low tar and nicotine was the notion that tars cause cancer and nicotine leads to addiction. Claims of low tar and nicotine were fundamentally unlike earlier health-oriented advertising. Tar and nicotine were known by scientists to cause disease, and the level of these substances a smoker ingested had significance for his or her health. Earlier claims had been mere hype, made up by advertising copywriters with no scientific significance whatsoever—e.g., "Not a cough in a carload."

But neither type of health claim was very good for an industry that desperately wanted the public to forget about the fact that smoking caused disease. Except for those few brands that actually offered low tar and nicotine, health claims were deadly. But for these, health claims were the breath of life. Certainly, no new low-tar brands could break into the market without using health claims.

There is a federal agency whose mission is to ensure that advertising is not misleading and deceptive. It is the Federal Trade Commission. The chairman of the FTC in 1959 was Earl Kintner, a former commission staffer who had been appointed by President Eisenhower to fill the unexpired term of the former chairman. Kintner was much loved by the advertising industry because he believed in as little government intervention in the marketplace as possible. Kintner also believed in consulting with groups that were regulated by the FTC. And he believed that industries had a responsibility to police themselves.

Nevertheless, the FTC filed charges against Brown and Williamson for its Life cigarette advertising campaign in 1959. The low-tar claims were not substantiated and the advertising was misleading, the commission charged. A year earlier the FTC had asked the cigarette industry to develop uniform specifications for testing tar and nicotine levels, but it had not done so. Apparently the TIRC had better things to do with its resources, like finding ways of blaming smokers for their own lung cancers.

The tobacco executives met with the Federal Trade Commission at the end of January, 1960, and made a deal. The commission would ban the following advertising claims: statements of tar and nicotine content; claims that a filter was efficient; all other health claims, even implied ones. The industry undertook voluntarily to obey the new rules. The agreement was seen as a part of Chairman Kintner's policy of encouraging industries to regulate themselves.

The 1955 "guides" had prohibited tar and nicotine claims that could not be backed with scientific proof. The 1960 ruling declared that these claims could not be made *even if* there was scientific proof that they were accurate.

The reaction of the industry to this new "regulation" could be described as restrained jubilation. The health incubus had been lifted from its shoulders by government fiat. For the first time since the major health scare of 1953, the industry did not have to worry about trying to produce a safer cigarette. Even Brown and Williamson, whose Dukes were hurt by the new rules, expressed satisfaction. William P. Blount, president of the company, said in October of 1960 that although the rules destroyed the basis for high-filtration cigarettes, "basically these depend on a health appeal and the ruling probably was good for the industry itself. People smoke for pleasure, pure and simple."

The advertisers who made money from cigarettes also were happy with the new rules. *Printer's Ink,* the preeminent magazine of the advertising business at that time, editorialized that the FTC ruling "undoubtedly contributed to an improvement in cigarette advertising." No longer would the public be presented with dull numbers about milligrams of tar and nicotine. Once again advertisers would be free to express their creativity.

Why would the FTC give such a major boost to the cigarette industry? This remains unclear. It is interesting, though, that Kintner's partial term as chairman ran out in 1960 and his Senate confirmation for a full term was held up pending results of the 1960 presidential election. He was clearly the Republicans' choice for the job and would have stayed there if Richard Nixon had won. There was even talk that as a respected FTC insider he might be acceptable to John Kennedy, if the Massachusetts senator was elected. Kintner was known to want reappointment badly. Certainly the cigarette companies, with their ties to Southern tobacco-state Democrats, could help him.

Again, it is possible that tobacco industry documents developed in product liability litigation shed light on these events. The important ones may never be made public. The rules were quietly shelved in 1966 and the public was once again allowed to consider tar and nictotine levels in the cigarettes it was buying.

Throughout the 1950's, the tobacco industry demonstrated a remarkable ability to respond to the most fundamental challenge to its legitimacy. In terms of marketing and advertising it learned to bob and weave with great dexterity and ended up fooling the public almost as much as before. But its greatest achievement was the development of an implacable unity. The cigarette makers did not succumb to the temptation to use the health issue to compete against each other. Instead they created the Tobacco Industry Research Committee and the Tobacco Institute, which were intended to fight for the best interests of the existing cigarette companies—and against the interests of the public.

# 3

DISSENT
IN TOBACCOLAND

Tobacco causes more deaths than all the toxic chemicals spewed out of our factories or mines, but it just doesn't seem as bad as things like DDT, EDB, PCBs, or asbestos. *Natural* and *farm* are good wholesome words, and *tobacco* fits with both of them. Tobacco is as American as apple pie, perhaps more so. No other toxic substance is so ingrained into our culture. Beverly Barbour, 1985 Southern Flue-Cured Tobacco Festival queen, could state in print, apparently without embarrassment, "My year as queen has given me so many wonderful memories that I will carry with me for the rest of my life. Tobacco has been part of my life and the community I grew up in for a long time. It has truly been an honor to represent this plant and the people whose lives revolve around it."

Tobacco is a source of great riches to the multinational companies that make cigarettes, but to the farmers it is a way of life. Tobacco has enabled the small family farm to survive in many places in the South and given a decent living to many who otherwise would be dirt poor. Of all the people involved in the business, it is the farmers who are the most remote from the glitter of the big money and the Big Lie of the cigarette companies. R. J. Reynolds worries about advertising bans and excise taxes, but the farmers worry about the root-knot nematode, which eats the roots of their plants.

As a Northerner from a big industrial city, I found tobacco growing as foreign as yak herding. My first view of tobaccoland was at Lake City, South Carolina, where I attended the 1986 Coastal Plains Farmer Show at Bowens Warehouse. It was early in the year, just before the farmers were to plant their tobacco seeds in specially prepared beds.

The cavernous warehouse (four acres under one roof), which is the scene of tobacco auctions in July and August, was lined with booths displaying all types of merchandise of interest to tobacco growers: pesticides, weed killers, tractors, irrigation devices, fertilizers, seed bed covers, equipment for flue-curing tobacco, and information on the latest methods of growing tobacco from the state of South Carolina and the U.S. Department of Agriculture. One booth gave out free copies of magazines entitled *Tobacco International* and the *Flue Cured Tobacco Farmer*. I got there too late to take in the entertainment, which included gospel singing and Jerry Clower, "everyone's favorite country comic."

United States Tobacco and several smaller smokeless-tobacco companies gave away free samples of snuff and chewing tobacco at their booths. There were signs that said YOU MUST BE 21, but I saw a mother take half a dozen packages of Copenhagen snuff and then pass them out to her kids. She had, no doubt, never heard of Sean Marsee, the Oklahoma high school athlete who had died of oral cancer after "dipping" Copenhagen for six years. And U.S. Tobacco, which was being sued by Sean's mother, was not about to tell her.

R. J. Reynolds was the only cigarette company represented. Its booth was gaily decorated with posters for the "Pride in Tobacco" campaign, which is intended to make the growers feel part of one big tobacco family. An older lady with frosted hair and a friendly smile gave out thick plastic shopping bags colorfully imprinted with the Camel logo.

Before introducing me to some farmers, "Moat" Truluck, proprietor of the warehouse, made a show of looking at my left ear to make sure I wasn't wearing an earring. He then reached into a box and pulled out a baseball-type cap that had the company name on it over a tobacco leaf. "They'll talk to you better if you wear this," he said.

The farmers, and others who worked with them, were only too anxious to talk. At that moment, the tobacco price support program, which had virtually guaranteed them a living if they were willing to work for it, looked like it was about to collapse. The government-pegged price of tobacco, which included a twenty-five-cent-per-pound assessment that the farmers were obligated to pay to fund the program, had fallen below the cost of growing the crop. They had to begin planting within a few weeks at the latest, but they did not know what the price support level would be for this crop. It seemed likely that the more tobacco they planted, the more money they would lose.

It quickly became obvious that the lives of these rural Southern farmers were embedded in a complicated national and international economic and political system. The growers and their neighbors believed in the mythology of rugged individualism and distrust of government, especially the federal government. But the reality was that their economy depended not on the local weather, but the vagaries of the political winds in Congress.

Most important, the growers are tied into the cigarette companies, which are their main customers. The companies, particularly R. J. Reynolds, like to play up the connection; it is their largest constituency, besides smokers, and the farmers have been in the past their most reliable and powerful allies. But these are no longer Southern companies—they have become giant multinationals. Their need to earn ever-increasing profits every quarter, regardless of consequences to the growers, has created tensions that may soon destroy the alliance that has worked so well to protect the companies from the anticigarette forces.

Edward Horrigan, chief tobacco executive of RJR/Nabisco, is fond of telling people that the various groups associated with tobacco are like an Irish family: "We fight like hell with each other," he says, "but we close ranks when an outsider threatens one of us." To many farmers who have seen the recent changes in the tobacco price support legislation, changes that favor the companies at the expense of the farmers, Horrigan's boast is nothing but big-city public relations. Richard Jenks, a prominent North Carolina tobacco farmer, said to me in the spring of 1986 about the cigarette companies, "We thought they were patting us on the back, but they were really cutting our throats."

The cigarette companies would like very much to present to the outside world the image of a monolithic tobacco family, one united group of farmers, workers, leaf dealers, wholesalers and retailers, and of course the manufacturers themselves doing good things for everyone. But this image has become a distortion of reality, a myth perpetuated by the manufacturers to buy themselves goodwill with the public and with the farmers themselves.

Unlike the other groups who make their living from the deadly weed, farmers have a kind of legitimacy that the tobacco companies want and desperately need. Tobacco farmers are something special: They convey the image of a happy agrarian society; with their small but profitable farms they are the last and best example of a sturdy American-style yeomanry. Most important, the growers have had clout on Capitol Hill far beyond their numbers for the past fifty years. Tobacco is grown in only 51 of 435 congressional districts, but in 27 of these, tobacco is king. The tobacco district representatives have tended to pursue their constituents' interests with great tenacity and considerable legislative sophistication.

Whatever legitimacy smoking has, whatever sanction of tradition claimed by the industry, comes from the growing of tobacco in the South. Tobacco was cultivated by American Indians even before Europeans colonized North America. John Rolfe, the husband of Pocahontas, was the first major grower of tobacco; it was the first important cash crop of the American colonies. One of the major reasons for the American Revolution was the British prohibition on direct sales of tobacco to foreign countries. Generations of Southern families have tilled the same land to produce tobacco. The weed is embedded in American legend.

The cigarette companies like to harken back to this heritage, but the mass marketing of cigarettes is in fact a relatively recent phenomenon. The tradition of tobacco before cigarettes is very different from the story of cigarettes, in terms of both economics and health. While tobacco has now been proven conclusively to be unhealthful, it is far less dangerous if the smoke from burning tobacco is not inhaled, and pipe and cigar smokers do not usually inhale. Chewing and dipping snuff have never been done by the great masses of people who learned to smoke cigarettes. The vast numbers of people dying from tobacco are victims of cigarettes.

Until the end of the nineteenth century, cigarettes were mainly poor hand-rolled things used by people too impecunious to buy cigars. The original R. J. Reynolds himself, like other Southern men of his era, despised cigarettes, although he built his fortune on them.

The history of the mass marketing of cigarettes began in 1881 when James Albert Bonsack invented the first practical, economical cigarette-making machine. At age twenty-two he had a device that, when perfected, could produce 120,000 cigarettes a day, equivalent to the output of forty expert rollers working twelve and a half hours.

This new technology allowed James Buchanan Duke, the son of a North Carolina tobacco farmer, to create a cigarette monopoly that has never been equaled in size or power—except perhaps by the Chinese government's current monopoly, which is based on a similar principle of eliminating all competitors. With a grasp of possibilities that seems a hallmark of the great entrepreneurs, Duke understood what the Bonsack machine could do to the cigarette-manufacturing business, and he knew how to capitalize on it.

Duke tied Bonsack to a series of unbreakable contracts guaranteeing that while his machines could be sold to competitors, the price and royalties Duke paid for them would always be 25 percent lower than what the other cigarette manufacturers paid. Through a combination of aggressive price cutting and expanded advertising and marketing, Duke managed to subdue all of his important competitors and achieve in the tobacco field what Rockefeller had done in petroleum and Carnegie in steel—he created a trust that totally dominated the business.

The trust turned on the tobacco farmers with the same rapacious self-interest that it had shown its competitors. For as long as anyone in tobaccoland could remember, the price of tobacco had fluctuated between seven and nine cents per pound. That was when there were buyers competing with each other. By 1900, the trust offered three cents per pound for premium leaf—take it or leave it. Faced with economic ruin, the tobacco farmers of Kentucky and Tennessee decided to fight back. They formed an association to buy their tobacco and hold on to it until the trust was willing to pay a price they considered reasonable.

This strategy was to be used again later by other farmers in other states, but it always led to failure. The problem for organizers of a voluntary producers' association is to get everyone, or at least a large majority, to volunteer. There are always those who have no compunction about taking advantage of their neighbors' misfortunes, and there are also those who fear that the association will simply not work and they will be driven out of business.

The trust courted the renegade farmers. Those who sold their tobacco got the highest prices in memory: twelve to fourteen cents per pound. The members of the association starved—and got madder and madder. Violence flared; night-riding horsemen put the torch to warehouses storing trust tobacco. Finally, the association dissolved, unable to keep its members united. But the trust itself was destroyed, busted by the U.S. Supreme Court, which ruled in 1911 that its existence was in violation of the Sherman Antitrust Act. Disgorged from the belly of the trust were companies whose names are still familiar: R. J. Reynolds, Lorillard, Liggett and Myers, and the American Tobacco Company, which was the legal successor to what was left of the trust.

James Duke and his trust had not just gobbled up the component parts of the cigarette-manufacturing business, they had expanded the total market for cigarettes tremendously. At the same time, Duke had demonstrated that tobacco farmers could be picked off one by one and that the price of tobacco could be held down by determined action on the part of the manufacturers.

While the manufacturers became bigger and bigger, the agricultural base changed little. Tobacco continued to be grown on family farms, some as small as one acre or less. By 1930, tobacco farmers were back to where they had been during the heyday of the trust. A tobacco cooperative association created in the 1920's, this time in North Carolina, had failed and once again the manufacturers were offering less for tobacco than the cost of production.

The Great Depression and Roosevelt's New Deal changed everything and set up a system that would endure for nearly fifty years. The Depression had no real adverse effect on the cigarette companies, which were among the most successful businesses in the country in the 1930's. It was noted at the time, when the concept of addiction was not yet applied to smoking, that people would give up food rather than cigarettes.

But tobacco growers did not share in the cigarette manufacturers' prosperity. Like most other American farmers, they were in dire straits. In 1933, at the urging of the Roosevelt administration, Congress passed the Agricultural Adjustment Act, which set up mandatory limits on production of basic agricultural commodities and minimum prices for them.

The political power of the tobacco farmers came into sharp focus in 1933. It was not clear to everyone that tobacco was a "basic commodity" like wheat or dairy products. It was not a food product and certainly not necessary to sustain life. Furthermore, it was a regional crop, important only in six states. But those states had a habit of returning the same congressmen and senators term after term, and because of congressional seniority they held powerful committee chairmanships. Although there were not very many congressmen for whom tobacco was important, for those from tobacco-growing districts it was all-important. No other issue compared. Also, there were no significant rivalries among the growers of this commodity, as there were among others. These factors taken together ensured the political potency of tobacco.

The clout of the tobacco representatives was demonstrated in the choice of the base period for setting the support prices. The original proposal called for using the period 1909–1914, but the tobacco representatives got that changed for their crop to the period 1919–1929, during which prices had been much higher. None of the other commodities got this special treatment; they were relegated to the earlier period. Marketing agreements were negotiated with the cigarette companies to buy from the large 1933 crop, which had already been planted before the AAA was passed.

The Agricultural Adjustment Act was found unconstitutional in 1936 by the Supreme Court that attempted to wreck so much New Deal legislation. The North Carolina Farm Bureau was formed to secure tobacco production control in the breach, but a new and similar law passed again in 1938 and endured in the same basic form until 1981. Its overriding importance was in its extension of government intervention in the production and marketing of tobacco. In 1980 a student of tobacco wrote, "The federal government accepted an open-ended commitment to ensure that the flue-cured growers were paid a decent price for their tobacco. It was a responsibility that the government has maintained to the present day."

Of all the aspects of the tobacco world, none is more misunderstood by outsiders than the tobacco price support program. Its basic outlines are not complex, however. Tobacco can be grown in the United States only on farms that have an "allotment," a kind of government license. This allotment can be leased or sold, but only within the same county. At harvest time, the farmers bring the tobacco to a tobacco warehouse, where it is sold at auction.

Each year the U.S. Department of Agriculture sets a maximum quota for all tobacco that can be grown and a minimum price for it. If there are no bidders for the tobacco, or if the bids are less than one cent over the minimum price, the crop is taken by one of the farmers' cooperatives and the farmer is given a "loan" for the minimum price of the tobacco. The cooperative then tries to sell the tobacco (which keeps in good shape for five to ten years). The cooperative gets the money to lend to farmers from the Commodity Credit Corporation, which is effectively a part of the U.S. Department of Agriculture. Until 1982 the "loan" given to the farmer was a "nonrecourse loan," which is another way of saying that the farmer did not have to pay it back.

There have historically been some differences in the way the price support program works for the flue-cured tobacco growers of the Carolinas as opposed to the burley growers of Kentucky, but the basic framework is the same.

The tobacco price support system has cost taxpayers much less than supports for other commodities. Department of Agriculture statistics show that of all the commodity programs, tobacco has been by far the least expensive. According to the Commodity Credit Corporation, less than $200 million of public money was spent on tobacco between 1933 and 1984. This compares with more than $12 billion for dairy supports in the same period.

Circumstances conspired over the years to make tobacco easy to support. First, until recent years there was no significant foreign competition for the type and quality of tobacco grown in the United States. Indeed, America is the world's largest exporter of tobacco. And then the number of smokers grew and grew in the United States until the peak of the mid-1960's, when the average annual per capita consumption of cigarettes topped four thousand per year. Demand for what Henry Ford had called "the little white slaver" seemed insatiable. Most important was the restriction on the amount of tobacco that could be grown, which continues to this day. Mandatory production restrictions were abandoned for other commodities with the coming of World War II, but they continued for tobacco.

The halcyon days of smoking in America ended in 1964. No one could think of cigarettes quite the same way after the first surgeon general's report that officially proclaimed them a cause of lung cancer. However, predictions of the swift demise of the industry were overly optimistic. Instead there began a long and continuing war of attrition.

After 1964 the image of cigarettes began a long, slow decline and smoking, which had once seemed on its way to becoming almost universal, came under attack from the medical community and the government. At the same time the United States started to become a much more health-conscious society. The more people gravitated to the ranks of the antismokers, the more necessary it seemed for the cigarette industry to pull the wagons in a circle and assume a defensive posture. The cigarette companies needed to associate themselves closely with the tobacco farmers in order to cloak themselves with the farmers' legitimacy, and also to make sure that the farmers' congressional representatives represented them as well.

R. J. Reynolds instituted the Pride in Tobacco program. The company regularly sponsored picnics for the tobacco farmers. Free barbecue for the family; all the beer and whiskey you could drink, no charge. "We're all one big family," the manufacturers announced; from the growers in their tobacco beds to the executives in their Winston-Salem or Park Avenue suites, we're all good ole boys together, one for all and all for one. But the companies were thinking of the challenges that affected them—new excise taxes, restrictions on smoking in public places, government-mandated health warnings and restrictions on advertising.

It was only natural for the farmers to assume that if they supported the companies on these issues, they would get the companies' help on the one issue that was important to them, the tobacco price support program. For the farmers, there was a big psychological boost in being part of the "tobacco family." They thought that it meant that they were not alone; they had powerful friends. The growers were only a generation or two removed from "Tobacco Road." But the companies were rich; they had platoons of public relations people, squadrons of lobbyists, treasure troves of money to finance the tobacco battle.

By the early 1980's the cigarette companies were under regular and sustained attack by health advocates. Finally, it was the farmers' turn. In 1981, Senator Mark Hatfield of Oregon introduced a bill to abolish the tobacco program. Congressman Thomas Petri of Wisconsin introduced a similar bill in the House of Representatives. Why, it was asked, should the taxpayers subsidize the growing of a crop that kills people?

The tobacco price support program seemed totally illogical to those who knew little of its history or the implications of its abolition. A medical association lobbyist expressed this naïve view when he testified at a congressional hearing (at a later battle, in 1985), "The American Medical Association finds it unconscionable to use Federal resources for supporting tobacco growing while Federal health policy clearly recognizes the health hazards of smoking and while Federal health care programs and other areas in critical need are suffering budget cutback."

But the purpose of tobacco price supports, and what they have actually done, is to keep the price of tobacco higher than it would be in an unregulated market. Furthermore, the program limits who can grow tobacco and keeps the size of tobacco farms small.

The real issue is what the consequences would be if the program were eliminated. If this happened, much more tobacco would be grown. The cigarette companies could contract with a small number of large farmers, or operate their own farms. The price of tobacco leaf would plummet and the companies would be in total control of their suppliers. The result of all this would be either cheaper cigarettes or higher profits for the industry. Since higher cigarette prices are associated with a reduced number of people smoking, especially young people, the tobacco price support system is consistent with good-health objectives.

While it is clearly in the growers' interest to preserve the program, it is not so clear that the manufacturers need or want tobacco price supports. When the program came under attack in 1981, the big brothers of the "tobacco family" looked the other way.

In the early 1980's, there were many tobacco farmers who just did not understand why their program was under attack. The North Carolina grower Richard Jenks asked Senator Walter Huddleston of Kentucky in a hearing in 1982, "This is something that has often bothered me . . . why are we as a commodity being picked out, and none of the other commodities are being picked out, you know, being attacked."

Huddleston's response to this was disingenuous. He said, "That's a paradox. There's no question about that. But as Robert Frost started one of his famous poems with 'Something there is that don't like a fence [sic],' to paraphrase that, 'something there is that don't like tobacco.' "

At a hearing in his home state of Kentucky on March 15, 1982, "Dee" Huddleston got an earful from an old tobacco farmer that might have told him why something doesn't like tobacco. James Sharp, who had grown tobacco since the 1930's, told the senator in a local hearing, "Now if the guy that smokes has been told all the warnings on earth that it is going to kill you, and I think the same thing. I think it is going to kill you. I think any fool that takes smoke down in his belly is going to suffer. I have never smoked a cigarette in my life. I have made a fortune on it. . . . The only way that we built this country is by selling the rest of the fools in the world tobacco.'' Huddleston, of course, made no response to this outburst of candor from an old man who had nothing to lose any longer. One critical difference between Sharp and Jenks is that Jenks is a smoker.

Since the 1930's the tobacco farmers had friends in high places whom they could count on. In 1981 they thought they had as their champion one of the nation's great power brokers, Senator Jesse Helms of North Carolina. Darling of the New Right, Helms was adept at going for the jugular when it came to pushing his conservative agenda. With the advent of the Reagan presidency and the Republican capture of the Senate in the 1980 election, Senator Helms became a vitally important insider.

Everything conspired to augment his power. A Southern Republican in a party that was courting the South as the key to its future, a conservative with ironclad right-wing credentials, and the guru of a major right-wing constituency, Helms was no ordinary legislator. And tobacco farmers were among his major constituents. Time and again he had pledged support for what had historically been North Carolina's chief cash crop. The farmers knew that he was in line to become chairman of the Senate Agriculture Committee and really in a position to help them. And they believed that he was close to the Reagan White House.

But there was an inherent dilemma for the Reagan-Helms axis in supporting the growers. The tobacco farmers were among the most valuable of supporters, not least because they had shown themselves willing to abandon the Democratic party of their forefathers and lead the way in breaking up the solidity of the Democratic South. Yet the tobacco price support program that ensured their economic health was an example of government at its most interventionist.

Most unforgivably (to the conservatives), the program did extremely well what it was supposed to do, keep the price of tobacco high by limiting production and ensure that small tobacco farmers were able to make a decent living. Furthermore, the program was run by the farmers themselves and had their almost unanimous support. Conservatives from non-tobacco-growing states loathed the program. David

Stockman, former Office of Management and Budget chief, in his 1986 autobiography, *The Triumph of Politics,* complained that the tobacco price support program was an example of government power that made Russian communism pale in comparison.

Stockman proposed eliminating the program, but the spirit of politics that the former budget director deplored, the pragmatic concern that if you cut off the living of thousands of your supporters they might decide to support someone else, prevailed. There was to be an election in 1982, and Senator Helms was in for a slugging contest with popular governor James Hunt. So the administration's proposals to eliminate the program were quietly shelved, in deference, Stockman wrote, to the political needs of Jesse Helms.

But "something there is that don't like tobacco," as Dee Huddleston said. The liberals took over the attack when the conservatives held back.

So when the ascendant conservatives were attempting to wring the vegetables out of school lunch programs, the liberals turned on the tobacco price support program. As Senator Hatfield said on September 17, 1981, "Let the tobacco farmer stand on his own two feet as we are asking the welfare recipients and the poor and the needy and the minorities and all the others in America because we are prone to cut the programs upon which they depend. I suppose that many people, including myself, find it unconscionable to allow Americans to go hungry while supporting an inedible and unhealthy crop like tobacco."

The tobacco farmers were fortunate to have as their champion in the House a consummate politician, Congressman Charlie Rose of the Seventh District of North Carolina (the southeastern corner of the state). Rose explained to me that it was the 1981 "Gramm-Latta" budget that soured the liberals: "The budget cut more urban than rural programs in ways that really got the city boys upset. The farm bill came to the floor of the House in a very angry atmosphere; the city boys were saying, 'Hey, don't ask us for any favors. It was you Southern Democrats who joined with the Republicans to pass this budget.' "

Jesse Helms had the habit of going around tobacco country and getting his audiences to chant, "There is no tobacco subsidy." This came back to haunt Representative Rose: "These boys in the House had heard him saying that and they said to me, 'Look, all we are asking you to do is put your money where your mouth is.' ''

But Rose was a congressional insider, with the strongest of ties to the House leadership. He had carefully cultivated liberal representatives from the urban North and from California. And the North Carolina Democratic delegation had not joined their fellow Southerners in deserting the party on the budget.

Congressman Rose also gets high marks for candor, unlike most other tobacco advocates. He told me, "I don't smoke; I don't want anyone in my family to smoke; it'll kill you." But his position is carefully formulated to be acceptable to a broad spectrum of legislators outside the tobacco culture: "As long as they're making a potful of money selling cigarettes, I want American tobacco farmers to get the right to grow that tobacco." When he proposed a compromise, he was accorded a great deal of respect. The compromise was accepted by Congress in 1981 and resulted in the so-called no-net-cost program.

Throughout the struggle to preserve the price support program, the cigarette companies did nothing to help the farmers. Indeed, according to both Rose and Heidi Pender, staff director of the Tobacco and Peanut Subcommittee of the House Agriculture Committee, there were leaf dealers (companies that buy tobacco for most of the manufacturers) advising Congressman Petri, who had introduced a bill to abolish totally the tobacco price support system, allowing him to claim that he had been visited by people from North Carolina and even they didn't want the program. Petri's assistant who was most involved in promoting the bill, Steve Weikert, later went to work for a Wisconsin paper company that was a subsidiary of Brown and Williamson's corporate parent, BATUS.

After 1982, the tobacco price support program was to be run at "no net cost" to the taxpayers. This meant that the government would pay only for the administrative costs associated with the program. The ultimate responsibility for tobacco price supports would be shifted from the government to the farmers themselves. This would be accomplished by requiring the farmers to repay the Commodity Credit Corporation loans that had formerly been nonrecourse loans. The farmers, through their cooperatives, would be responsible for tobacco that was not sold at auction. In order to pay for this, the farmers were to be charged an assessment on a per-pound basis. Prices, which had been continually going up for the previous fifteen years, were to remain relatively high.

The no-net-cost program proved to be a disaster for the growers. Events beyond their control piled one burden upon another. Some factors affected all farmers: The increased price of oil drove up the cost of gas for farm machinery as well as fertilizer; the inflated interest rates of the early 1980's made the customary yearly loans almost unaffordable for many farmers and drove them out of business.

Then there were the special tobacco factors. The use of filters and the development of special processes for puffing tobacco have led to a major reduction in the amount of tobacco used in each cigarette. In 1955 it took 2.75 pounds of tobacco to make one thousand cigarettes; by 1985 it only took 1.75 pounds. Also, each year in the last decade saw a higher percentage of that tobacco coming from abroad. Of all the factors, it was imports that hurt most in the past five years.

Historically the United States has been the world's greatest source of high-quality tobacco. From the time when the first national cigarette brand (Camel) swept the country until the triumph of the low tars, Americans overwhelmingly preferred the taste of American tobacco. The mixture of Carolina flue-cured and Kentucky burley was irresistible. Furthermore, the tobacco price support program guaranteed a reliable source of the commodity every year.

After 1980 there was a phenomenal growth in imports of tobacco from two faraway sources, Brazil and Zimbabwe. Most foreign tobacco had formerly been either the wrong type for American tastes or of very poor quality. But this began to change in the 1980's. The reason for the change was simply that American cigarette companies had embarked on a program of improving foreign, especially Brazilian, tobacco in order to import it to the United States.

The advantage of foreign tobacco from the cigarette companies' point of view was simply price. Brazil has no tobacco price support program and no restrictions on the amount of tobacco that can be grown. There are none of those bothersome governmental regulations that protect farmers and workers. Also, the unique flavor and quality of American tobacco is no longer unbeatable. Low-tar cigarettes depend for their flavor as much on additives as on tobacco.

Several American tobacco farmers journeyed to Brazil in 1985 to see the situation there for themselves. They were accompanied by Heidi Pender. The delegation found a surprising mixture of the modern and the primitive.

Pender says the leaf-processing plants, where the raw tobacco leaves are prepared for curing, were highly organized and extremely clean, with equipment as modern as anything in the United States. "The plants could have been in America." These were owned by Universal Leaf, which is the company that buys tobacco for Philip Morris (RJR buys its own). The Brazilian farmers were being carefully taught how to grow high-quality tobacco by agronomists who had been trained at North Carolina State University's School of Agriculture. A North Carolina tobacco farmer told me that there was one agronomist for every sixty farmers.

But the Brazilian tobacco farmers themselves were poor, dirt poor. They plowed their fields with oxen and for transportation used carts that according to Pender looked "prehistoric." Raw sewage ran through the front yards of the farmers' huts and everyone in the villages was barefoot. Pender says that many of the farmers and their families were covered with open festering sores and even the ones that were said to be "wealthy" looked undernourished. Most of the adults were missing teeth. These were farmers under contract to R. J. Reynolds.

The Brazilian tobacco was cheap, probably no more than half the price of American tobacco and possibly less. Heidi Pender says that she saw invoices in bonded warehouses (where the tobacco is held until it is taken by the manufacturers, at which time they pay the tariff) in the United States that stated the price of the tobacco at $0.36 per pound. This was when American tobacco was pegged at about $1.70 per pound. There are no limits to imported tobacco, although the main source of imports, Brazil, does not itself permit imports of tobacco. Furthermore, there are no official sources of information about the price of imported tobacco—only the cigarette companies know for sure.

Conditions in Zimbabwe are, if possible, worse. There tobacco is grown by black workers on white-owned plantations. A crew from National Public Radio went there in September of 1986 and found a typical farm where five hundred workers lived jammed together in a compound the size of a football field. There was one source of water for all these people, a rusty tub, and one toilet, which was overflowing with excrement. The government had recently decreed an increase in workers' wages, from eighteen to fifty dollars per month.

As imported tobacco began to arrive, it proved impossible for American farmers to compete in terms of price. The cigarette companies reduced their purchases of American tobacco so that a large percentage of it went under loan to the farmers' cooperatives. Before 1980 it had been very rare for as much as 10 percent of the crop to go under loan. In 1984, some 18.8 percent of the flue-cured crop and a whopping 28.8 percent of the burley crop went under loan. A huge surplus of tobacco built up between 1982 and 1985, nearly 800 million pounds. This surplus, which included tobacco grown between 1976 and 1984, represented an indebtedness of $1.9 billion, which the farmers owed the Commodity Credit Corporation.

There was little incentive for the cigarette companies to buy tobacco at or above the official price at auction when it could be bought for a lower price from a cooperative desperate to unload tobacco at a later date. It could be expected that only what was needed immediately would be bought at auction time. In earlier times, the cigarette companies had been forced to compete with each other to get the best tobacco at the auctions, because they could not be certain of fulfilling their needs later in the year. With the glut of tobacco in the cooperatives' warehouses and the flood of imported tobacco, supply would now be no problem.

In 1982 the price support was pegged at $1.69 per pound and the assessment (the amount collected to cover the costs of the new no-net-cost program) was $0.03 per pound. By the time the 1985 crop came around, the assessment had increased to $0.25 per pound. The growers I talked to in South Carolina in early 1986 feared that the assessment would go to $0.50 per pound.

Attention turned anxiously to Washington. The tobacco price support program was in trouble. If something wasn't done in Congress, there was a good chance that the farmers would vote against the program and it would simply collapse.

The tobacco legislators in Washington had been aware of the

growing problem for some time. And buried within the anguished discussions were intimations that all was not well with the "tobacco family." The farmers knew that the cigarette companies' profits had continued to soar while the farmers' woes grew apace. For behind all the rhetoric and the politics of tobacco and health was the overriding fact that the demise of the tobacco price support program would benefit *only* the cigarette companies.

In 1985 there were two competing versions of federal legislation that addressed the tobacco farm crisis. Democratic Congressman Rose proposed that two cents of the cigarette excise tax be earmarked to subsidize the tobacco price support system (he later reduced it to one cent), while Republican Senator Helms championed a bill that would lower the price supports but allow for a cigarette company buyout of the surplus. American tobacco, the Helms people declared, had been too expensive and should be cheaper so that it could compete with foreign leaf.

Charlie Rose's bill was more than controversial in the tobacco world—it was nothing short of heresy. Excise taxes on cigarettes are one of the manufacturers' major bugaboos, ranking right up there with the surgeon general. Horace Kornegay, chairman of the Tobacco Institute, wrote to Rose telling him that "cigarette taxes are not in the interest of anyone in the tobacco family."

Especially disturbing to the companies was the notion of earmarking a part of the tax for a specific purpose. There have been proposals for the last decade to earmark a part of the cigarette excise tax to pay for the health costs of smoking incurred by Medicare, Medicaid, and welfare. If public costs for smoking-related diseases were paid out of excise taxes, the price of cigarettes might go as high as three dollars a pack. The companies were probably afraid that any earmarking might be an opening wedge for this. Of course, the industry is much too powerful on Capitol Hill at present for cigarettes to be made to pay their own way, but like the kind of people who fear that paying for lunch will obligate them later, the manufacturers don't want to take a chance.

It was hard for growers to take these concerns about taxes seriously. In 1983, when there was a move in Congress to increase the excise tax from eight to sixteen cents, the cigarette companies mobilized the Tobacco Action Network (TAN) to fight the increase to the death. Growers, wholesalers, and retailers wrote letters and called their congressmen and senators to protest the projected increases. One of the major arguments they were told to use was that increased taxes were regressive; they hurt most those who could least afford them.

The tobacco people lost the battle, and a certain amount of cynicism developed in the "tobacco family" when the response of the manufacturers to the increased excise tax was . . . to increase prices! One tobacco distributor wrote a letter to the *U.S. Tobacco and Candy Journal* and said what, no doubt, many others were feeling. He called the cigarette companies "profiteers."

Congressman Rose told me that in his judgment the cigarette companies have forgotten all political considerations in a blind scramble for short-term profits. "I think they've sowed the seeds of eventual destruction," he said, "by raising the wholesale price of cigarettes some forty to fifty percent in the last five years, while at the same time they are beating on state legislatures and beating on local farmers to beat on state legislatures to please don't tax us at the local level because that cuts consumption."

While the Rose bill, HR 2600, was adamantly opposed by the cigarette companies, it was embraced by many farmers who saw it as the only way out of ever-increasing assessments that would make it impossible to continue growing tobacco. In the fight for this bill, the historic antagonism between growers and manufacturers surfaced and broke the facade of the happy "tobacco family."

In hearings for the bill, farmers' grievances began to be aired as they hadn't been for many years. One farmer said, "I have voiced my concerns about the tobacco program to representatives of both Reynolds and Philip Morris. They appear indifferent to the plight of tobacco farmers." Another farmer said, with more eloquence, "Tobacco farmers do not want to be serfs or slaves of manufacturers. We do not believe manufacturing interests when they say 'trust us.' We do not believe that." This was a counterpoint to the theme struck by George Dunlop, Senator Helms's chief agricultural adviser, who advised the farmers, "I know that it is fashionable to 'bash' the companies, [but] we've got to trust them."

Meanwhile, the Helms bill was the subject of intense negotiations in Senate offices. Most legislation is the outcome of bargaining by interested parties. In many cases the legislators merely acquiesce in the final agreement, or if there is no agreement, they may endorse the proposals of the strongest party. A critically important factor is, obviously, who is part of the negotiations.

At first the only grower representatives invited were from an organization called the Tobacco Growers Association. This was a group that had been formed in 1982. The organization received funding from the cigarette companies and agreed with the cigarette company proposals in most details. The leader of the group is Carlton Blaylock, a retired North Carolina State University official. Congressman Rose says that the organization should be called the North Carolina Cigarette Manufacturers, Leaf Dealers, and Growers Association, because "the dues and salaries of those people are not paid for by little old dirt farmers, as the name leads you falsely to assume. Big hunks of seed money have been put in by Philip Morris, RJR, Brown and Williamson, and Lorillard."

The two groups that really represented the majority of tobacco farmers, the North Carolina Farm Bureau and the North Carolina Grange, were not invited, but quickly made it clear to the senator's staff, led by archconservative George Dunlop, that they had to take part. They each had hundreds of thousands of farmer members, while the Tobacco Growers Association represented a few hundred. Both were finally allowed to be part of the negotiations. The negotiator for the grange was a man named James Oliver, who was an extremely effective advocate for the tobacco farmers, according to several former associates. Oliver leaned toward the Rose proposal for excise-tax earmarking.

The Helms bill and the Rose bill proceeded through hearings and negotiations at roughly the same time. But it was clear to many farmers that the Helms bill would benefit the cigarette companies at their expense. Tobacco growers who had been fervent Helms supporters, and who had expected that as chairman of the Senate Agriculture Committee he would be able to help them, were dismayed by his actions. "There's a lot of feeling that the senator is listening to the companies and not the farmers," Robert Jenkins, president of the North

Carolina Farm Bureau, told me while the legislation was still pending. One prominent tobacco farmer said to me, "Helms is leading us down the primrose path."

Congressman Rose was disturbed by the way the negotiations over the Helms bill were conducted. The North Carolina House delegation was not invited or welcomed to participate. "The companies were represented by their top executives and attorneys. Some of their lawyers were the highest-priced in Washington, Covington and Burling [one of the most prestigious law firms in the capital] senior partners. Those high-powered execs were negotiating with staff assistants from Senate offices, not the senators themselves. Now, that ain't a fair match. Charlie Whitley [a fellow North Carolina Democratic congressman] and I will tell you that if we're going to negotiate with the companies, we're not going to send staff assistants or interns to negotiate with Covington and Burling, we're going to get in with our hands on and do it ourselves. . . . It was a setup job."

The warning of tobacco farmer Richard Jenks at a congressional hearing in 1982 was prescient: "We as farmers are going to need some protection from the economic and the political powers combined with bureaucracy for financial gain of people who buy farmers' products." It was becoming all too apparent that they would not get that protection from Jesse Helms.

The maneuvering in Washington was matched by events in North Carolina. The Tobacco Growers Association, which claimed to represent the poorest of the farmers, sent out a mailing to every tobacco farmer in the state urging passage of the Helms bill. The TGA had already started a monthly newsletter and hired a journalist to write and edit it. These actions indicated a level of funding far beyond the reach of newly started grassroots organizations.

Many farmers I spoke with agreed with Rose that the TGA was representing the interests of the cigarette companies. Some thought that the organization's goal was to work for the eventual abolition of the price support program without appearing to do so. The farmers who led the TGA were the largest of the tobacco farmers and they were suspected of wanting to become major contractors for the cigarette companies once the program was gone.

Richard Jenks thought that the farmers who supported the TGA were being seriously misled. He told me, "The cigarette companies are brainwashing those boys. But you watch. If the program goes, the tobacco companies'll chop their heads off." The leader of the TGA, Carlton Blaylock, is an intelligent and extremely articulate man and a very convincing representative of his point of view. But many farmers no doubt agreed with the view of one J. H. Poplin when he wrote to the editor of the *Flue Cured Tobacco Farmer*, "Mr. Carlton Blaylock (may his soul rest in hell) says the farmers demand a cut in price and quotas. Never has a greater prevarication been foisted on the public. . . . Then one of our domestic companies goes to South America and gets the people to produce tobacco to drive the price down. This is not new but increasingly worse. We need friends."

In the fall of 1985, the grange had its election for state master. James Oliver, the extremely effective profarmer lobbyist, was running for his second two-year term. It had been the custom for many years to reelect the master, but this time there was active opposition. Rumors that were very negative about Oliver were being circulated by farmers who were close to the manufacturers, according to a grower who was at the scene. It was being said that Oliver had not followed grange policy when he supported the Rose earmarking bill. This despite the fact that there was no official grange policy on this issue. Oliver was unable to clarify his position and the reasons for it, since grange procedure does not allow speeches before the balloting. He was defeated by a 58-to-49 vote of the executive committee and Robert Caldwell, who was not a tobacco farmer, was elected.

Robert Jenkins of the North Carolina Farm Bureau believes that Caldwell was elected not because of the rumors about Jim Oliver, but simply because Caldwell's family had led the grange for many years before Oliver's tenure as master. Nevertheless, immediately after his election the first person Caldwell met with was Carlton Blaylock. And several months later a column appeared in the *The Tobacco Grower* (the official publication of the Tobacco Growers Association) under Robert Caldwell's name, entitled, "The Grange's Policy on Tobacco."

In this column, Caldwell acknowledged, "For the past several months there have been some questions as to what the policy of the

North Carolina State Grange is as it related to tobacco. I am pleased to give you the following position. . . ." He went on to express an unalterable opposition to excise taxes on cigarettes, especially earmarked excise taxes, and his belief in cooperation with the cigarette companies. With Oliver removed from the office and no longer part of the negotiating process, the tacit alliance between the grange and the farm bureau to oppose the cigarette companies was dissolved.

The Rose earmarking bill passed the House Ways and Means Committee and then the full House, but ran into a brick wall in the Senate. The senators from North Carolina and Kentucky were behind the companies' bill. And when it came down to a head-on conflict between the manufacturers and the growers in Congress, there could be little doubt about who would win.

The tobacco farmers don't have their own lobbyists; for a long time they've relied on the company lobbyists. The growers don't have the inexhaustible pile of money that enables the companies to contribute generously to everyone in Congress who may benefit them. And the growers don't have fat jobs in the Tobacco Institute or big corporations that they can offer to defeated or retired congressmen or senators. And in this case the growers didn't have any support from the Reagan White House.

There had to be some legislation, or the price support program would collapse under the weight of the no-net-cost assessment. Faced with a fifty-cent-per-pound assessment, the farmers would probably have voted the program out of existence and taken their chances on the open market. The smallest and most marginal of the farmers would quickly have been driven out of business either way. Rose and his allies in the House had little choice but to go along with the companies' bill.

The Democratic congressmen tried to get some concessions from the manufacturers (the bargaining was done directly with cigarette companies; Senator Helms stayed aloof from the process), but were not very successful. "In the final analysis," Congressman Rose said, "when we traded away the one-cent earmarking all we really got in return from the companies was that the price support level would be about a dollar forty-four instead of a dollar forty, and that allotments could not go down more than six percent per year for the next four years. The companies and the senators cut a poor deal for the growers. I don't think Jesse's interested in being tough. Nobody was ever tough with the cigarette companies. They just cut their own deal.''

Senator Helms may have been dozing in his office when he should have been doing some hard negotiating with the cigarette companies, but he certainly knew how to swing into action to get his promanu-facturer bill through the Senate. Knowing that he could not get the bill through the Agriculture Committee, he turned to his friend Senator Robert Dole, then the majority leader. According to a key Senate staff member, Senator Helms "called in all his chips" (he had helped Senator Dole get his leadership position). The majority leader assigned the bill to the Finance Committee, where it was buried in the com-prehensive budget-reconciliation bill. No senator would vote against the reconciliation bill because of this relatively minor issue, so what should have been called the "Cigarette Companies' Relief Act" breezed through Congress.

The 1985 amendments to the tobacco price support program capped a long-term effort by the manufacturers. Charlie Rose told me, "What the leaf dealers and the companies wanted, they ultimately got in 1985 from Jesse Helms. Back in 1981 they tried to get it through the Petri amendment, but it didn't work because we came up with the no-net-cost amendment.'' Most surprising about the politics of the 1985 amendments is that Jesse Helms, who was popularly thought to be the farmers' champion, betrayed them to the cigarette companies.

And the farmers felt betrayed. I sat in Richard Jenks's barn in Apex, North Carolina, one long hot afternoon in June of 1986, while many of his neighbors, fellow tobacco farmers, drove up in their pickup trucks and stopped to buy fertilizer or pesticides. Jesse Helms, who had been their hero, was definitely not in favor. The conversation turned to the Senate primary, which had been the day before. Former congressman James Broyhill had trounced a Helms protégé named David Funderburk in the Republican primary for the seat that was to be vacated by Senator John East—who himself had been elected be-cause of his connection with Helms's Congressional Club.

The Helms coattails were no longer worth much, at least in tobacco country. Jenks told me that a friend of his who had supported Democrat Jim Hunt against Jesse Helms in 1984 had recently taunted him about it. Jenks, who had been a fervent Helms supporter, now regrets it.

The Helms bill gave the manufacturers the whip hand in tobaccoland. According to Robert Jenkins, the cigarette companies now monopolize the entire system of selling tobacco. "They're calling all the shots" he says. "The manufacturers can make or break the North Carolina tobacco economy." Heidi Pender says that the companies' power is legitimized: "Now the cigarette companies are dictating policy; before they had to exert their influence by the back door."

Under the 1986 law, the secretary of agriculture must set the quota, the maximum allowable amount of tobacco grown in the United States, based on a complicated formula. But the key element is what the manufacturers say will be their requirements for the next year. As part of the compromise with Congressman Rose, the legislation allows them to reduce the amount of American tobacco they buy by no more than 6 percent per year for the next four years. After that they can reduce it by up to 10 percent per year and then by whatever amount they want. The farmers—by law—can grow only the amount of tobacco the cigarette companies want them to grow. In the first year of the program the secretary of agriculture has ordered the maximum 6 percent reduction—pursuant to the companies' instructions.

Part of the deal was that the companies will buy out the surplus tobacco over a five- to eight-year period. The buyout follows a complicated formula, but is certainly a bargain sale. The tobacco from the years before the no-net-cost program went into effect, pre-1982, is being sold at a 90 percent discount. Since the farmers are not legally responsible to pay for this, it is only the taxpayers who are being shortchanged—for about $1 billion. It is ironic that a hard-core conservative like Jesse Helms is responsible for this boondoggle.

In exchange for the buyout, the growers accepted a lower price support level. In 1985 the minimum price of tobacco was about $1.70 per pound, while in 1986 under the new law it was $1.44 per pound. The manufacturers agreed to split the assessment equally with the farmers. The assessment was about $0.025 per pound in 1986.

Pender says that the real issue is how much wealth was transferred to the companies and what the farmers got in return. The companies complained that the price of American tobacco was too high compared with foreign tobacco. But according to Pender, the price of tobacco worldwide is pegged to the American price. When American tobacco goes down, the price of foreign tobacco declines also. American tobacco can never be as cheap. Charlie Rose says, "My farmers can't compete with Brazilian farm labor; the Zimbabwe tobacco workers will never receive what I've got to pay tobacco farmers to grow it in North Carolina."

The political ramifications of the new law are far-reaching. Ironically, 1986 turned out to be an excellent year for American tobacco farmers. Market prices were higher than they had been the year before. But the reason for this had ominous implications for the future. Because of bad weather, 1986 was a very bad year for the Brazilian tobacco crop and the tobacco companies were forced to buy American. But when Brazil rebounds, we may see the beginning of the end for American growers.

If cigarette companies continue to rely more and more on foreign sources for their tobacco and starve the American growers, we can expect to see decreasing support for the companies from Southern congressmen. Tobacco's most effective spokesperson in Congress, Charlie Rose, makes it clear that his loyalty is not to the companies but to the growers. He told me that he says to the manufacturers, "Don't come to Washington and ask me to become known as Mr. Tobacco and then spend all my Green Stamps saving your butts from people who would raise your taxes, increase the number of places you can't smoke, and double the kinds of health warnings that's out there about smoking, and then watch you go off and cut the income on all my growers. . . . If my farmers go broke, I'm not going to raise a finger to help the cigarette companies."

But while the companies still need Charlie Rose, they are laying the foundation for a much broader political base. The cigarette companies are becoming the centers of diversified financial empires. They are outgrowing the South and planting roots in congressional districts across the country. Rose told me that the Tobacco Institute, which used to concentrate on Southern tobacco-district congressmen, has in recent years become more concerned about representatives from other areas. "For whatever reason, they've started a more vigorous outreach program, and clearly diversification enables that to happen."

Whether tobacco will continue to be an important cash crop in the South depends on the buying practices of the cigarette companies. If they procure more and more of their tobacco from foreign sources, American tobacco farmers will continue to be driven out of business. At some point there will be a push to abolish the price support program so that tobacco growing can be rationalized, i.e., grown on a small number of large farms using hired labor. If this happens, the small tobacco farmer will become a historical curiosity and the companies will take over the growing of tobacco. When the companies are diversified enough so that they no longer need the farmers, they will complete the slow process of economic strangulation and nothing more will be said about the "tobacco family."

# 4

## LAWSUITS–
## A POTENT CURSE

Tobacco is an important part of the American economy and a "social issue," but it is also a very personal matter. Those who are most intimate with it, those who take its burning smoke into their lungs, are at once victim and perpetrator of their own demise. Until three or four decades ago, the civil law prevented lawsuits by those who had some responsibility for their own condition. No more.

New Yorker Rose Cipollone began smoking Chesterfields around the same time my mother began smoking them, in 1942. This was wartime and women who were not necessarily daring suddenly found it acceptable to smoke. Like almost all smokers, Rose began when she was a teenager, at sixteen. Her reason to smoke was also typical: "I thought that it was cool to smoke, and grown up, and I was going to be glamorous or beautiful. I thought I would be Joan Crawford or Bette Davis," she later recalled.

Rose Cipollone was one of the millions of women who were targets of cigarette company advertising that was meant to get them to smoke. She changed brands in later years, going through L&M, Parliament, Virginia Slims, and True. In 1984 she died of lung cancer. But before she died, she did something few of her contemporaries would have thought of—she sued the cigarette companies that had made the cigarettes that eventually killed her.

It's cold comfort to her widower, Antonio Cipollone, that her name has achieved a kind of posthumous fame among personal injury lawyers. After three years of litigation the case hung fire before the U.S. Supreme Court simply on the issue of whether there could be a trial. Still, although the case is likely to go on for another decade, through trials and appeals, it and cases like it may do more to attain the surgeon general's goal of a smoke-free society by the year 2000 than anything else. Such is the nature of the American legal system that Rose Cipollone's claim had to strike more fear in the hearts of cigarette company executives than would ten angry senators and a militant Federal Trade Commission.

Tobacco may be a way of life for hundreds of thousands of people in the South, but it is a way of life on trial. The livelihood of farmers and others in the tobacco economy is the death of hundreds of thousands of others. It is not surprising that ex-smokers are suing the cigarette companies because of lung cancer and other diseases that resulted from smoking.

The industry has bought a kind of limited immunity from government interference in Washington and in the nation's statehouses. Great wealth and a powerful constituency are hard for legislative bodies to overcome. Nevertheless, the fact that the cigarette companies are still allowed to market their deadly products aggressively strikes many people as just plain wrong. When there is no public legal remedy, there is usually a "private law" remedy. Americans are used to going to court to assert their rights. This is a time-honored tradition in American society. With us, lawyers usually have the last word.

The recent spate of cases started in about 1983. But there was an earlier attempt to sue the tobacco companies, in the late 1950's and early 1960's. These were successfully resisted by the industry and as yet no tobacco company has paid a cent in personal injury damages.

But the new cases take place in a totally different and, for the tobacco companies, far more dangerous legal environment.

First, the law has changed considerably since the 1960's. The trend in the laws of all the states has been to hold manufacturers more and more liable for the effects of their products. Also, the legal defense of "contributory negligence" is now defunct in most places. According to this old rule, if the plaintiff had any responsibility for his own injuries, he could not win the case. Under this rule, anyone who had any knowledge at all that smoking was harmful could not win a case.

This was replaced by a defense called comparative negligence. If the plaintiff has some responsibility for his injuries, that doesn't defeat the claim; it just reduces the amount of the award, proportionally to the percentage of the plaintiff's fault. If the plaintiff smoker is found by a jury to be 40 percent responsible and the manufacturer 60 percent responsible, the manufacturer has to pay roughly 60 percent of the total damages. This leads to a rather artificial determination of fault, but it does permit a person who had some understanding of the hazards of smoking to prevail.

Some states have a "pure" comparative negligence law. Theoretically, even if a cigarette company is no more than 10 percent responsible, a plaintiff could win.

Another big change in the law is the development of very strong doctrines of "strict liability." Manufacturers no longer have to be found to be "negligent" (this can be hard to prove). Like the simple rule "Use a gun, go to jail," strict liability means essentially, "Market a dangerous product, pay for damages." Many appeals courts have extended this concept to mean that manufacturers should pay for the damages their products inflict even if they did not know that the products were dangerous when marketed. Some courts and legal scholars have said that manufacturers should be held responsible even if they *could not have known at the time* that their products were dangerous.

Under this theory, what the plaintiff knew or didn't know about the hazards of smoking is legally irrelevant. Of course, juries don't always confine themselves to fine legal points, so as a practical matter plaintiffs' lawyers prefer clients who became addicted to smoking before 1965, when the first government-ordered warnings were put on cigarette packs.

The changes in the law came about because of another development that has made the courtroom a source of great danger to the industry—the litigation that decimated the asbestos industry.

Between the early 1930's and the middle 1970's, the asbestos products manufacturers became major suppliers of materials for everything from ships to skyscrapers. Asbestos is a mineral with wonderful properties. Relatively cheap and totally fireproof, it can be mixed with other materials to be fashioned into any shape that is needed. Its only drawback is that it emits microscopic particles that can be inhaled and can cause lung cancer, as well as a fatal lung disease called asbestosis. Some of the top asbestos company executives knew about this hazard in the early 1930's but concealed the facts from their workers. Unlike smokers since 1964, the asbestos workers had no way of knowing they were at risk.

During World War II, thousands of workers toiled in shipyards on both coasts feverishly constructing warships and freighters, and were exposed to massive doses of asbestos that were used to insulate steam pipes, boilers, and fireproof bulkheads. Asbestos-caused diseases have a long latency period. Thirty years later, lung cancer and asbestosis began to claim many of these people. Because workmen's compensation laws forbid employees to sue their employers (the shipyards were responsible only for workmen's compensation payments, which are based on rates in force at the time of exposure), these disease ex-workers seemed to have no legal recourse—except against the manufacturers of the asbestos products.

One of the key legal theories of the asbestos litigation was that the manufacturers had a duty to warn those who would be exposed to their products of their dangerous properties, but had failed to warn.

Alerted to their rights by a network of occupational health activists, thousands of exposed workers became clients of eager personal injury lawyers across the country. The half-dozen major asbestos producers, and the twenty or so minor producers, were barraged with cases. Asbestos litigation itself became a major industry.

As an attorney, I represented workers who sued asbestos manufacturers on account of lung cancer or asbestosis, and noted the fearful reaction of giant companies (which often contrasted oddly with the bravery of dying plaintiffs). I saw Johns-Manville, one of the nation's largest corporations, devote a major part of its resources to litigation, hiring literally hundreds of law firms around the country to handle thousands of cases. And I watched as one day it declared bankruptcy, froze all payments to creditors, and eventually underwent a total upheaval, emerging as a corporation whose main mission was to pay off claims far into the future.

The asbestos litigation was a school in mass lawsuits for personal injury lawyers. And the graduates had a stunning success. A few hundred plaintiffs' lawyers achieved what would never have been done by Congress or the federal bureaucracy. They virtually destroyed the asbestos industry in the United States.

The asbestos litigation did not merely serve as a model for the cigarette litigation; there is more than a legal relationship between asbestos and cigarettes. The two together act synergistically to cause lung cancer. The worker exposed to asbestos who smoked had a far greater risk of developing the fatal disease than the worker who did not smoke.

Indeed, cigarette companies have been drawn into a few asbestos cases on the theory that the synergistic effect of smoking and asbestos was the cause of the plaintiff's disease. However, most lawyers involved in the asbestos litigation are reluctant to open this particular can of worms. They know that theoretically the cigarette companies should share liability with the asbestos manufacturers, but have not wanted the cigarette companies to be added as defendants, fearing to complicate already difficult cases.

Executives of tobacco companies must have thought long and hard about the fate of the asbestos industry. For, like Scrooge, they have much to fear of ''Christmas Future.'' Compared to the damage done by cigarettes, asbestos affected a relatively small number of people. By the surgeon general's reckoning, about *3 million Americans* have died of smoking-related diseases in the past decade. The toll taken by smokeless tobacco, especially snuff, is still unknown, but it is likely to amount to a significant number of shortened lives.

From a lawyer's point of view, there are striking similarities between asbestos litigation and tobacco litigation. Both pit individuals against large corporations. Although there are large numbers of people involved, these are not class action suits. Each individual has a separate case that must be individually resolved. And the plaintiff's lawyer is opposed not just by other lawyers but also by the huge bureaucracy of one or more multinational corporations. The request for records may be answered first with a legal steeplechase of objections and then with the delivery of a truckload of documents.

Also, both involve complex medical issues that require of an advocate two qualities: a firm grasp of the scientific basis for the claim (the causation issue), and the ability to communicate the science to a jury of laypeople.

But there are some major differences. The asbestos defendants, with the exception of Johns-Manville, were much smaller firms than the tobacco companies. And the litigation took them by surprise—there was no precedent for mass tort litigation. The tobacco companies have been dealing with threats and enemies for many years. And they have the example of the asbestos litigation to guide them. Their resources are far greater than those of the asbestos companies.

But their wealth also makes the cigarette companies tempting targets. Personal injury lawyers, a breed noted for their entrepreneurial zeal, have long been aware that the law now favors suits against the tobacco manufacturers.

The cigarette companies and the snuff manufacturer United States Tobacco are vulnerable not only because of developments in the law, and the growing expertise of personal injury lawyers, but also because of the economics of the tort system. Personal injury lawsuits, a variant of which is product liability, are among the most lucrative types of business for plaintiffs' lawyers. Fees are not tied to an hourly rate, but are a percentage of the amount won by the plaintiff through either negotiation or litigation. The percentage varies from 33 percent up to as much as 50 percent of the award. The higher percentage is usually charged when a case goes to trial. Some aggressive lawyers who do good trial work can make as much as the most high-powered corporate executives—hundreds of thousands, even a million or more dollars per year.

This kind of suit is also good news for clients. They do not have to pay the lawyer—all costs and fees are paid out of the award. And if the lawyer loses the case, the client pays nothing.

But there is great risk for plaintiffs' lawyers, because they usually advance the costs of the lawsuit and these can involve major outlays. New Jersey lawyer Marc Z. Edell is one of the foremost plaintiffs' lawyers in the tobacco litigation arena. He is a partner in a major law firm (a firm that represented Johns-Manville in the asbestos litigation) but is very concerned about the costs of getting the cigarette cases to the point where they begin to pay off: "The entry level is extremely costly. The first two years are exorbitant—the discovery that you do, the blind alleys that you run up, the education that you get, the experts that you cultivate. To get the *Cipollone* case to trial it will cost over four hundred thousand dollars' out-of-pocket expenses and over two million dollars in lawyers' time."

Of course, if litigation against the tobacco companies begins to pay off for plaintiffs, the cost per suit will go down—but it will never be cheap. It can never be done economically unless it is done on a large scale. Successful plaintiffs' lawyers in the asbestos litigation had hundreds of cases; a few had thousands of cases. There were several hundred plaintiffs' lawyers involved in those cases. Tobacco litigation has the potential to be much, much larger.

Product liability law is the most entrepreneurial kind of business for the lawyer. There are great monetary rewards for the smart, brave, and lucky, and quick economic extinction for the others. Lawyers in this field must be particularly smart to succeed for, unlike other businesspeople, lawyers have a well-defined set of responsibilities to their clients. They must choose their cases carefully from the very beginning, because once accepted a case cannot be dropped unless the client voluntarily leaves, no matter how difficult and expensive it proves. The potential penalty for ignoring or mishandling a case is a legal malpractice suit brought by another lawyer. There are lawyers who specialize in these.

The increasing number of lawyers in the United States (there were almost seven hundred thousand as of late 1986) makes for a more competitive situation than ever before. Lawyers are actively seeking out business and taking greater risks than ever before. Suing the tobacco companies is a high-risk endeavor, but it will make the fame and fortune of the first lawyers to succeed at it.

The tobacco companies have been braced for this litigation for a long time. George Braly, attorney for Betty Marsee, whose son Sean died of oral cancer after seven years of dipping snuff manufactured by U.S. Tobacco, believes that the tobacco industry perfected its legal strategy as long ago as the 1950's. An important element of this is a policy of absolute intransigence. At the same time, the companies have outlitigated plaintiffs' lawyers in all the cases brought against them. It is likely that it will take at least ten years for a case to go through all possible pretrial, trial, and posttrial procedures and appeals. So far no plaintiff's lawyer has been able to stay the course.

Marc Edell told me, "I think the defense strategy has been the same always, and it's the same today. They litigate these cases hard as hell and they make it financially impossible to deal with the litigation. They make you re-invent the wheel in every case. They have protective orders [gag orders] entered in every case, you can't share information among plaintiffs' lawyers, and they try to paper you to death and outspend you, which they're quite capable of doing."

Although they have had the upper hand so far, the companies are extremely vulnerable because they cannot afford to lose even one single case. Personal injury lawyers across the country are intrigued by this new business potential. The legal sharks are circling, and if one of the corporate whales starts to bleed, there will be a feeding frenzy such as has never been seen before.

Indeed, there is evidence of great concern among jurists that tobacco litigation, if it takes off, will be too much for the courts. Federal judge Harold Ackerman said in the spring of 1986, "It's not overly pessimistic to suggest that any attempt to try these cases back to back will bankrupt the state and federal system."

The cigarette companies not only have to worry about losing legal cases, they also are concerned about their secrets leaking to the public. Company documents bearing on the knowledge cigarette executives have had about the relationship of their products to a variety of diseases might have been uncovered in the product liability suits. Possibly there are documents that prove coordinated industry strategies to conceal the bad news about smoking. Public revelation of these secrets would further tarnish an already poor image. It's no wonder that the companies have fought to impose gag orders on all papers that have emerged in the legal process of discovery. Of course, if such documents have been found by plaintiffs' lawyers, they would be devastating if used at trial.

This may be one of the reasons the companies are most anxious to prevent the cases from going to trial. They have been successful in delaying trials by claiming that federal law "preempts" state court lawsuits against them.

The companies that made the cigarettes Rose Cipollone smoked, the Liggett Group (formerly Liggett and Myers), Philip Morris, and Loews Corporation (owner of Lorillard), had good reason to fear a trial in her case. The lawyers representing the Cipollones were a consortium of three important New Jersey firms. One had represented Johns-Mansville and the other two had represented plaintiffs in asbestos litigation. Formerly adversaries, these lawyers had banded together and had among them an enormous amount of experience. Furthermore, New Jersey product liability law is among the most favorable to plaintiffs in the country.

When the cigarette company lawyers made a motion in the spring of 1984 to U.S. district court judge Lee Sarokin asserting that the federal cigarette-labeling act prohibited the lawsuit, few thought they would prevail. The industry lawyers claimed that the warning required by federal law was not merely the only warning they were *required* to give consumers, but the only warning they were *allowed* to give consumers. Furthermore, they said, since Congress had made a law in this area, it meant, by implication, to forbid any lawsuits under state law against the cigarette companies for personal injuries.

The companies said that the following language in the federal law forbade people like Rose Cipollone from suing them:

(a) No statement relating to smoking and health, other than the statement required by Section 1333, shall be required on any cigarette package.

(b) No requirement or prohibition based on smoking and health shall be imposed under state law with respect to the advertising or promotion of any cigarettes the packages of which are labelled in conformity with the provisions of this chapter. [15 United States Code, Section 1334]

Judge Sarokin took about six months to prepare a thoughtful sixty-page opinion that carefully reviewed the legislative history and analyzed the precedents. He concluded that Congress intended only to prevent states from imposing their own warning requirements on cigarettes; the government-mandated warning was merely a minimum and "legal minimums were never intended to supplant moral maximums. Nor were they intended to eliminate pride in quality and craftsmanship or self-imposed standards of health and safety." He denied the defendants' motion and it looked as if Rose Cipollone would get her day in court.

But the cigarette lawyers appealed, and this time they won. On April 7, 1986, the Third Circuit Court of Appeals, which ranks just below the U.S. Supreme Court in reviewing cases from three mid-Atlantic states, overruled Judge Sarokin's decision. In a cursory three-page opinion, the court decided that the federal cigarette-labeling act "preempted" product liability lawsuits against the cigarette companies. Remarkably, the court refused to look at the legislative history of the law they were construing. Marc Edell, who was the plaintiff's lawyer for this case, says that a federal judge from another court told him, "If you read between the lines, what the Third Circuit is saying is that they don't want these cases in our system."

The appeals court ruled that the cigarette companies could not be sued under state law for failure to warn consumers of the dangers of smoking, because Congress had already occupied this field of law. The court said, "The Act preempts those state law damage actions relating to smoking and health that challenge either the adequacy of the warning on cigarette packages or the propriety of a party's actions with respect to the advertising and promotion of cigarettes."

The court's reasoning was very shaky. There was certainly no intent on the part of the legislators who passed the cigarette-labeling act to prevent product liablity suits, and congressional intent should control in questions of preemption. But the court refused to consider the legislative history, saying, "We find the language of the statute itself a sufficiently clear expression of congressional intent without resort to the Act's legislative history."

A few months after this decision, Marc Edell found out that Judge

James Hunter III, who had written the opinion for the three-judge panel, had represented the American Tobacco Company from 1964 to 1966. Edell thinks that Judge Hunter should have disqualified himself from deciding the case. There is no agreement on this point among legal scholars, but there is near-universal consensus that Judge Hunter should have disclosed the information about his background before taking on the case. The legal standard for disqualification is set forth in federal law; it is whether a reasonable person "would have a doubt about whether the judge was completely impartial in his decision making process." Edell filed a motion with the court to disqualify the judge and have the court decide the case again. The motion was denied.

This court's decision is binding only in New Jersey, Pennsylvania, and Delaware, but the same issue has gone to three other federal appeals courts. If there is disagreement among the circuit courts, as is likely, the Supreme Court may decide to rule on the matter and bring order out of chaos. In any case, there will not be many trials of cigarette cases until the preemption issue is settled.

Edell, like other plaintiffs' lawyers, was very surprised by the appeals court decision. He says it doesn't make sense: "It's very difficult to conceive that that's what the law is; that a manufacturer can discover that its product causes a certain disease that nobody else knows about, and yet the manufacturer doesn't have an obligation to warn of that disease. . . . That's the logical conclusion." Under the court decision, the cigarette companies would not be responsible for warning of anything other than what is mandated by federal law. Since the cigarette companies managed to lobby hard enough to delete the word *death* from the 1985 cigarette-labeling act, the court decision means that they cannot be held responsible in a court of law for not telling consumers that cigarettes can kill—despite the conclusive evidence that cigarettes do kill about 350,000 Americans each year.

The effect of the Third Circuit Court's decision was to bar the use of the "failure to warn" cause of action. The plaintiffs can still sue on the bases of both strict liability and negligence. Rose Cipillone's case will proceed, but without the critical charge that the cigarette companies failed to warn her of the dangers of their product.

Smokeless tobacco plaintiffs do not face the same problem, because until 1986 there was no federal legislation requiring warnings. The law mandating them, which passed in that year, contained language that made it crystal clear that federal law did not preempt product liability suits under state law. It said, "Nothing in this chapter shall relieve any person from liability at common law or under state statutory law to any other person." Dr. Win Froelich, aide to Senator Orrin Hatch, chairman of the Senate Labor and Health Committee when the law was passed, told me that the drafters of the snuff warning legislation were aware of the preemption issue and wanted to avoid the fate of the drafters of the cigarette-labeling act—being misinterpreted by the courts.

The cigarette companies did allow one case to go to trial in recent times. Indeed, observers believe they dragged this case to trial before the plaintiffs were ready because it looked like a sure winner for the defense. This trial took place in Santa Barbara, California, in 1985. The man who started the case was an insurance company official named John Galbraith (no relation to the famous economist). When he had begun to smoke in the 1930's he heard no talk of addiction, of course, or of lung cancer. Galbraith, a college graduate, prided himself on being well informed. He was, says his widow, Elayne, "a very intelligent man about almost everything in life except smoking. He discussed everything else openly, but not smoking."

John Galbraith was diagnosed as having lung cancer in 1979 and died in 1982. When he had come to believe that his fatal disease was caused by smoking, his attitude changed. Becoming reflective, he looked at his smoking in the same cool way he had always regarded other issues. He finally admitted the truth smokers find so hard to face—smoking had not really been a matter of free choice for him. "I wouldn't be dying now if I hadn't been addicted to cigarettes," he told his wife.

Before he died, Galbraith contacted well-known torts attorney Melvin Belli, who was at the time looking for a cigarette victim to represent. Suing the cigarette companies had a lot of personal meaning to Galbraith. His widow told me, "He begged me time and time again to follow through with the lawsuit, not to drop it."

Galbraith's attitude about the cigarette industry had gone through a major change in the year before his death. He was a conservative; probusiness all the way, Elayne says. He had always trusted in the basic decency of businesspeople, including those in cigarette companies.

But one day in the hospital, his widow recalls, her husband pointed out all the glossy advertisements for cigarettes in a copy of *Newsweek*. A businessman himself, he could appreciate how well done the ads were, how convincing they were. The required health warnings were so cleverly disguised that most readers would miss them. Galbraith thought he had been taken in by ads just like these, that he'd been sold a bill of goods. He didn't want it to end there; he wanted to warn others.

Elayne Galbraith now finds it hard to believe that cigarette advertising is permitted. "They don't have a right to advertise," she says. "It's as if we would allow heroin and cocaine to be advertised. Tobacco kills and is addictive."

Lawsuits, courtrooms, and trials have always been fascinating. But the reality of being a plaintiff is the opposite of glamorous—it is usually a harsh and degrading experience. The tobacco lawsuits have a pronounced David-and-Goliath aspect. Elayne often had to remind herself of her husband's wish that she continue the suit.

Long before trial she had to submit to depositions (informal court proceedings that allow the parties to hear the other side's point of view before trial). The first one lasted a total of fifteen hours, the second about seven hours. The tobacco company lawyers had done a great deal of investigation. They asked Elayne Galbraith about every conceivable aspect of her husband's life that might be construed negatively—regardless of its relevance to his smoking and smoking-related cancer.

The industry lawyers wanted to know all about a business John Galbraith had been involved with that had failed, and the resulting depression he had gone through. He'd been married once before and divorced in 1941. They wanted all the details of that marriage and actually went to Texas to interview Galbraith's first wife, who had not seen him for more than forty years before he died.

Elayne told me, "They took a good man's life and tried to tear it to pieces. They will stop at nothing to protect themselves. They don't care that people are dying. . . ."

The manufacturers did themselves a service by dragging this case to trial. John Galbraith had had a variety of other very serious diseases besides lung cancer and the jury could not be convinced that cigarettes had killed him. The trial judge, Bruce Dodds, commented afterward, "I can't imagine a weaker case for the plaintiff in that situation. It was the worst possible set of facts." Interviews with jurors after the trial indicated that they simply did not buy the addiction argument.

Nevertheless, the jury took the case very seriously, taking a day and a half to reach a verdict. Much to the surprise of the judge, three jurors voted for the plaintiff.

There was muted criticism of Melvin Belli. In an interview in a publication called *Tobacco on Trial*, Judge Dodds commented, "I get the feeling that Belli set the thing back quite a ways. . . . It's got to be well done; it's got to be done right." But when Judge Dodds was asked about the statement of a juror who had said that someday, somewhere the right plaintiff would win, he replied, "I agree with her 100%."

In this case, as in most cigarette cases, the victim was an older person who had been smoking for many years. The most difficult thing in such cases is to convince a jury that it is the cigarette company that is responsible, not the smoker. The issue of addiction is a particularly difficult one for lawyers to handle, yet it is extremely important. If smoking is purely a matter of free choice, and smokers understand the risks they run by smoking, why should they be allowed to come back and sue the cigarettes companies for what was, after all, their own fault?

Marc Edell says that the addiction issue must be handled with great care. Regardless of the mounting scientific evidence that tobacco is one of the most addictive of substances, juries probably won't buy the notion that cigarettes, or smokeless tobacco, is in the same category as heroin, or even alcohol. He says that his approach is to call smokers not addicts, but "weak people"—individuals who are not strong enough to give up smoking. This approach is consistent with a fundamental principle of law: The tort-feasor (civil wrongdoer) takes his victim as he finds him. If a company makes its profits by selling deadly products to people, it should not be able to get off the hook by claiming that the consumer should have been strong enough to resist the company's blandishments.

Advertising is a critical issue in cigarette liability cases. In order for the plaintiff to make an effective case, it is necessary to show the jury the marketing practices of the cigarette companies. The jurors need to learn that the companies did everything they could to lull smokers into a false sense of security. Advertising implicitly negates the health warnings on cigarettes. Images of healthy young people splashing in the surf, or an athletic middle-aged man in the locker room with a cigarette in his mouth, or a lithe dancer taking a smoking break from her workout are meant to reassure smokers, to make them associate smoking and healthfulness, to turn their minds away from the idea that smoking is harmful.

But the jury in Galbraith's case was never presented with evidence of cigarette advertising. According to Marc Edell, Melvin Belli and his young associate Paul Monzione did not offer into evidence advertising that had been published before Galbraith developed his lung cancer. The judge refused to admit 1985 ads, because they could not have contributed to his decision to continue to smoke and were therefore not legally relevant. Belli could have offered evidence of advertising that Galbraith had seen and relied on when he was a heavy smoker, but he didn't.

Judge Dodds said, "Advertising is important . . . because it essentially overcomes any possible warnings. That's the kind of testimony I think was missing in this trial. It would be very very effective. Then you could no longer argue 'look, we told you right on the package.' If the plaintiff could say 'yeah, but look what you did to hook everybody and to hook me.' "

Cigarette litigation is still dogged by the preemption issue. In some parts of the country plaintiffs are not allowed to show that the cigarette companies failed to warn of the dangers of smoking since they did have the government-mandated warning labels. When this issue is finally settled (only the United States Supreme Court can do that), we can expect to see many more cases going to trial.

But there has been a preview of things to come. Tobacco went on trial in Oklahoma City in late May of 1986, not in the form of cigarettes, but in one of its smokeless forms—snuff. The trial, *Marsee* v. *United States Tobacco Company*, was a classic battle of the kind the tobacco industry will be facing for the next decade or more. It will be a duel to the death—the death of the tobacco companies or the end of litigation against them. Death in fact is the motif of the trials—the death of plaintiffs or their loved ones, and hovering in the background the death of hundreds of thousands each year from tobacco-related diseases.

The legal system is a less than perfect arena for dealing with the important issue of smoking and health. It is costly and fraught with delay and arbitrariness. The personalities of judge and jury are important, too important. The skill of lawyers counts for much more than the rightness of their cause. Perhaps most important, in trial the cigarette companies can make the case that the hazards of smoking are not proven. Although almost all doctors and scientists believe the case is closed, in a trial it looks like there is still a debate about this, that there are two equally serious scientific points of view about whether smoking causes disease.

But to point out the irrationality of much of the legal system is not to deny its power and influence. Trials and courtrooms have an enduring fascination, just because they flout rationality. The decision of a jury after a trial carries a weight, a legitimacy, that no other institution can match. The surgeon general, the American Medical Association, the World Health Organization—all say tobacco is harmful, but with only modest effect. But if a jury of laypeople were to find it unhealthful, it would constitute a potent curse on the industry.

The tobacco people understand this very well. They know that they must not be defeated on the legal front. They are hoping that they can escape disaster by picturing themselves as normal, business-as-usual corporations. The great danger for them is to be unmasked, revealed for what they really are. Timothy Finnegan, a lawyer for United States Tobacco Company, warned corporate staff at a meeting in 1987 that the industry was safe ''as long as juries do not see us as merchants of death.''

# 5

## TOBACCO ON TRIAL

United States Tobacco makes snuff (moist tobacco that is placed in the mouth), not cigarettes. But it shares the cigarette industry's risk of being engulfed by product liability lawsuits. The impact of a verdict against one product will spill over to the other. The stock market is very sensitive to this litigation, and a verdict in favor of a plaintiff in any tobacco-related case will dramatically affect the stock of all tobacco companies. Also, public opinion will not differentiate much between cigarettes and smokeless tobacco. A verdict against one will bring the other into disrepute as well.

In July of 1986, the nation's largest manufacturer of smokeless tobacco won a trial in a suit brought against it in 1984 by Betty Marsee, but this was probably only Round One—and it was a costly victory. So much damning evidence was revealed, and more suggested, that it is only a matter of time until further lawsuits are filed against the company.

The trial itself was a fascinating interplay of personalities, science, and law, all against the backdrop of the tragic suffering and death of Betty Marsee's son Sean. This was a high-visibility story. The case was followed avidly by the press and a variety of interested parties. Much of the trial was attended by reporters from four or five newspapers as well as the wire services. There were at least a dozen other regulars who refused to be identified for the record. They included financial analysts, attorneys in firms representing cigarette companies in product liability litigation, and shadow jurors (people who are paid by one side or the other to watch the trial and tell the lawyers each day their reaction to what has happened in the courtroom).

The *Marsee* case was a classic David and Goliath story. U.S. Tobacco is one of the Fortune 500 (it proudly joined this exclusive group in 1985 when it was listed as the 476th-largest industrial corporation in America). The company manufactures Copenhagen and Skoal, the world's best-selling brands of snuff. In 1985, in the United States alone, the company sold 480.8 million cans of snuff. Sales were over $480 million and the company's return on average shareholders' equity was a spectacular 30.9 percent.

The snuff business began to boom in the middle 1970's. Moist snuff, which had in recent years been used mainly by old people in the hollows and bayous of the South, began to spread. It started to become the favorite tobacco product of young men from Los Angeles to Boston. In a historical irony of some note, United States Tobacco has profited from the rising awareness among young people of the dangers of smoking. Many young people turned to snuff as a safe alternative to cigarettes, not knowing that there were dangers in snuff as well.

The smokeless tobacco industry thus turned the tables on the cigarette makers, after a defeat of monumental proportions in the early part of the century, when there had been a similar health-related movement *away* from smokeless tobacco. Snuff and chewing-tobacco manufacturers had lost a great deal of business to the cigarette companies when people started to become aware of the dangers of tuberculosis in sputum. Spitting out tobacco was recognized as a significant health hazard.

Betty Marsee, Sean Marsee's mother, was an unlikely adversary for United States Tobacco. She came from a small-town family that had migrated from Ohio to the Dakotas and most recently settled in Talihina, Oklahoma, on the edge of the Ozarks. During most of her married life, she and her children lived in houses that did not have a street address. Her husband died of a heart attack in 1982. Her son Sean worked during the summers and sometimes when he was in school, and his jobs smacked of a rural life that most of us think is gone. Sean painted picket fences; he worked on a dairy farm; he baled hay. In school he was a star athlete. A runner from the age of thirteen (a year after he had begun dipping snuff), he was voted Talihina High's outstanding athlete of the year in 1983. In 1984, at the age of nineteen, he died of oral cancer at home in the town's mobile home park, Lot 150.

After his death, his mother sued the U.S. Tobacco Company of Greenwich, Connecticut, which made the Copenhagen snuff that Sean had used, claiming damages of $147 million because, she said, her son had been killed by the tobacco that the company sold.

Betty Marsee said in her complaint, filed with the U.S. district court in Oklahoma City, that the company knew that its tobacco could cause cancer and that it had purposely concealed that knowledge. In its annual report for 1985, U.S. Tobacco blandly noted the *Marsee* case and another that had been filed against it, saying, "The Company intends to contest these lawsuits vigorously."

On June 20, 1986, the jury found for the defendant, denying Betty Marsee's claim. She has appealed, and may win another trial, and next time perhaps a victory. The company, and the tobacco industry, bought a reprieve, but at great expense. It may not be so lucky next time.

The case began shortly after Sean's death, more than two years before a federal jury heard opening arguments in the trial. But the story began long before that, when a twelve-year-old boy who was typical of that part of Oklahoma, part Western, part Southern, went to a rodeo and got a free sample—of Copenhagen snuff. U.S. Tobacco often passed out free samples at selected sports events.

It took him some time to become a regular snuff dipper. Moist tobacco is a little tricky to use. You wad the stuff up and put it between your cheek and gum. You keep the "quid" there by nudging it occasionally with your tongue. It's hard at first to keep the quid from disintegrating, but with experience you learn how to do it. Beginners may also feel a burning sensation if they keep the quid in their mouths too long, but they'll get over that eventually and be able to keep tobacco in their mouths all day, replacing the worn-out quid with a fresh wad.

As Sean grew up, snuff became a regular part of his life. Like other boys of his age in Oklahoma and increasingly throughout the country, he carried a can of snuff in his back pocket as a sign of manhood, a proof of masculinity. And Sean was glad that there was nothing unhealthful about snuff—or so he thought. He didn't drink because he was an athlete and wanted to stay in condition. He didn't smoke; everyone knew that smoking was bad for you. There were warning labels on cigarette packs and you didn't see ads for cigarettes on television. But snuff had no warning labels and was actively promoted on television by the sports figures Sean admired so much, athletes like Walt Garrison, former running back of the Dallas Cowboys.

The federal law that mandated warning labels on snuff and banned advertising of it in the broadcast media was passed in 1986, almost two years after Sean died.

Sean didn't know that snuff was addictive; many people say that it is even more addictive than cigarettes. The nicotine that marks the tobacco's "strength" is absorbed through the delicate mucous membranes of the gums and swiftly reaches the brain. Some of the nicotine in cigarettes escapes into the air, but all of the nicotine in snuff is absorbed into the body.

It's too bad Sean, or his teachers or coaches, didn't read the statement of Dr. Vincent DeVita, director of the National Cancer Institute, about snuff and the companies that sell it. DeVita said:

I'd like to have the tobacco industry explain a couple of things about the business of chewing tobacco and dipping snuff. Something like 10 to 15 per cent of oral cancers in this country are directly related to snuff dipping. They're increasing that market and I understand that some high level tobacco offical in one of the tobacco companies has been quoted as saying, ''When the kids chew tobacco and they get hooked on the nicotine, you've got them forever.'' That means they'll be hooked on nicotine and they more likely will smoke cigarettes after that. I'd like to hear an explanation of how one could justify that. I'd be very interested.

Recent data, for example, from our institute show that snuff dipping among populations in the South—where they have been doing this for a long time—is associated with such a very high incidence of cancers of the oral cavity and mouth. A relationship is unequivocal. We do have cancer mortality maps and the spots stand out on the map so brightly that we had to go down there and find out what was going on in the areas with the high incidence of oral-cavity cancer. We found out it was due to snuff dipping. I don't understand how they can look us squarely in the eyes and tell us that we should have an open debate when they're packaging chewing tobacco in packages that resemble bubble gum so they can attract teenagers to chewing tobacco.

By the time Sean found out something was wrong, it was already too late. His mother took him to the doctor because he had a whitish sore on his tongue, near the right side of his mouth where he kept his quid of Copenhagen. It was a leukoplakia, the precursor of tumor. The first specialist they went to was pessimistic. Betty Marsee refused to take Sean back to him—he offered no hope. The ENT doctor in nearby Ada, Oklahoma (population seventeen thousand), Dr. Carl Hook, thought the cancer might be cut out, but he put off the first operation for six weeks so that Sean could compete in a big track meet and graduate from high school.

On May 16, 1983, Dr. Hook removed about one third of Sean's tongue. He was scheduled to receive radiation therapy to the floor of the mouth and neck, but a mass arose in the neck before he was able to start the treatments. On June 19 he was admitted to Valley View Hospital in Ada so his doctors could remove all the lymph nodes in his neck. The surgery revealed that the mass was definitely metastatic sqamous cell carcinoma and that there were nine lymph nodes positive for tumor all along the jugular vein.

After this operation, Sean underwent radiation to the neck and upper chest five days a week for five weeks. This was very rough on him. He developed pneumonia and became dehydrated; his throat and mouth grew extremely sore. He couldn't eat and the treatments had to be stopped twice to allow him to recover enough from the side effects to continue. In late August, Sean went back to the hospital for ten days to be treated for the side effects of the radiation. By October, Sean was feeling a good deal of pain on the right side of his jaw and getting bad headaches.

Soon after Thanksgiving, Sean was admitted to Oklahoma Memorial Hospital in Oklahoma City for another operation. A mass at the right base of the tongue was removed, as was a large right submandibular mass. Since he could not eat normally any longer, the doctors performed a tracheotomy and inserted a feeding tube in his neck. About a week and a half after the operation, Sean developed a fistula, or abnormal passage, that ran from the oral cavity to the right side of his neck. A few days before he was discharged (just before Christmas) the fistula closed, but he still had residual damage to his neck and mouth.

On January 19, 1984, Sean was admitted to Oklahoma Memorial again. He had a noticeable mass on the *left* side of his neck. The biopsy showed that it was the same kind of cancer as on the right. He had lost ten pounds in the previous ten days and the doctors noticed that he was lethargic and drowsy but occasionally suffered from restlessness. He had constant nausea and vomiting and had difficulty breathing. The complaint filed by Betty Marsee's lawyers summarized the rest:

He was diagnosed to be suffering from hypercalcemia [excess calcium in the blood], secondary to the cancer. The hypercalcemia was treated to alleviate the nausea and vomiting. Excess secretions were treated in order to facilitate breathing. Sean was provided with a suction kit and was taught how to use it to keep his airway clear. Sean was then put on a chemotherapy regimen which again caused some nausea and vomiting. He was discharged on January 26, 1984, as it was felt that the new tumor was inoperable. Sean was relegated to breathing and eating through tubes. It came to the point where he could no longer orally communicate and was forced to use hand signals and scribbled messages.

Sean was again admitted to Valley View Hospital on February 10, 1984, with a rectal temperature of 103, enlargement on both sides of the neck and face as well as a swollen and painful right arm. There was increasing redness and enlargement of the tracheotomy site. At that time he was not able to open his mouth for examination of the oral cavity. On February 18, 1984, Sean Marsee was sent home to die. He passed away February 25, 1984. At the time of his death he was nineteen years of age and weighed less than 94 pounds.

Dr. Hook felt that Sean's cancer was caused by the snuff he had used, nearly a can a day for six years. For the first six months of his ordeal, Sean still had hoped he would recover, and one of his dreams was to go around the country with Dr. Hook talking to other young people and telling them not to dip snuff. His mother, a registered nurse, also wanted to get the message out. The need to prove that a loved one has not died in vain is a strong motivation, and a lawsuit is one of the most forceful ways of doing it.

So after Sean died, Betty Marsee traveled the ninety miles to Ada, Oklahoma, and went to see George and Dania Braly, a husband-and-wife team of lawyers. The Bralys knew they had a big case on their hands, but they could not know how much of their lives would be devoted to it. They were not veterans of large-scale product liability litigation.

The complaint filed on March 21, 1985, by the Bralys alleged that U. S. Tobacco had failed to warn Sean Marsee of the deadly danger of its moist tobacco and that the law required that the company be held strictly liable for the resulting injuries.

In the "prayer for relief," which sets out what the plaintiff hopes to win by the lawsuit, Betty Marsee's lawyers asked for punitive damages because of the "willful, wanton, or reckless disregard for the safety of the deceased and the public in general.'' The punitive damages requested were $136,540,000, U.S. Tobacco's net earnings for 1983. ''Such punitive damages are sought for the purposes of punishment, to set an example, and to deter other manufacturers from similar conduct.''

Punitive damages, which are rarely awarded by juries, are the grail for plaintiffs' lawyers, and the nemesis of civil defense lawyers. Their theoretical purpose is to punish civil wrongdoers and they are the real wild card of litigation. In a 1986 Texas suit between Texaco and Pennzoil, a jury awarded punitive damages of $10 *billion* to plaintiff Pennzoil. Even a giant company could be destroyed by punitives. And since they are intended to punish, the jury is entitled to hear details about the defendant's conduct that might otherwise be excluded as irrelevant. *Marsee* v. *United States Tobacco Company* was the first tobacco case ever where the issue of punitive damages was allowed to go to the jury.

Most of the work of litigation is done during the period of time after filing the complaint and before the trial starts. The vast majority of lawsuits never get beyond this stage. Trials are not supposed to contain surprises; modern legal theory holds that each side should be able to discover all of the legal points that are to be used against them as well as the facts that will be used to establish these points. The names of all potential witnesses must be disclosed, as well as the gist of what their testimony will be. Of course, lawyers try to conceal as much as possible from their opponents while making the other side reveal as much as possible.

Large corporations like U.S. Tobacco have many ways of avoiding discovery. Delay is usually the most effective tactic. The company's answers to interrogatories (written questions that must be answered under oath) were as terse as possible—so brief as not to answer the questions. Twice the Bralys had to go to court to ask federal district court judge David Russell to order the company to answer more fully. And the company kept delaying handing over documents from its files that had been subpoenaed. Finally, in the legal equivalent of blitzkrieg, two days before the trial the company delivered to the Bralys eighty thousand documents.

When the *Marsee* trial finally came, in late May of 1986, it was closely watched by the tobacco community, on both sides of the issue. Most knowledgeable observers believed that this case had the best chance of producing a verdict for the plaintiff of any of the recent tobacco cases. There was no issue of government-mandated warnings and the "decedent" (as lawyers say) was young and ill informed enough to avoid the charge of voluntarily assuming the risk of injuring himself.

Because a very large amount of money hinged on the outcome of this trial, the defense preparations were extraordinary. George Braly told me that he had heard that the defense attorneys had held a complete mock trial of the case in Kansas the month before. Before the actual trial began, U.S. Tobacco rented a large suite of offices in Oklahoma City. Braly said that the company had forty lawyers working on the case at one time.

The jury was picked after a list of questions suggested by lawyers for both sides were asked by the judge. Among these was the question "Do you have a settled opinion whether tobacco causes cancer?" The wife of a surgeon who did believe this perfectly reasonable proposition was excluded by the judge.

The federal courthouse in Oklahoma City was one of those 1950's "modern" buildings, the kind that are so bland that you can't tell what they are meant to be. It could have been a high school or a government office building. The courtroom itself was windowless and unimpressive. The air conditioning more than made you forget the muggy atmosphere outside; when the lights were turned down for the videotaped testimony there was the cold dark feeling of a cave. For a month the eyes of the tobacco world focused on this room. Following is a record of three days of the trial in Oklahoma City in June, 1986.

## MONDAY, JUNE 2

The morning routine is invariable. Three men with hand trucks wheel in twelve large boxes full of documents, which they put in the corner near the defense (U.S. Tobacco) lawyers' table. The more avid spectators are in the courtroom before the offical starting time of 9:30 A.M. Betty Marsee's lawyers, George and Dania Braly, come in separately.

George Braly is a little portly, with reddish thinning hair, a large mustache, and large glasses. When the jury is out of the room he usually seems a little distracted, but when they can see him he becomes somehow tougher, almost angry. He's relatively young, a member of Brown University's 1970 graduating class. As Oklahomans go, he comes from old stock. His grandparents settled there when it was Indian Territory.

Dania Braly is a different type altogether. Where he is a little diffuse, she looks highly focused, sharp. Today she is wearing a blue pinstriped suit with a tight skirt and four-inch heels. She wears navy-blue stockings. Her blue eyeshadow contrasts with her deep-red lipstick. Her opponent, Timothy Finnegan, a New York lawyer and partner in the firm of Jacob, Medinger, and Finnegan, also is wearing a blue suit with pinstripes, but his are thinner and finer—more Eastern.

Betty Marsee sits at the plaintiff's table and is so unobtrusive you could almost forget that she is there and that all the complex trappings of the court proceedings were instigated by her. A stocky woman with short frosted blond hair, she wears the kind of glasses with temples that dip down below the eye, where they join the front of the frame. Plain, homey, and not unintelligent, she is middle America personified.

The defendants have their own folksy figure. Walt Garrison, former running back of the Dallas Cowboys and now a vice president of United States Tobacco, sits at the defense table wearing cowboy boots, Wrangler blue jeans held up by a thick belt with a large brass buckle, and a gunmetal-gray windbreaker with epaulets. Next to him sits Andy Coats, a slender gray-haired man who just happens to be the mayor of Oklahoma City. He is local counsel for the company. There is another defense lawyer in addition to Finnegan; Alston Jennings of Little Rock. Jennings is a sepulchral figure—his face is almost as gray as his suits. He speaks with a soft Southern accent, without the trace of harshness found in the West. He pronounces *tobacco* as if it ended with an *a*.

The judge is not from central casting. Some men look the part (regardless of their judicial skill or temperament), like former chief justice Warren Burger, but not so David Russell, federal district court judge for the Western District of Oklahoma. The judge looks more like an accountant or a branch bank manager. He has the indecisive manner of a not completely seasoned jurist. Judge Russell is always polite to both sides, and he often has a somewhat perplexed air.

The jury, upon whom all hopes and fears rest, is composed of four women and two men along with three alternates. Juries of twelve are now required only in felony criminal cases. One of the women, a young blonde, wears glasses that are the opposite of Betty Marsee's; the temples turn up to meet the front just above the eyes. Two other women are blond and they are all attractive and under thirty-five. The fourth woman is slightly older, a speech pathologist with short curly brunet hair. She is the jury foreman.

The only jury member who is certifiably blue collar is a man who often wears jeans with a big *G* on the belt buckle. He works in the local General Motors plant. The defendants tried to keep the one black man, a retired chemist who is the oldest on the panel, off the jury, but had already used up their peremptory challenges and could find no cause to remove him (lawyers consider blacks likely to favor plaintiffs). Taken together, the jury looks relatively young, trim, and healthy.

The Bralys are beginning their third week of presenting the plaintiff's evidence. The first witness this morning is Dr. William Lijinsky, head of the National Cancer Institute's research facility in Frederick, Maryland. Dr. Lijinsky has a pronounced British accent and a quizzical manner. He seems slightly nervous on the witness stand. George Braly establishes the fact that the doctor is a British subject. It is better to bring out this kind of thing in direct examination instead of giving the opposition the chance to bring it out in an embarrassing way on cross-examination.

Last week the Bralys showed the videotaped depositions of two researchers who testified that the cancer-causing substance in U.S. Tobacco's snuff was the class of compounds known as nitrosamines. Now Dr. Lijinsky tells the jury that nitrosamines were first noticed to be carcinogenic in 1956. He goes on to say that while some carcinogens act only on a very narrow range of organs or species of animals, nitrosamines act extremely broadly. They have been shown to produce tumors of the oral cavity, lungs, tongue, trachea, and esophagus in forty-five species of animals including monkeys, hamsters, mice, rats, frogs, snakes, chickens, and cats. No species tested was found to be resistant to the cancer-causing potential of nitrosamines.

Just when Dr. Lijinsky is making the critical point that compounds that are carcinogenic but thousands of times less potent than nitrosamines are banned from the marketplace by federal law, a spectator comes into the courtroom and sits down. Three members of the jury gaze over at this minimal activity as if even that is more interesting than what the scientist is saying. Dr. Lijinsky pronounces the word *laboratory* with the accent on the second syllable, reminiscent of Boris Karloff.

Dr. Lijinsky goes on to explain the dose-response relationship in terms of nitrosamines. He says that the development of cancer does not depend on the length of the life of the experimental animals, but on the size of the dose of nitrosamines given them. This is a critical point since the U.S. Tobacco attorneys will claim that there is no medical evidence that shows a relationship between snuff and oral cancer in young people (until the 1970's, snuff dipping was seen mainly among older women in the rural South).

The lowest dose of nitrosamine that has been shown to cause cancer, Dr. Lijinsky says, is 7 micrograms per kilogram of body weight per day for two years. He then estimates that a typical snuff dipper would be exposed over a six-year period to 16.6 micrograms per kilogram of body weight per day. As he says this, the mayor of Oklahoma City moves back comfortably in his chair at the defense table and closes his eyes, looking like he's going to take a nap.

Unaware of the mayor's mental defection (he never looks at the defense table), Dr. Lijinsky goes on to explain that nitrosamines in the average person's diet from smoked meats, beer, and liquor represent perhaps one microgram per day.

George Braly then asks Dr. Lijinsky if he knows of any industry that markets such a potent cancer-causing agent other than the tobacco industry. The defense could object to this question on the grounds that it is irrelevant and unduly prejudical, but Jennings is too canny for that. An objection would be likely to fix the question firmly in the jurors' minds. Finally Braly gets down to the question of the reliance on animal tests. Would it be ethical, Braly asks, to give nitrosamines to humans for experimental purposes? "Not outside a Nazi concentration camp," the doctor replies.

It's now Alston Jennings's turn to ask the questions. Surprisingly, Dr. Lijinsky does better on cross-examination than direct. His slight nervousness evaporates and he seems to revel in being challenged. Jennings tries to get the doctor to admit that the substance that affects humans is a metabolite of nitrosamines, but Dr. Lijinsky says, "Yes, but the metabolites are themselves nitrosamines." They go around like this for a few minutes and I wonder what the jury is thinking about. Lunch, probably. Jennings brings out the fact that Dr. Lijinsky is being paid fifteen hundred dollars for his testimony and he spent seven hours with George Braly before giving his deposition and four before trial. This is standard cross-examination stuff; it is supposed to discredit the witness in the eyes of the jury.

On direct examination, Dr. Lijinsky talked about the "Ames test." Named after Berkeley scientist Bruce Ames, this test shows whether a substance is mutagenic (mutation causing). The Ames test was perfected in 1973, but U.S. Tobacco didn't get around to testing its snuff until the spring of 1984. The results were negative. Internal company documents that the Bralys obtained showed that this round of testing had been faulty. The test was repeated on August 22, 1984, and this time it showed that the nitrosamines in the snuff were mutagenic. Seventy to 90 percent of all mutagens are carcinogens also, so this finding should have set off alarm bells. On cross-examination, Jennings makes much of the fact that the reason the original test was negative was that toxic chemicals in the snuff neutralized the nitrosamines before they could be effectively measured for mutagenicity. Jennings refrains from pressing home the point, because he is walking a fine line. He has to imply that in actual use the nitrosamines in snuff are neutralized by other chemicals, but he cannot admit that nitrosamines are cancer causing.

After Dr. Lijinsky has finished, the five or six journalists in the room follow him out to the hallway, crowding around him. We know that he has said something important, but don't really understand exactly what it was. The Ames test in particular seems crucial, but the connection between mutagenicity and carcinogenicity is obscure. This makes me wonder how much the jury could have understood. Through a glass darkly, indeed.

After the day's proceedings, I walk back to my hotel through the deserted streets of downtown Oklahoma City. The Bralys have an uphill fight on the causation issue, I decide, because it is easy to confuse the jurors about it. A politician once told me that when people are confused about a ballot issue, they tend to vote no.

## TUESDAY, JUNE 3

Walt Garrison is the only officer of U.S. Tobacco to attend the trial. All the others have refused. They cannot be subpoenaed for the trial because a witness in federal court proceedings cannot be required to travel from a distant state. This is a rule that protects from oppression poor old people and Fortune 500 executives with equal solicitude. But witnesses can be required to testify by deposition if the other party goes to them. So before the trial the Bralys went to the offices of U.S. Tobacco and deposed some key corporate officers. The important depositions were videotaped (at the Bralys' expense, or Betty Marsee's, if she wins) as well as transcribed verbatim.

The purpose of a deposition is essentially discovery. The lawyer calling for it tries to find out as much as he can, while the lawyer for the witness tries to limit the answers as much as possible. The rules of evidence apply as in court, and the witness is obligated to answer the questions, under oath, unless he is instructed by his lawyer not to answer. The great difference between testimony at trial and in a deposition is that there is no judge present at a deposition. Objections are noted for the record, but for the most part they don't lead to withdrawal of the question.

But George Braly's task was more than discovery. Since the corporate officers would not appear at trial, he had to combine the discovery function of the deposition with the more important function of cross-examination. This is an exceedingly difficult task. The normal procedure is to depose a witness and then be prepared at trial for any inconsistency in his testimony. A good trial attorney can use this to make the witness look either deceitful or incompetent. "Isn't it true, Mr. X, that in your deposition you said the memo was prepared in 1980, and now you say 1982?" But Braly couldn't do that—he had only one crack at the U.S. Tobacco executives.

Today we see the videotaped deposition of Dr. Richard Manning, U.S. Tobacco's vice president in charge of research and development. Videotaped testimony is new to the courtroom—five years ago it was extremely rare—but it now seems essential. The courtroom is a maze of wires and monitors. There is a full-time technician, paid for by the Bralys, who sits at the plaintiff's table. The alternative, which is used for less important witnesses, is to read the verbatim transcript of the deposition out loud. Mac Braly, George's brother and himself a lawyer, would sit in the witness box and read the answers; George or Dania would read the questions. This is as tedious as it sounds.

Most of the day is spent watching Dr. Manning on the screen. His background is unexceptionable. He got a Ph.D. in organic chemistry from the University of Arkansas and was hired by the company in 1969. He appears furtive and evasive.

George Braly's first line of questioning concerns a U.S. Tobacco interoffice memorandum that turned up in discovery. This showed that the company was carefully calibrating the level of nicotine in its snuff so that the snuff marketed to beginners—i.e., young people —had the least amount. Most of the tobaccoish taste of tobacco products comes from nicotine; the more nicotine, the more tobacco taste. The apparent idea was that children would start with a very mild product called Happy Days, move on to Skoal, and then graduate to Copenhagen. The company slogan was a blatant "Sooner or later it's Copenhagen."

But Braly can get nowhere with Manning. The man's stonewalling is amazing. He refuses to answer even the most basic questions. I think most people would be too embarrassed to do what he's doing

Q. Has the U.S. Tobacco Company conducted any research on the safety of its products?

A. I don't know what you mean by the use of the word *safety*.

Q. Has U.S. Tobacco done any research to determine whether its snuff was dangerous?

A. I don't know what you mean by the use of the word *dangerous*.

Q. Is it safe for a purchaser of Copenhagen snuff to use Copenhagen snuff?

A. I don't know what you mean by *safe* in that context.

Q. Is it dangerous for a purchaser of Copenhagen snuff to use Copenhagen snuff?

A. I don't know what you mean by *dangerous* in that context.

Q. What does the word *dangerous* mean to you, doctor?

A. It has many different meanings in many different contexts.

When asked what the relationship is between mutagens and carcinogens, Dr. Manning replies, "I don't know." Braly asks Dr. Manning whether U.S. Tobacco has conducted research to see if snuff is mutagenic (of course he knows that the company has—this was the Ames test). Dr. Manning says, "I need to know what you mean by mutagenic." Braly tries to clarify, but gets nowhere with the witness.

The questioning then turns to nitrosamines. Braly is obviously becoming more and more frustrated and Dr. Manning isn't giving an inch.

Q. What is the significance of the presence of nitrosamines in tobacco?

A. I don't understand the meaning of the word *significance*.

Q. Well, is there anything about nitrosamines that human beings would want to know before consuming them?

A. I'm not qualified to know what human beings want to know.

Q. If a product contained nitrosamines, would you want to know about it before you put it in your mouth?

A. I don't know if I would want to know about it or not.

After several hours of this it is time for a break and the jury is told to leave the room. The lawyers and the judge now discuss the deposition. Braly wants the jury to see the rest of it, which would take several more hours. But Judge Russell is impatient: "I think the deposition has effectively made the point you wanted to make," he says.

But the plaintiff's lawyer argues that there are other company documents that he wants to introduce into evidence and this is the best way to do it. He does offer to delete about twenty-six pages (the videotape is calibrated in relation to the typed transcript of the deposition). Judge Russell turns to defense lawyer Finnegan and asks him if there is anything he wants the jury to hear in those twenty-six pages "I don't think so," he says with a laugh.

The jurors are called for. They file in and sit down in their customary places. The older black man is flanked by the two blond women in the front row; in the back the GM worker sits on the right and the two women next to each other. There are also two alternate jurors on the right in the front row. The jurors rarely talk or even look at each other in the courtroom.

Dr. Manning is summoned to the screen once again. This time we see only excerpts and they have a choppy feel. It's very hard to follow the questions and answers because they jump around with little apparent logic.

This is a mercifully short day. Tuesdays are half days in this trial, because the judge is allowing Andy Coats to fulfill his mayoral duties on Tuesday afternoons. In the afternoon I go over to the U.S. Tobacco press room in the Sheraton Hotel, coincidentally the same hotel where I am staying. I find two exceedingly friendly people, a youngish woman from a New York public relations firm and her assistant, an Oklahoma woman who had the habit of saying, "Well, God bless you!"

There is a table groaning with documents—all of the pretrial papers. Many of them are marked confidential. The PR people tell me I can have any that I want; they will make copies for me. After spending a few hours looking them over, I take back to my room a rather thick package. They also give me a packet of press clippings, most of which are unfavorable to the company. That night I get a frantic call from Larry Allen, a U.S. Tobacco public relations man, who tells me that many of the documents that they gave me are covered by the judge's gag order. Giving them out was an unwitting violation of the order. After copying what I think is important, I give him back the papers.

The answers to interrogatories that I have seen tell some interesting stories. One has to do with marketing to young people. The company's 1984 advertising budget tells it all. A total of only $2,696,000 was spent to advertise all brands of snuff—with the exception of the starter brand Skoal Bandits. This product, made specifically for beginners, was advertised to the tune of $7,239,000. The other important information was that the company had stopped using an ingredient that was a known carcinogen (coumarin) in 1982.

## WEDNESDAY, JUNE 4

More of the Manning deposition. At one point the judge excludes the spectators, including the press, from the courtroom, saying that trade secrets are about to be discussed. The judge, who is invariably polite to everyone, seems almost apologetic about this.

I'm a little unnerved about the closure. The First Amendment requires that trials be conducted in public unless there is a compelling interest that requires exclusion of the public—and the press. U.S. Tobacco's claim of trade secrets seems laughable to me. The company sells 90 percent of the snuff used in the United States at present and it is unthinkable that any other company would enter this liability-strewn market.

Nevertheless, when I peer through the window in the courtroom door to look at the monitor that faces the spectators' section, one of the defense lawyers, Finnegan's partner Edwin Jacob, pushes his way in front of me and starts making threatening noises. But just as he seems to be about to either hit me or push me, I can't tell which, he thinks better of it. So he calls an eager young gofer lawyer on the defense team and tells him in a choked voice to get the U.S. marshal. But before the marshal can get there, the monitor is turned off and the confrontation is diffused. Of course, I wouldn't have been able to make out anything even if I had been able to watch, since reading lips has never been one of my strong suits.

I go down the hall and call the Reporters Committee in Washington and talk to Bob Becker, a lawyer who specializes in the First

Amendment. He tells me that I can protest the closure of the trial and request an immediate hearing on this issue. If I do, the judge is supposed to make a finding on the record that the interest he is protecting is more important in this context than the First Amendment rights of the press. I can then appeal to the circuit court of appeals. Nevertheless, Becker tells me, the U.S. Supreme Court has not ruled on this yet and in Oklahoma the judge might not have to follow this procedure. In practical terms it's all beyond me, and I try to enlist the wire service reporters to get their organizations interested. Nothing comes of it and by this time the courtroom is open again. Later George Braly tells me in Tim Finnegan's presence that there was nothing consequential in the secret testimony.

Back in the courtroom, it's Dr. Manning again. More stone-walling:

Q. What is a carcinogen?
A. I really don't know what a carcinogen is.
Q. Has U.S. Tobacco ever tested any of its products for muta-genicity?
A. Yes, the Ames test.
Q. Why would U.S. Tobacco want to conduct an Ames test?
A. I don't think I said that U.S. Tobacco wanted to conduct an Ames test.

Braly then asks Dr. Manning how long he has prepared for the deposition. He has been well prepared—he spent fifteen to twenty hours over a period of five or six days with four of the defense lawyers.

The deposition is over. The monitors are blank but the marshal has forgotten to turn the lights up. George Braly walks slowly over to Betty Marsee, takes off his coat, and gently puts it over her.

The jury is sent out of the room and the judge begins on U.S. Tobacco's objections to the next videotaped deposition. This will be the testimony of Per Eric Lindquist, U.S. Tobacco's vice president of marketing "worldwide." Judge Russell says that he wants to save time.

Finnegan's first objection is to the questions and answers that relate to a company product that was called, with unwitting irony, the "good-luck portion pack." This contained three brands of snuff, Happy Days, Skoal, and Copenhagen. George Braly argues that this testimony is needed because it is the best way to introduce a company document clearly showing that the company knew that it was selling nicotine. U.S. Tobacco kept testing and retesting to see what the levels of nicotine were in the different brands of snuff.

Without waiting for a reply from the defendants, Judge Russell sustains the objection, saying, "I've sustained motions in limine [motions made just before a trial starts] excluding products other than Copenhagen. I'm going to sustain the objection to this one." The judge agrees with the defense that evidence of the company's misconduct regarding products other than the Copenhagen brand is irrelevant, because there is no evidence that Sean used any other brand.

Next is the part of the deposition where Braly questioned Lindquist about a company document that says the satisfaction of tobacco use is based on the "nicotine kick." Braly says that this shows the company knew that the tobacco was addictive. Finnegan opposes this feebly, and Judge Russell sides with Braly. The objection is overruled and the jury will hear the testimony.

The "Lotus Project" is now considered. This was the name U.S. Tobacco gave to the effort to develop snuff in a kind of bag similar to a tea bag. One of the problems the smokeless-tobacco company faced in expanding the snuff market was that its products were not easy to use. And since snuff dipping had almost died out or had never been practiced in some areas, there were no elders to show young people how to use it (unlike cigarettes).

Loose snuff isn't easy to keep wadded in a neat little quid; it takes some practice. So little bags were produced and called Skoal Bandits. The document that Braly wants the jury to hear about is a memo of a meeting in the office of the president of the company. The target market for the product is mentioned. It is people fifteen to thirty-five years old.

Judge Russell says that this evidence concerns a product other than Copenhagen and is therefore irrelevant. In his customary, rather hesitant manner, he says that he will sustain the objection—"for now." His tone of voice allows for more and Braly hammers on, trying now to get him to change his mind. The attorney says that the purpose of offering the testimony for consideration by the jurors is not to prove that the company planned to market a bag-type snuff to young people, but to show that the company officers lied under oath by testifying that they did not intend to market snuff to young people. The truthfulness, or lack thereof, of a witness is always relevant. Judge Russell is not convinced, however.

As George Braly gets more and more frustrated, Tim Finnegan seems to get sleeker and even more ingratiating. The lights are still dim and the courtroom frigid with air conditioning. The spectators, many of whom have a stake in the outcome, are riveted by the sight of Braly trying to preserve the case he's worked so hard to create.

Finnegan has objected to the part of the deposition that discusses the company marketing strategy for 1984. The judge sustains the objection because it relates to a time period after Sean's death. Braly wants to include questions and answers about an important study that showed the hazards of snuff, which was published just before U.S. Tobacco launched a $10 million campaign to promote Skoal Bandits. He wants to show that the company relied on statistics that had an 80 percent confidence level in mapping out its marketing strategy, so that he can contrast that with the company's refusal to credit medical statistics showing the dangers of snuff with a 95 percent confidence level.

Judge Russell says blandly, "That may or may not be appropriate conduct, but we're limiting our case to Sean Marsee and what happened to him." Braly pleads with the judge not to "gut the deposition" when the corporate witnesses refuse to be present, but Judge Russell is unmoved.

Finally the judge rules that the fact that the company formed a task force to combat the bad publicity about the health effects of snuff cannot be told to the jury, since it was done after Sean's leukoplakia had developed and was therefore "irrelevant."

The judge and the lawyers have spent about two and a half hours arguing over a deposition that is not much longer than that. The jury is now summoned and the monitors light up with the pale Swedish face of Per Lindquist. He speaks English with a slight accent and, although he seems a little stressed, he doesn't seem quite as sneaky as Manning appeared. Because the material covered by the objections is so extensive, the deposition is very choppy and hard to follow.

Braly makes little headway on the nitrosamine issue; Lindquist keeps insisting on narrowing his range of his responsibilities and excluding anything that smacks of research. He admits that U.S. Tobacco products marketed in Sweden, where smokeless tobacco has been used for a long time, have had warning labels, by law, since 1975.

Lindquist is asked about a company memorandum regarding its program of giving out free samples of snuff at colleges. Braly has Lindquist read the part that says, "Avoid high sampling visibility at parent- or college-official-oriented events." Now, why should you do that? Braly asks. Lindquist replies in a dignified tone, "We should avoid a situation where sampling would be interfered with by parents or college officials. There is a health controversy about our product. What this says to me is that it could be a situation for concern or irritation on the part of parents because of the health controversy." Several of the jurors look as if they're going to nod off.

Finally a live witness is brought out, and she's on Betty Marsee's side. She is Saundra Hunter, Ph.D., from Louisiana State University. Her field is medical sociology and she is working on a major study of life style and health habits among young people between the ages of eight and seventeen. The study, which is funded by the U.S. government's National Institutes of Health, has tracked all of the children in Bogalusa, Louisiana, since 1972. Dr. Hunter says that there was a tremendous increase in the use of snuff among young people between 1976 and 1981. In some age groups the increase was 600 percent. The increase was noted in children below age seventeen. At that age, many snuff dippers graduate to cigarettes.

Alston Jennings gets up slowly to cross-examine the professor. He tries to get her to admit that what's true in Bogalusa is not necessarily true of anywhere else. She disagrees, of course, but Jennings makes his point more clearly than she defends the representative nature of Bogalusa and her study. Jennings turns to the numbers she has been discussing.

"Didn't you say that the percentage increase in snuff dippers was from five to fifteen percent and that this represented a threefold increase?''

''Yes,'' she replies.

''But fifteen is ten more than five, and ten is twice as much; therefore the increase is two hundred percent, not three hundred percent as you had said, isn't that right?''

Dr. Hunter is immobilized. She obviously doesn't know how to respond. Finally she says that she didn't develop the numbers; there were statisticians who did that. As Jennings drives home his point, the blond juror on the right in the front row gives the defense lawyer a large admiring smile.

A little later the reporters stand outside in the hall and talk about Jennings's mathematics. There is no agreement about whether he was right or wrong.

The rest of the day is spent with witnesses favorable to Betty Marsee who each have some single point to make. Calvin Smith owns a grocery store in Ada. A mild slender man, he is nervous on the stand. Dania Braly questions him and when she asks, to preempt a charge of bias and to add a homey touch to the testimony, ''Isn't it true that your children play with our son?'' he answers ''No, ma'am.'' The attorney gets him to say that he sells U.S. Tobacco's snuff in his store and has been visited at least once a year for many years by a representative of the company. The point is that the company rep never once told him that U.S. Tobacco's products were not to be sold to minors. Jennings asks him if he sells the snuff to young people, and Smith says no.

Kim Henley, one of the Bralys' secretaries, verifies two photographs of the U.S. Tobacco booth at the World Championship Quarter Horse Show, which is held in Oklahoma City. The pictures were taken a week apart, but it was a fateful week, the week the lawsuit in this case was filed in federal court. The later picture is identical to the first one except that on the table of the company booth is a sign missing in the first picture. The sign says, FREE SAMPLE ONLY TO THOSE OVER 18. There is no cross-examination.

Next on the stand is John Zotas, a young construction worker from Texas. He is here to tell the story of his brother, Pete, a college rep for U.S. Tobacco and a snuff dipper. Pete got very worried when he developed a sore on his tongue. Walt Garrison himself came to see Pete and took him and John out to lunch. According to Zotas, Garrison said that the company would send Pete to the best doctors and pay for all his medical care. But there was one more thing. "There's no need to tell the world about this," Garrison cautioned Pete Zotas.

The monitors are turned on again and this time we get to see more than a talking head. It's a driver education film produced by U.S. Tobacco for high school courses. Starring is race car driver and U.S. Tobacco celebrity representative Harry Gant. There are many shots of him driving his race car with the words *Skoal Bandit* painted all over it. Gant talks about driver safety and there are interviews with high-school-age kids—some look as young as fourteen—about the importance of safe driving. The film ends with exciting scenes of the *Skoal Bandit* in a race. We then see a string of U.S. Tobacco commercials featuring Harry Gant in his race car. Much of this looks like the same footage as the driver training film.

One of the plaintiff's "shadow jurors" later explains what he got from the driver training film. It left a strong impression that Harry Gant was concerned above all with safety, and anything he was associated with would have to be safe.

The day ends with George Braly reading a letter to U.S. Tobacco that he found in a mountain of documents that had been handed over to him. Kevin Fowler of Jasper, Alabama, is complaining about the high price of Skoal in a letter to U.S. Tobacco. "There are a lot of us who play high school sports and use five or six cans a week. I can't quit Skoal. . . ." The company's response was to send the boy a complimentary set of cans of snuff.

The rest of the plaintiff's case continued in a similar vein. The videotaped deposition of U.S. Tobacco's then president, Louis Bantle, was chopped to pieces like Lindquist's. Bantle did say that "it's a social policy that you just don't market tobacco products to teen-agers. We never have and we never will." This despite his being quoted in a newspaper article in the 1970's saying, "We've gotten excellent sales from young people. In Texas today, a kid wouldn't dare go to school even if he doesn't use the product, without a can in his Levis.'' Bantle also tried to sidestep the impact of a written report by a company consumer-marketing representative complaining that many retailers had begun to refuse to sell snuff to minors: "A lot of our consumers are under 18 and have been smokeless tobacco users for years and now they are being turned down." The company president responded to this by saying, "I think the word 'a lot' is a bad word to use. I don't think he really knew."

Louis Bantle doesn't have the slickness of the cigarette company executives. A year before the trial he went to see Surgeon General Koop, one of the nation's leading opponents of tobacco. Dr. Koop told me, "I'll tell you how crass that guy is. He came to my office with a little leverage from somebody in Congress to tell me to lay off. He said that they had a lot of money and they'd be pleased to work with us in this research, and after all smokeless tobacco was a health benefit because you didn't get cancer of the lung, and of course the material we had on other types of cancer was absolutely without foundation. There was a strong hand there. . . . It wasn't exactly a threat. . . . Then he took out a sterling silver snuff box and put a Skoal Bandit in his mouth. I couldn't believe it. Crass."

Bantle had brought with him Nicholas A. Buoniconti, who succeeded him as president of U.S. Tobacco in 1985. Surgeon General Koop said of Buoniconti, "Here's a guy that was involved with Parents for Drug Free Youth, who received and accepted from them an award . . . and here he is prostituting himself and foisting on the youth of America the most addictive drug in our society."

Judge Russell subsequently refused to let the Bralys show the jury toy cars emblazoned with the Skoal Bandit logo. (When I got back to New York after covering the trial I found myself one day with my children at a major record store. There was a sale bin filled with caps. One that fit my six-year-old, Sam, nicely and sold for one dollar had written all over it: COPENHAGEN/U.S. TOBACCO.)

The defense case relied on a week's worth of medical experts, only two of whom were medical doctors. The thrust of the case was that the cause of tongue cancer in young people is not yet known; that it is an extremely rare and obscure disease.

The first question for the jury to decide was causation in very specific terms. Had U.S. Tobacco Company's Copenhagen snuff caused the cancer that killed Sean Marsee? The degree of certainty required in a civil case is different from that in a criminal case. From courtroom drama we are all familiar with the need to prove guilt "beyond a reasonable doubt." This is a high standard since it requires a verdict for the defendant even if the jurors strongly suspect he is guilty—as long as some doubt could remain in a reasonable person's mind. This is *not* the standard for a civil case. Here the jury should find the defendant "liable" (not "guilty") if the "preponderance of the evidence" is against him. This means that if it is more likely than not that the plaintiff has proven his case, the jury should find for the plaintiff.

George Braly felt that the jury held Betty Marsee's case to a higher standard of proof than the simple "preponderance of the evidence." Despite procedures meant to minimize it, bias plays a crucial role in legal cases, and this was a jury of people none of whom started with a settled opinion that tobacco causes cancer. No reputable scientist could agree with this, of course. The line between 50 percent and 51 percent proof of causation is sure to be found in a different place for those who have not yet accepted the overwhelming evidence that tobacco is cancer causing.

The Bralys based their appeal to the Circuit Court of Appeals for the Tenth Circuit (headquartered in Denver) on Judge Russell's refusal to let the jury see some crucial evidence. Young people in the United States did not start using snuff in a big way until the 1970's. Because it is in some ways a new product, epidemiological evidence conclusively linking snuff to oral cancer does not yet exist. There are not yet enough young snuff dippers who have died of oral cancer to prove the causal chain.

As always, the medical studies lag behind the events. But the Bralys had heard of other young snuff dippers around the country who had developed oral cancer and they were prepared to introduce evidence of eight other cases similar to Sean Marsee's. The medical records of these other young people had been made available to the Bralys' expert witnesses and they were prepared to testify that there was an epidemic of oral cancer in the making, caused by snuff. Judge

Russell would not let the jury see this evidence, saying that it was not relevant.

One thing the Bralys could do nothing about anymore was the deposition of Dr. Manning. His testimony was outrageously unresponsive; he should have been ordered by the judge to answer at least some of Braly's questions. But since the plaintiff's attorneys had not asked for this already, it could not be the subject of appeal. George Braly told me that the defense had postponed the deposition until three days before the cutoff of discovery. The Bralys had been fearful that if they asked for an order compelling Dr. Manning to be responsive, it would have delayed the trial.

Dr. Manning's testimony was extraordinary for a judicial proceeding. This was not a case of invoking the Fifth Amendment against self-incrimination—it was simply an example of resolute corporate intransigence. Furthermore, it was not an idiosyncratic response of Dr. Manning alone. He had been very carefully coached by the company lawyers—he admitted to many hours of training for the deposition. His behavior had to be the result of a carefully thought-out legal strategy. One reasonable explanation is that the director of U.S. Tobacco's research and development knew facts that were so damaging to the company that a radical approach had to be tried to avoid revealing them.

If the court of appeals agrees with the Bralys, it will probably order a new trial. The litigation could go on for years. But even if Betty Marsee loses, there will be other smokeless tobacco cases and other juries. U.S. Tobacco is exceedingly vulnerable; if it loses a single case, plaintiffs' lawyers around the country will pounce on it. Its stock will decline in value and its image will be damaged, perhaps beyond repair.

The publicity about the *Marsee* case has probably discouraged many young people from using snuff. Nevertheless, more and more boys, and girls, are turning to the product. Ironically, they see it as a safe alternative to cigarettes.

The government has finally done something about the dangers of smokeless tobacco. In the spring of 1986, Congress passed a law requiring health warnings on snuff cans and banning television advertising for snuff. Harry Gant and his ilk will no longer be telling young people to "put a pinch between gum and cheek"—at least on TV. But the magazine advertising, the college promotions, the U.S. Tobacco–sponsored rodeos and automobile races will go on.

Ironically, the Smokeless Tobacco Council, which represents U.S. Tobacco and the other snuff and chewing tobacco manufacturers, supported the federal legislation. This was not an act of altruism. Without themselves admitting that snuff can kill, they will now be able to say in future product-liability trials that people like Sean Marsee were warned and assumed the risk of using their product.

# 6

## ADVERTISING ADDICTION

Cigarettes and advertising have always gone together. Unlike soap or cereal, cigarettes would probably never have achieved a true mass market in the United States without advertising. But cigarette advertising has become an anomaly. It is so familiar that we take it for granted—not least because it's ubiquitous. Like corn flakes and baseball, the Marlboro man and his imitators flying helicopters or sitting pensively on motorcycles are embedded in the American psyche. But the familiar images carry warnings of dread diseases. The glamorous, gorgeous Virginia Slims models advertise lung cancer as well as "pleasure."

Cognitive dissonance now emanates from cigarette promotion like thick smoke. It's hard to think of the Newport theme, "Alive with pleasure," without thinking of the opposite statement, "Dead with pain.'' A 1986 Kent advertising campaign showed dark silhouettes of people wind surfing, riding a snowmobile, and dancing in a field, all against full-color backgrounds. The slogan was ''The experience you seek.''

The pictures were severely criticized by advertising professionals because the silhouettes looked like ghosts, or the outlines of accident victims that police draw on the ground, or the shadows of vaporized humans in Hiroshima. Anyway, the ads seemed to suggest death. This is a touchy subject for cigarette marketers. *Ad Week* critic Barbara Lippert described the silhouettes thus: ''Like Casper . . . these are active friendly ghosts . . . they suggest a pleasant stylish return from the hereafter.'' She wrote facetiously that the ads represented a new approach to market segmentation—aiming at ''that great untapped market: those seeking an active sporty afterlife.'' Lorillard responded to the criticism by withdrawing the ads.

Although never as much as now, cigarette advertising has always had a lot to overcome. Even when the general attitude toward smoking was favorable, it was difficult to say just why one cigarette was better than another since brands are not very different. Within the basic types—filters, low-tar filters, standards, menthols, and long cigarettes—there is little to distinguish one brand from another . . . except the differences that are invented by the creative departments of advertising agencies.

In recognition of this, the major advertising firm of Wells, Rich, Greene created a new unit in 1986, which was called the image group. Its purpose was to sell products through emotional appeals rather than product benefits. *The New York Times* said that this agency ''knows that the future belongs to the sizzle, not the steak.'' One of the members of the group, Marsha Bell Grace, told the *Times,* ''I like doing cigarette advertising. It's advertising in its purest sense—no product difference, but a perception of difference in the product.''

Many advertising professionals refuse to work on cigarette accounts, but others have no moral qualms about it. Richard Flack, who worked on the creative side of the Salem account a few years ago, told me, ''If the stupid asses want to smoke, let them. I gave it up twenty-five years ago.'' Norman Muse, former chairman and CEO of the Leo Burnett agency, said with more circumspection, "I don't smoke. I did smoke, but I don't now because it affected me. I didn't feel as healthy when I smoked." Muse, however, continues publicly to follow the cigarette manufacturers' line about cigarettes and disease.

Advertisers have never had much more to sell than the "sizzle" of cigarettes. Smokes are not like candy, or liquor, which have their own payoff. Cigarettes taste horrible to people who have never smoked and the nicotine kick is anything but euphoric. It takes a certain amount of perseverance to learn to smoke, so young people have to be motivated by peer pressure, which is generated, at least in part, by alluring advertising.

Cigarettes also present problems for habituated smokers. The minor annoyances smokers have always endured include throat irritation, shortness of breath, and a sharp decline in sensitivity to tastes and smells. Smokers who have a cold have to experience the pain of hot tobacco smoke scratching their already sore throats. To wake up in the morning with a mouth tasting like stale tobacco is one of life's small torments. On top of all this, cigarette smokers now have to put up with growing social disapproval. Hostile stares and remarks, as well as banishment to porches and hallways, are becoming the standard lot of smokers. And then there's the fear of lung cancer, emphysema, heart disease . . .

But for cigarette marketers there is one factor that counterbalances all of the negative facts about smoking. Users of Dalkon Shields got rid of them with alacrity when they were discovered to be dangerous. Everyone now shrinks from asbestos. But cigarettes continue to sell because they are addictive, and it is for that reason alone that more than 50 million Americans still smoke.

One theory of addiction holds that addictive behavior actually displaces ordinary emotions. Affective responses are all experienced through drug (in this case, cigarette) use. The cigarette at the end of the meal becomes more important than the meal itself; sex is a means to a cigarette; whenever you feel stress, happiness, fear, or pleasure, you crave a cigarette. According to this theory, smoking becomes a way of life, a substitute reality.

Advertising that taps into the addictive qualities of cigarettes can be very powerful. Put together the addict's craving and an image that reinforces it, and you have the most powerful combination known to marketing. Philip Morris has, perhaps unwittingly, given the substitute reality a name, Marlboro Country, and located it in a place that has a kind of dreamlike familiarity. The slogan "Come to Marlboro Country" is an invitation to the lotus land of addiction. The Marlboro cowboy doesn't look at the camera; he always looks off into the distance with an expression reminiscent of smokers when they light up after enforced abstinence, the self-absorbed look of an addict getting his fix.

With a few temporary exceptions, the campaign has not changed since it began in the late 1950's and it has made Marlboro the single largest-selling packaged product in the world, surpassing even Coca-Cola. Marlboro Country has made the brand the most popular in the world among both male and female smokers of all ages. The ads seem to have a powerful appeal to young people. While Marlboro had a 22.9 percent share of the U.S. market overall in 1986 (twice as much as its nearest competitor, R. J. Reynolds's Winston), it had a staggering 37 percent share of smokers under thirty-five. Marlboro is by far the most popular starter cigarette.

Philip Morris's competitors have been trying for years to come up with a formula that would have the effect of the Marlboro campaign, but without success. R. J. Reynolds, in particular, has tried macho men in all types of settings, but none of them caught on. The company even hired a former Marlboro man, Bob Beck, whose rugged looks and curly dark-blond hair were meant to make Camels a genuine competitor to Marlboros, but to no avail.

But even the only moderately successful campaigns, even the genuine failures of cigarette advertising, serve the industry as a whole. Cigarette advertising, simply because it is allowed, allays the fear of health consequences in addicted smokers and discourages them from quitting. Advertising also continually reminds people who have quit of the joys of smoking and encourages them to succumb to their nicotine cravings.

The cigarette industry was built by modern advertising and has spent vast sums to push its products. Cigarette advertising was very big business long before there was any scientific evidence linking smoking to a variety of diseases. In the period from 1925 to 1930, American Tobacco spent $75 million (in 1930 dollars), while R. J. Reynolds spent $92.9 million for ads. Half a century later, in one year, 1984, cigarette companies spent over $2 billion on advertising and promotion, more than $35 for each of the nation's 56 million smokers.

Philip Morris, with its General Foods subsidiary, now controls the largest advertising budget of any American company, over $1 billion per year. The tobacco company that is now called RJR/Nabisco is close behind. Just the tobacco advertising of these giant companies together amounts to close to $1.5 billion per year. Three other companies, Loews Corporation (Lorillard), American Brands (American Tobacco), and BATUS (Brown and Williamson), are among the top one hundred advertisers in the country.

Television advertising swallows dollars in great gulps, but Congress banned cigarettes from the airwaves in 1970. The billions go into the print media, and into promotion as well. So it is not surprising that cigarette manufacturers are the single largest group of advertisers in American newspapers and magazines, accounting currently for over 15 percent of newspaper product advertising and 10 percent of magazine advertising.

Cigarettes are also the most heavily advertised single product on billboards. Of the seven companies with the largest advertising expenditures in outdoor media in 1985, six were the members of the American cigarette oligopoly.

Major brands are "supported" by major advertising budgets. Eighty-four million dollars was spent to promote Marlboro in 1984 (a few million more than the annual budget of the City College of New York), while Kool (Brown and Williamson) was supported by a budget of over $43 million. Introducing brands costs really big bucks. Philip Morris spent $100 million, almost the entire annual ad budget of third-place Brown and Williamson, to introduce Players (not related to the English brand). RJR spends about $80 million to introduce a new brand, according to James W. Johnston, former company marketing vice president. Poor little Lorillard could afford only $40 million to introduce a women's brand named Satin.

Most new brands do not succeed, but the cigarette companies keep trying. A brand that manages to capture a 1 percent share of the market will be highly profitable, despite the huge advertising expense.

Advertising for cigarettes has taken place within a unique social context. The dire news about smoking that began as a trickle in 1950, and since then has grown into a virtual scientific tidal wave, had a paradoxical effect on the industry. In its relations with the outside world, the health news was a catalyst that drew the cigarette manufacturers into the united front of the Tobacco Institute and the Council for Tobacco Research. But the health news also rekindled fierce brand competition and led to a scramble for market share among the six companies. The biggest winner was Philip Morris, which shot from last to first place among the manufacturers.

*Forbes* magazine noted in January of 1968 that smokers could be expected to stay with the same brand for a lifetime, unless provoked to change, and "the health scare was such a provocation." Ross B. Millhiser, then president of Philip Morris, told the magazine, "The filter revolution caused more switching than all the cigarette manufacturers with all their money could have induced." Millhiser did not, of course, add that the reason for the rush to filters was the vain hope of finding some protection from the dangers of smoking.

It was because of the health scare that Philip Morris introduced, or rather re-introduced, a brand called Marlboro in 1954. The marketing dilemma faced by the company was that male smokers were alarmed by the smoking–lung cancer link and were rejecting their customary Camels and Lucky Strikes—and the brand called Philip Morris. But at the same time, filter cigarettes were seen as effeminate. Philip Morris turned to Chicago advertising executive Leo Burnett, who decided that the solution was to create an ultramasculine image to associate with the new PM filter. The cowboy was chosen as a universally recognizable figure. Thus began the Marlboro man, the lonely and rugged figure inhabiting Marlboro Country. Ironically, the brand name chosen by the company had been used before, in the 1920's and 1930's, for a women's cigarette promoted with the slogan "Mild as May."

The advertising response of the industry to the health news was either to address the issue by emphasizing low tar and nicotine or to distract smokers with images that had nothing to do with health. Both approaches had worked in developing market share, but there was much worry in the industry that anything that reminded smokers of the possibility of disease was box office poison.

Although Marlboro advertising had no association with the health issue, nevertheless Philip Morris was acutely aware of these health worries and for a while modified the ad campaign to try to deal with them. Marlboro advertising changed in response to the 1957 *Reader's Digest* article that rated cigarettes according to the amount of tar and nicotine they delivered. Marlboro was exposed as one of the dirtier filters. To counteract this, Leo Burnett launched a series of ads that showed the cowboy in poses that exuded repose, relaxation, unconcern. This was called the "settleback" campaign. John Benson, former account executive at Leo Burnett, said, "We went to 'settleback' supposedly to offer a little reassurance." The approach did not seem to work; Marlboro sales faltered. After about two years of experimentation, the Marlboro man went back to roping steers.

There are two basic purposes of advertising: brand competition and increasing the total number of consumers of a product. Competing for an increased share of the market is the main goal of the smaller brands. But advertising theory recognizes that the goal of the best-selling brands must be to increase the total number of consumers of a product as well as to hold their own against competitors. This means getting young people hooked. Starting to smoke is something middle-aged people rarely do. Most starters are in their teens.

Replenishing the pool of customers is especially important for cigarettes, since they kill 350,000 people each year, other smokers die from natural causes, and many quit each year. The manufacturers must recruit young smokers, or the industry will face extinction.

Industry spokesmen routinely deny that they market cigarettes to young people. Those who believe that there is a genuine scientific controversy about the link between smoking and disease and those who have never seen cigarette ads (which in America could only mean the blind) might believe this.

Dr. Ronald M. Davis, now director of the U.S. Office on Smoking and Health, wrote in the *New England Journal of Medicine* of March 19, 1987, "Cigarette advertisements continue to appear in publications with large teenage readerships. In 'Glamour,' one fourth of whose readers are girls under 18 years of age, cigarette advertising expenditures were $6.3 million in 1985. . . . R. J. Reynolds is the exclusive advertiser in 'Moviegoer,' a 'customized' magazine distributed free in hundreds of movie theaters nationwide. About half of those who attend movies today are less than 21 years of age. 'TV Guide,' which receives more cigarette advertising revenue than any other magazine ($36 million in 1985), informs its advertising clients that each issue reaches 8.8 million teenagers 12 to 17 years old.''

Although most of the market research that has been done by the cigarette companies regarding young people is a nest of closely guarded secrets, a few documents did surface in the late 1970's. The Federal Trade Commission issued a report on cigarette advertising in 1979 that was based on documents subpoenaed from the cigarette companies.

The report found, ''The marketing plan indicates that a primary theme for the promotion of Salem has been to associate the cigarette with the lifestyle of 'young adult males' who are 'masculine, contemporary, confident, self-assured, daring/adventurous, mature.' Marketing plans for other cigarettes are similar. A Doral campaign sought to project the image of 'an independent, self-reliant, self-confident, take-charge kind of person.' A Winston man was projected as 'a man's man who is strong, vigorous, confident, experienced, mature.' ''

Adman Richard Flack told me that the two brands in particular that try to get kids to smoke are Salem and Newport. The Salem ad graphics were purposely youth oriented, made so that they would look good in *Rolling Stone* or a record-oriented magazine. The ''Salem spirit'' campaign, which showed people who looked in their early twenties, at the oldest, having fun, was intended to make young people look at it and think, ''I want to be right there in the middle of that scene.''

The *Louisville Courier-Journal* quoted a Brown and Williamson marketing man who said, ''Nobody is stupid enough to put it in writing, or even in words, but there is always the presumption that your marketing approach should contain some element of market expansion and market expansion in this industry means two things, kids and women. I think that governs the thinking of all the companies.''

In order to deflect criticism, the cigarette companies have long agreed not to show models younger than twenty-five years old in their ads. But John Benson could not resist boasting, "I think the Marlboro cowboy dispels another myth. In order to attract young people, you've got to show young people. That's not true, not true at all." Other brands, particularly Newport, have not learned this lesson, however. Many of their models, whatever their actual age, look like teenagers.

Indeed, it was because of the youth market that Marlboro became the number one brand. In the early 1960's, when the new filter brands were jostling for market position, Marlboro's ad campaign just happened to fall into sync with the zeitgeist. John Landry of Leo Burnett says that Marlboro Country was a friendly place to young people, ages eighteen to thirty-four; it resurrected a way of life that wasn't complicated. During the Vietnam era, Marlboro was the countercultural smoke. Young people were reaching out for something, someone they could identify with, Landry says, and "Marlboro Country fit these desires, this search" that people were going through. What Landry does not say is that the inchoate yearning he refers to is a perennial condition of adolescence.

Using sports to promote products is extremely effective in selling to young men, including teenagers. *Sports Illustrated*, one third of whose readers are boys under eighteen, earned a whopping $29.9 million from tobacco advertisements in 1985 alone. United States Tobacco has consistently increased its snuff sales by hiring football players, race car drivers, and soccer stars to endorse Skoal or Copenhagen, its two largest-selling brands. Cigarette manufacturers have agreed not to use sports stars, as they used to, to endorse their products. But if the manufacturers cannot use sports stars, they can and do use sports. Cigarette billboards are clearly visible in stadiums across the country, some placed so that they will often appear on television, thus defeating in one small but important field the purpose of the ban on broadcast advertising of cigarettes.

RJR/Nabisco boasted of its "leadership in sports marketing" in its 1986 annual report: "During the year [1986], an estimated 25 million spectators attended the more than 1,400 events sponsored by R. J. Reynolds Tobacco USA. The company is a leading corporate sponsor of American motor sports—stock cars, sports cars, drag racing, and motorcycle racing.'' Reynolds also sponsors golf, including the Vantage Cup events. The firm is particularly proud of its association with NASCAR, the stock-car-racing association: ''Under a long term agreement, the company sponsors the Winston Cup Series, including the $1 million Winston Bonus. Instituted in 1985, the Winston Bonus goes to any driver winning at least three of the four major events on the NASCAR Winston Cup circuit—the Daytona 500, the Winston 500, the World 500, and the Southern 500.''

Camel was the sponsor of the World Cup soccer championship in Mexico City in 1986. Nabisco is a major supporter of tennis, sponsoring the Nabisco Grand Prix, a seventy-three-tournament tour.

The companies use sports to promote their products. An example was the case of the ''Camel Scoreboard.'' In 1981, R. J. Reynolds decided that Camel ads in newspapers would be in the form of the Camel Scoreboard. This was a listing of team rankings for a variety of sports printed in an elaborate scoreboard format that was actually a Camel advertisement. The ad would include statistics that were normally in the sports pages. Hundreds of newspapers were presented with this plan in 1981. Some newspapers did not like this plan, perhaps because it was such a blatant pitch to teenaged boys. But they were no match for R. J. Reynolds. The Camel Scoreboard was a take-it-or-leave-it proposition. There would be no other Camel ads for those newspapers. The Camel Scoreboard must have worked. Philip Morris later came out with the Marlboro Sports Calendar.

If young people are essential to the future of the cigarette industry, women are critical to the present. Tobacco use has historically been predominantly a male habit, and when cigarettes were mass-marketed in the early part of this century it was simply assumed that most smokers would be men. Until the late 1920's it was considered illicit to advertise cigarettes to women, as it is now to advertise to young people. One of the first ads aimed at women coyly showed a young woman without a cigarette, but with a man (presumably a boyfriend) who was smoking; she says, ''Blow some my way.''

By the late 1920's women had become what an earlier generation would have called brazen. The cigarette companies started going after women with unashamed, if often inept, marketing strategies. In the late twenties it appeared that women were resistant to the color of the Lucky Strike pack, a dark shade of green. George Washington Hill, then czar of the American Tobacco Company, was advised to change the color of the pack. He refused and instead embarked on a campaign to make women like green. He tried to make the fashion industry adopt green as the color most preferred by fashionable people.

One of the well-publicized events in this campaign was a Green Fashion Luncheon with a menu that featured green beans, asparagus salad, pistachio mousse glacé, and crème de menthe. There were other aspects of the campaign that proved how fertile were the imaginations of the tobacco marketers. American Tobacco supported symposia of psychologists to discuss the implications of the color green in the area of mental health. All the implications were said to be favorable. Artists gathered to discuss the use of green in the works of the great masters and found that they approved heartily of the use of the color. Mrs. Frank Vanderlip, a prominent socialite, sponsored a Green Charity Ball—paid for by American Tobacco—at which all who attended had to wear green gowns.

Ultimately the strategy did not work. Women could not be made to like the green pack. But when World War II came, American Tobacco saw its chance to change the color of the package. The company held a large parade in New York where it proclaimed that "Lucky Strike green had gone to war." The implication was that the dye used for the green packs was being sacrificed to dye uniforms. This was pure hype. The reason for the change was simply to get women to smoke Luckies.

The industry is finally getting close to reaching its goal of female equality in smoking, albeit in a reduced pool of smokers. The percentage of females as well as males who smoke continues to decline, but the decline is much more precipitous among men. In 1965, some 52.4 percent of men over twenty years old smoked, while in 1986, the percentage had dropped more than twenty points, to 29.5 percent. Among women over twenty, some 34.1 percent smoked in 1965, while by 1986 the figure had dropped only about ten points, to 23.8 percent.

Until the late 1970's, women of all age groups smoked proportionally less than men, but this trend has been reversed. Among people up to age twenty-four, including teenagers, the percentage of female smokers now is higher than male smokers. Among graduating high school seniors in 1985, about 21 percent of girls smoked, while only 18 percent of boys did so. Among college students the disparity was even more glaring. Eighteen percent of females smoked, compared to only 10 percent of males.

Lung cancer rates have already begun to reflect the change in smoking patterns. The rate of this deadly cancer has begun a significant decline among white males, while increasing among both black and white females. In 1985 lung cancer surpassed breast cancer as the number one cancer killer of women in several states, including California.

When women's liberation began to change women's perceptions in the early 1970's, Philip Morris was right in there with a new brand called Virginia Slims. The brand's slogan, "You've come a long way, baby," said it all. This ad campaign brilliantly associated smoking with exciting careers, sexual freedom, and all the improvements in women's lives promised by the women's liberation movement.

For those women who were not quite bold enough for Virginia Slims, there were other female brands with names like Silva Thins, More, Eve, Satin, and Ritz. The packages and cigarette papers are often designed to appeal to women. Eve has a flower design on its filter tip, Satin has a satinlike paper tip, and Ritz bears the logo of Yves St.-Laurent on its package and filter.

Although the women's brands are highly visible (they demonstrate the manufacturers' commitment to the women's market), most women smokers buy brands that appeal to men as well. Oddly, more women smoke Marlboro, that most "masculine" of brands, than any other cigarette. This despite the brand's calculated appeal to men.

Some of the creative people at Leo Burnett believe that women relate even more to the Marlboro man than men do. John Benson says, "We ran a 'country store' promotion [where the company advertises boots, spurs, jackets, and so on] and we had an order blank in it. We got a letter from three girls in Texas ordering a cowboy. I think that [Marlboro] advertising has great appeal to women."

Whatever the psychological subtleties of the appeal of feminine or masculine ads, there is no ambiguity about the business rationale for targeting women. When sales of an R. J. Reynolds brand called More, a brown cigarette, lagged, the company decided in 1980 to "reposition" the brand to make it appeal to women. Sales then took off. Among the promotion tricks was the Ebony Fashion Fair, which traveled around the country showing the latest fashions to women, especially black women, and at the same time promoting More cigarettes. *The Wall Street Journal* reported on October 6, 1986, that free More cigarettes were given out to spectators and the brand was pushed at every opportunity: "As model Kym Thomas makes her exit in a Jackie Rogers black and gold backless evening dress, she stops to take a puff. 'She smokes More cigarettes,' intones a sultry-voiced commentator in one of several plugs throughout the show."

As a women's cigarette, More had spectacular growth, according to RJR senior executive Gerald Long. In a further refinement, to appeal to younger women, the company produced a beige cigarette called More Light, and targeted the advertising at young women.

For all the money and thought spent on them, ad campaigns sometimes come up with unintended double entendres, in either image or slogan. The Satin slogan was "Spoil yourself with Satin." The American Council on Science and Health, an outspoken anticigarette organization, commended this in its newsletter as the first truthful cigarette ad, because "our dictionary defines 'spoil' as 'to damage seriously; ruin; to impair the quality or effect of.' What better way to describe a product which harms the lungs, heart and other organs, stains the teeth and fingers, promotes wrinkles, fouls the breath, and leaves an unpleasant odor on hair and clothing. Certainly the more than 300,000 Americans who died last year of smoking related diseases were 'spoiled' by cigarettes."

The cigarette companies, led by Philip Morris, have used promotions as well as advertising to create a favorable image of smoking among women. One of the most successful efforts has been the funding of women's tennis through the Virginia Slims tournament. This has earned the company, and the brand, a great deal of favorable attention. Most of us like to be fooled a little, to be convinced that people are a little bit better than they seem. It's appealing to see the Virginia

Slims tournament as an example of corporate generosity, but in fact it is just another example of clever marketing. Virginia Slims means tennis, which means health, fun, the outdoors.

In addition to women and young people, the merchants of death have singled out minorities for special treatment. Blacks are a good market for the cigarette makers. The National Center for Health Statistics showed that as of 1986, a higher percentage of blacks smoked than whites, 32.5 percent compared to 29.5 percent for men, and 25.1 against 23.7 percent for women. It's not surprising that blacks smoke in higher proportions than whites, because they are special targets of cigarette promotion. In all packaged goods these days, the name of the game is segmenting the market, and the cigarette companies have done an effective job of it.

Cigarettes are heavily advertised in black-oriented magazines such as *Ebony, Jet,* and *Essence.* In 1985 cigarette companies spent $3.3 million on advertisements in *Ebony* alone. According to *The Wall Street Journal,* between 1980 and 1986 neither *Ebony* nor *Essence* published an article directly about smoking and health, although the subject has been mentioned in general health articles.

Philip Morris has published a *Guide to Black Organizations* filled with cigarette ads featuring black models. The tobacco industry has used its charitable contributions to make many friends among black leaders. "What's more important; that the United Negro College Fund receives hundreds of thousands of dollars in contributions from R. J. Reynolds for scholarships or that it advertises in one of the fund's publications?" James Williams, a spokesman for the NAACP, asked a *New York Times* reporter.

The vulnerability of nonprofit organizations to such blandishments is obvious. "I don't see any of the people who are criticizing us for accepting money beating down a path to our doors offering contributions," said Williams.

The use of the small "eight-sheet billboard," which measures five by eleven feet, is a very effective way to reach minority groups, according to Dr. Ronald Davis, head of the U.S. Office on Smoking and Health. It is usually placed low and close to the street. Children, in particular, are much more likely to see billboards than magazine ads. In 1985, Dr. Davis has written, tobacco companies spent $5.8 million for advertisements on these billboards in black communities, accounting for 37 percent of total advertising in this medium.

Three brands account for more than 60 percent of the total of cigarettes smoked by blacks. They are Kools, manufactured by Brown and Williamson; Newport, a product of Loews Corporation's Lorillard subsidiary; and Salem, an R. J. Reynolds product.

The cigarette companies have also been heavily involved in civic, cultural, and entertainment promotions aimed at blacks. Brown and Williamson sponsors the Kool Achiever's Award for adults who are working to improve life in the inner city. The prize for this award is a donation of ten thousand dollars to the nonprofit organization of the winner's choice. Black organizations, including the NAACP, have been involved in selecting winners of the award. In November of 1985, Philip Morris hosted ninety-three publishers of black newspapers in New York for a forum on preserving freedoms in American life.

According to Dr. Alan Blum, founder of an antismoking organization called DOC (Doctors Ought to Care), this was one of several such meetings in recent years arranged by Philip Morris at which it presented its case for continued support. When the giant cigarette maker placed $25 million in life insurance with a black-owned Harlem-based insurance company, it could not fail to win friends.

It's no wonder that the members of the Black Newspaper Publishers' Association went on record opposing a ban on cigarette advertising even before their white counterparts. But the decision was taken after a long meeting and it could not have been comfortable for many publishers. It should be noted that Burrell Advertising of Chicago, one of the largest black-owned-and-operated ad agencies in the country, refuses any cigarette accounts on grounds that it does not want to promote an unhealthy habit among blacks.

The cigarette companies have also targeted Hispanics in their advertising and promotion. In fact three cigarette brands with Spanish names have been introduced in recent years. They are Rio, Dorado, and L&M Superior. Of the top ten companies advertising in Hispanic markets, two are cigarette companies: Philip Morris is number one and R. J. Reynolds number ten. In 1985 cigarette companies spent $1.4

million for advertisements on eight-sheet billboards in Hispanic neighborhoods, more than twice the amount spent for liquor advertising, which was the next most heavily advertised product. The brands most heavily advertised to Hispanics were Newport, Winston, Camel, and Salem. Philip Morris published a guide to Hispanic organizations filled with cigarette ads in both English and Spanish.

To the dismay of much of the print media, the cigarette companies have quietly shifted large hunks of money from advertising to promotion. In 1975, some 25.5 percent of the advertising and promotions budgets of the companies was spent on promotions, while by 1984, the figure had increased to 47.6 percent.

Cigarettes are sold not only by ads, but by a great variety of promotional techniques. The common goal of all promotions is to make friends for cigarettes and smoking. Promotions run the gamut from coupons for two dollars off a carton of Winstons passed out in the streets of Oklahoma City, to donations to the Metropolitan Museum of Art in New York.

The gifts always have strings, although they are not always obvious. Those getting the free coupons are giving the cigarette manufacturers their names and addresses for massive mailing lists that allow the companies to locate their markets and prepare for a possible ad ban. Museums that had received grants had been asked to lend their credibility to the cigarette cause by opposing local nonsmoking ordinances.

*The Philip Morris Magazine* is a single multimillion-dollar promotional effort. This glossy quarterly, edited by the staff of the *Saturday Review,* has a circulation said by the company to be 5 million. It is distributed free to more people than get *Time* or *Newsweek,* at a current net cost to the company of $1.75 million per issue. The purpose of the magazine appears to be to give comfort and support to embattled smokers (it's also probably a way of compiling a giant mailing list of smokers in case cigarette ads get banned).

Having its own magazine allows Philip Morris to promote the image of smoking, and it loses no opportunity to do so. When journalist Eric Sevareid, an elder statesman of the broadcast media, wrote an article for the magazine about the American spirit, it was accompanied by a photograph of Sevareid with a lighted cigarette firmly placed between the fingers of his right hand. Sevareid was appalled. He had quit smoking years ago and firmly believed that it was a deadly habit; he had never even seen the picture of himself with cigarette that *PM Magazine* had found in some photo archive. When I asked him why he had written an article for Philip Morris, he told me that he had wanted very much to write on the subject of the American spirit, that the magazine had paid him very well, and that Philip Morris was now a large diversified conglomerate, wasn't it, not just a tobacco company.

United States Tobacco, the snuff maker, has supported NASCAR, the National Association for Stock Car Auto Racing. The company sent exhibits to shopping malls that featured the *Skoal Bandit* exhibition race car on display, autograph sessions with driver Chuck Brown, and free samples of Skoal.

At the other end of the social spectrum, George Weissman, retired CEO of Philip Morris, was elected chairman of the board of New York's Lincoln Center for the Performing Arts. This giant arts complex on Manhattan's West Side is a mecca for music lovers from around the world. In February of 1987, a huge banner advertising the Marlboro Country Music Festival (Dolly Parton, Alabama, the Judds) hung in front of Lincoln Center. The banner had the red and white triangular logo of the Marlboro brand, the same typeface, and even a surgeon general's warning! A few years before, PM had pulled off one of the most prestigious PR events of all time, with its support of the art exhibit entitled ''Treasures of the Vatican.'' One photograph, proudly published in the *U.S. Tobacco and Candy Journal,* reaffirmed for the tobacco world its own legitimacy: Nancy Reagan, Terence Cardinal Cooke, Philippe de Montebello, director of the Metropolitan Museum, and George Weissman of Philip Morris, all smiling together.

Brown and Williamson, with less exalted contacts, merely sent a group of musicians around the country to twenty military bases to play a series of concerts called the Kool Super Nights.

The industry has formed something called the Tobacco Heritage Committee, whose members are the chief executive officers of the seven largest producers of tobacco products (the cigarette six and U.S. Tobacco). According to the Tobacco Institute's publication, the *To-*

*bacco Observer*, this committee has "underwritten the architectural creation of a Treaty Room and its antechambers in the Department of State building." The companies subscribed $1.2 million toward the total $2 million cost of the Treaty Room suite. "The new rooms feature carvings of tobacco leaves, blossoms, and seed pods at the base of the vertical moldings. . . ." To make sure official Washington knew of the tobacco largess, the committee members hosted an inaugural reception right there in the U.S. Department of State, on October 1, 1986. How to win friends and influence people . . .

The vast amounts of money spent by cigarette companies have had a profound effect on the reporting of the story of smoking and health. The facts about smoking and the power and actions of the tobacco industry are by any measure critically important news for the American public. In a country that is deeply concerned about potential exposures to toxic chemicals and intensely worried about cancer, one would expect that news about smoking would be ubiquitous and that every new study of its harmful effects and the efforts of the tobacco industry to promote it would be front-page news. Furthermore, the irony of the growing wealth of the tobacco industry contrasted with the great number of tobacco-related deaths should provide grist for innumerable editorial mills.

Yet we rarely read about the hazards of smoking. And it's not that everyone knows the whole story. While there is a general impression that smoking is bad for you, most people still do not know just how bad it is. According to the FTC, most people know that smoking causes lung cancer, but few know that lung cancer is one of the deadliest forms of the disease—few survive it. Most people do not know that more people die of smoking-related heart attacks than lung cancer. Not many people know of the more exotic dangers of smoking—the vascular damage that results in thousands of leg amputations each year, or the thousands of babies that die because their low birth weight due to their mother's smoking is the extra contributing factor that kills them. And the list goes on and on. . . .

Coverage of the industry itself has been very thin in magazines. One of the major tobacco stories of 1986 was totally ignored by the newspapers and magazines that one would expect to cover it. When

Laurence Tisch bought a controlling interest in CBS and became its chief executive officer, it represented in effect the takeover of a television network by a tobacco company. Tisch got the money for the deal from his Lorillard subsidiary, whose income dwarfs the other subsidiaries of Tisch's Loews Corporation.

There is nothing new about the kid-gloves treatment meted out by the media to the cigarette industry and the story of smoking and disease. There were charges as early as 1938, and continuing thereafter to the present time, that newspapers, magazines, and the broadcast media failed to report adequately about cigarettes. The *Columbia Journalism Review* twice (in 1963 and 1978) surveyed media coverage of the story and found it wanting.

The American Council on Science and Health (ACSH) conducted a survey of eighteen magazines in 1982 to determine how well they covered the hazards of smoking and to explore the role that cigarette advertising might play in editorial policy. The study showed clearly that of the magazines surveyed, the best coverage of smoking and health was presented in those that did not accept cigarette advertising.

In January of 1986, the American Council asked me to supervise another of these studies. The goal of the study was to assess the reporting of smoking as a health hazard in a select group of nineteen magazines, some of which accept cigarette advertising and some of which don't. The following magazines were surveyed:

| | |
|---|---|
| *Cosmopolitan* | *Prevention* |
| *50 Plus* | *Reader's Digest* |
| *Glamour* | *Redbook* |
| *Good Housekeeping* | *The Saturday Evening Post* |
| *Harper's Bazaar* | *Self* |
| *Ladies' Home Journal* | *Seventeen* |
| *McCall's* | *Time* |
| *Mademoiselle* | *US News & World Report* |
| *Ms.* | *Vogue* |
| *Newsweek* | |

Researchers looked at every issue of these magazines for a five-year period beginning on January 1, 1980. The number of articles about smoking was counted—as was the number of articles about other health topics. There was much hard news about smoking during this period. It became clear that lung cancer would soon overtake breast cancer as the number one cancer killer of women; the surgeon general went on record saying that smoking is the principal cause of heart attack and emphysema; smoking was shown to cause cervical cancer; it became generally accepted that smoking by pregnant women can harm a fetus. The danger of tobacco smoke to nonsmokers began to be taken seriously for the first time.

Of all the magazines surveyed, five had good coverage of the dangers of smoking. These were *Reader's Digest* (which has carried on an antismoking crusade for many years), *Prevention, Good House-keeping, The Saturday Evening Post,* and *Vogue.* Among these, only *Vogue* accepts cigarette ads.

The award for the worst coverage of smoking had to go to *Cosmopolitan.* This magazine had no articles, even small ones, about smoking in the survey period, but had fourteen articles about food and health. Some of the mentions of smoking in other articles were misleading. For example, in an article entitled "Uncovering the Secrets of Health and Disease" the author said that reduction in smoking (as well as cholesterol levels and blood pressure) does not reduce the risk of heart disease, which, he said, is caused mainly by stress. Scientists are in general agreement that the main cause of heart attack in middle-aged women is smoking. Furthermore, women who take birth control pills and who smoke run a very high risk of heart attack.

*Cosmopolitan* finally did run an article about smoking, in January, 1986. Although it was outside the survey period, it was particularly noteworthy because it was a "good news" piece. Once every few years a study is published that has something good to say about smoking. *Cosmo* picked up on a study that appeared to show that heavy smokers have a lower risk of endometrial cancer than nonsmokers. In its only pronouncement on smoking in five years, this women's magazine told its readers that female smokers can "take a modicum of comfort" from this study. There was no mention in the article of the fact that lung cancer is not only more prevalent, but far more deadly than endometrial cancer, nor of the great risks of contracting other diseases incurred by women who smoke.

*Ms.* magazine, for many the flagship of feminism, managed to report about smoking in one story that was less than half a page in length—in five years. In that same period, the magazine carried four long stories on food and health and six on stress and health. Even in articles that are not directly on smoking, but must mention the taboo topic, it was rigorously underplayed. In an article about heart disease and cancer, only two sentences were devoted to lung cancer. They stated accurately that "smoking causes about 85% of lung cancer among women, who are, despite such evidence, starting to smoke at a younger age." Nothing else was said. A 1984 article entitled "Do You Jog Beside a Freeway?" advised women to "limit the intake of cigarettes, alcohol, and saccharin"—making smoking seem harmless, if done in moderation. Another article warned, "It makes no sense to smoke or take pills to lose weight." These bland pronouncements contrast with the current congressionally mandated warnings, which are far bolder.

The case of *Ms.* is particularly disturbing because the magazine has set itself up to be a trendsetter in women's issues. In its initial policy statement in its first issue, *Ms.* declared that it would refuse ads for products that "might be harmful." In a self-congratulatory mood, *Ms.* once called itself "the undisputed leader in reporting on women's health."

Writer Marie Shear reported in the *Women's Review of Books* on March 6, 1985, that in the 151 issues of *Ms.* published to that date, there were *583* pages of cigarette ads—"but no articles or letters to the editor about smoking except for a single children's short story and a single letter from a child in 1976. (Therefore it is not quite true that *Ms.* has *never* published anything on smoking as some critics have said.)"

Of the newsweeklies surveyed, *Newsweek* scored the best. Of six stories about cancer, four mentioned smoking and two of these featured smoking very prominently. The magazine also published a story about smoking and other lung diseases, unlike the other newsweeklies. Nevertheless, given the fact that smoking is the number one preventable cause of death in our society, *Newsweek*'s reporting was scanty. Of course, it had a lot to lose; cigarettes were a major source of the magazine's advertising revenue.

*Time*'s coverage was not as good as its chief rival's. It did have four stories about smoking and health (two shorter than half a page), but smoking was rarely mentioned in other health-related articles. For example, in a total of twenty-two stories about heart disease, smoking was mentioned in only one. In a total of five stories about cancer, smoking was not mentioned at all. If one read only *Time*, one would never know that smoking can complicate pregnancy and adversely affect a fetus, since smoking was not even mentioned in any of the eight stories that *Time* ran on subjects relating to human reproduction.

In the earlier ACSH survey, the dollar amount of advertising revenue for each magazine was considered. But no correlation was found between the percentage of tobacco advertising in a magazine and its coverage of smoking and health. There was, however, and continues to be a strong indication that the fact of acceptance of cigarette advertisements has a significant effect on the coverage of the hazards of smoking.

The data of the 1986 survey show that magazines that accept cigarette ads are less likely than magazines that don't accept them to report on the hazards of smoking. A few editors have stated publicly that they do not want to offend their tobacco advertisers. Helen Gurley Brown, editor of *Cosmopolitan*, told *The Washington Post* (as reported on December 11, 1985), "Having come from the advertising world myself, I think, 'who needs somebody you're paying millions of dollars a year to come back and bite you on the ankle?' "

Most editors are not so frank. When charged with keeping the story of tobacco and health out of *Sports Illustrated*, editor Mark Mulvoy told the *San Diego Tribune* (November 21, 1986), "It's absolutely wrong." Yet his accuser, Dr. Gregory N. Connolly, director of dental health for the Massachusetts Department of Public Health, had overwhelming evidence of the magazine's complaisance toward tobacco. Dr. Connolly said that he had been invited by the magazine's baseball editor, Steve Wulf, to write an article about the decision of members of the Kansas City Royals to stop using smokeless tobacco. Wulf approved the article, but it was then rejected by Mulvoy, according to Dr. Connolly. What's more, Dr. Connolly reviewed *Sports*

*Illustrated*'s record of health-related articles and found them totally lacking in information about cigarettes or smokeless tobacco.

In a letter to Mulvoy, Dr. Connolly wrote, "From 1982 to mid-1986, *Sports Illustrated* ran 15 health stories of which five were on cocaine abuse, four on sports injuries, and two each on steroid use, heart disease and physical fitness. In the 15, tobacco was mentioned in only two. . . . In the story on physical fitness and adolescent health (2/7/83) lack of exercise and poor diet were cited more than 150 times as causes of cancer or heart disease, but tobacco was mentioned only 4 times. The story incorrectly stated that coronary bypass surgery is the main reason for the recent decline in deaths from heart attacks. According to the American Heart Association, the principal reason is the sharp decline in smoking by adult males."

Dr. Connolly's suggestion that the magazine publish a "front page picture" of Babe Ruth along with an explanation that the great baseball player's fatal oral cancer had been caused by his tobacco chewing was, of course, not well taken by Mulvoy.

When writer James Fallows proposed a story to *The Atlantic* on the influence of cigarette advertising dollars on the reporting of the story of smoking and health, it was turned down by his editor, supposedly because it was not "newsworthy." Editor William Whitworth told *Washington Post* writer Susan Okie that he would publish an article about smoking if it revealed something such as "smoking caused leprosy or something besides . . . heart disease and lung cancer." Stories about cigarettes or the tobacco industry seem to have to pass a higher standard of newsworthiness than other topics.

The connection between cigarette ads and the lack of stories on smoking was brought home to me very graphically in the course of the ACSH study. One day I was looking over the data sheets that had been filled out by the researchers and I noticed that the magazine *50 Plus* had a poor record of reporting about smoking: only four stories, all of them less than half a page, in four years. What made this puzzling is that *50 Plus* had been commended by ACSH in its previous survey for its excellent reporting on the subject. I called the magazine and found out from its advertising director, John Parker, that the magazine had begun accepting cigarette ads in January of 1982.

*Vogue* is an exception to the rule. Although it accepts cigarette ads, it has a good record of reporting on smoking and health. Its editor, Grace Mirabella, is married to thoracic surgeon William G. Cahan, who is a veteran anticigarette activist. Mirabella told me that everyone in the editorial department was aware of the hazards of smoking and concerned about it. But also, she said that she was completely insulated from the concerns of the advertising side of the business. What has often been called the "Church and State" separation was strictly observed at *Vogue*.

But *Vogue* is one of the nation's consistently most successful magazines. Unlike the vast majority of publications, *Vogue* needs the cigarette makers' ads less than they need the magazine. Interestingly, *Vogue* receives letters every day from readers protesting its accepting cigarette ads.

Not included in the survey, but more typical of marginal magazines that take cigarette ads, is *New Woman*. A health writer for this publication, Dr. Holly Atkinson, told me that her attempts to include smoking in her stories are scratched out by her editor's red pencil. "If I put smoking on a list of factors that cause heart disease, for example, my editor will either put it at the end of the list or drop it altogether. She was getting pressure from the folks in advertising."

Cigarette advertising exerts an irresistible influence on many editors. The story of smoking and health is grossly underreported not because of overt threats of retaliation from Winston-Salem or Park Avenue, but rather as a kind of self-censorship imposed by editors who are fearful of offending cigarette advertisers. The presence of cigarette advertising seems to exert a "chilling effect" on the free flow of information about smoking and health.

Indeed, it can cost a lot of money to be outspoken. *Newsweek*'s June 6, 1983, issue, which included a long article on the nonsmokers' rights movement, carried no cigarette ads. When the cigarette companies learned of plans for the story, they asked that their ads be removed. The magazine may have lost as much as $1 million in advertising for publishing that story.

Cigarette money doesn't just inhibit editors from printing articles about smoking, it also creates a barrier to antismoking advertisements.

Dr. Kenneth Warner wrote in the *New England Journal of Medicine* (February 7, 1985) that Grace Reinbold, president of Worldwide Media, reported difficulties in placing ads for antismoking clinics. Of thirty-six national magazines that she contacted, twenty-two absolutely refused to run the ads, but would not say why. *Psychology Today* told Reinbold, "We have a lot of money that comes in from tobacco companies, and frankly, we don't want to offend our advertisers." *Cosmopolitan* explained its refusal without adornment: "[A]m I going to jeopardize $5 or $10 million worth of business?"

The effect of all that cigarette money is a kind of creeping self-censorship that touches all aspects of publication. Between 1983 and 1985, *Newsweek* published three advertising supplements written by the American Medical Association. For *Newsweek,* the business purpose of these was to attract advertisers, like drug companies, that ordinarily would not advertise in the magazine. The first supplement was 32 pages long and included 16.3 pages of advertising worth about $1 million. The AMA earned about ten thousand dollars for writing each of these "advertorials," as they were called by the magazine. The theme of the supplements was how people could be healthy by choosing a healthy life style.

There was virtually no mention of smoking in the first and third supplements, and only five paragraphs in the second, about 4 percent of the text. In a section on heart disease in the third supplement, the decline in deaths from heart disease (25 percent since 1970) was attributed to "advances in medical technology and greater public attention to proper diet, exercise, and lifestyle." Any knowledgeable scientist or doctor would readily fill in "smoking" for "lifestyle" and place it where it belongs, at the top of list, but the ordinary reader could be forgiven if he gleaned from the text (officially prepared, after all, by the American Medical Association) that smoking has nothing to do with heart disease.

In the section on cancer, there is a relatively detailed step-by-step explanation of how women can do a breast self-examination to detect breast cancer. Way back near the end of the section is a short paragraph that mentions the increase in lung cancer among women and mouth cancer among teenagers—due to the increase of cigarette smoking among women and use of smokeless tobacco by young people. But the good old family doc of the AMA discreetly declines to suggest that people stop smoking. After all, the magazine has lots of cigarette ads and cigarette executives might get mad and take their money elsewhere.

Of course, many experts sent angry letters about the supplements to the AMA and to *Newsweek*. Dr. Elizabeth Whelan, executive director of ACSH, called the supplements "a classic case of disinformation. It is like representing yourself as an auto safety expert and writing a supplement on 'how to reduce your risks of death and injury on the road' and purposely avoiding any reference to seatbelts and the risks of drunk driving, instead focusing in depth on the desirability of getting your windshield wipers changed frequently."

Dr. Kenneth Warner, professor and chairman of the University of Michigan's School of Public Health, wrote to Dr. James Sammons, executive vice president of the AMA, "I have little doubt that hundreds of thousands of Americans are smoking today because the AMA has lacked the courage or conviction to have its most visible public actions conform to its formal policy, which is largely publicly invisible. As a public health professional, I am appalled. Were I a member of the AMA, I would be deeply ashamed." Dr. John Richards, Jr., assistant professor of family medicine at the Medical College of Georgia, wrote, "If an organization could be sued for malpractice, there would be a good case here to support gross negligence."

Self-censorship and toadying to the cigarette companies extend beyond magazines and sometimes find new and exotic forms. Barry Ackerly, owner of a radio and four television stations and, even more important, of one of the largest billboard companies in the country, proved his loyalty to tobacco in 1986. He sent out a memo to all his operations telling them to reject public service announcements of the American Heart Association and the American Cancer Society, because the organizations had called for a tax increase on cigarettes and a ban on all tobacco advertising.

There is another and more personal reason why the story of smoking and health is underreported. If publications are addicted to cigarette advertising revenue, many editors are addicted to cigarettes themselves. On being asked why he has never commented on the subject, a very well known conservative social critic wrote in a personal letter, "I have never addressed the issue of cigarettes and health, probably because I am something of a chain smoker and prefer not to think about it."

# 7

# BANNING CIGARETTE ADVERTISING–THE MAGIC BULLET?

The cigarette companies are now facing a challenge unthinkable only a few years ago—they may lose their right to advertise. The promotion of a product that is both deadly and addictive and has no redeeming value is starting to seem unjustifiable, almost obscene. The Virginia Slims woman with her saucy smile, the Marlboro man who looks like he would rather kiss his horse than the Virginia Slims woman, the happy crew of the Merit yacht, the Newport kids doing crazy things, and the Salem woman of whom we only see the legs—all these may be consigned to what the Marxists call the dustbin of history.

Although a few countries have already banned cigarette advertising, including Norway, which has a total ban, and France and Italy, which have partial bans, it seemed highly unlikely that such a move could happen in the United States—until December of 1985. Then the

House of Delegates of the American Medical Association called for a complete ban on cigarette promotion and committed the AMA to work for it.

This action had a great impact not only because the AMA is a formidable lobbying force in Washington, but also because it had never been a leader in the antismoking movement. Long considered overly cautious on smoking by some, it was thought to be downright friendly to the tobacco industry by others (the AMA had opposed warning labels on cigarettes initially, saying they weren't needed, and didn't divest cigarette company stocks until 1981). If the AMA advocated a ban, it meant that the idea had entered the political mainstream.

Some of the regular antismoking organizations, including the American Cancer Society and the American Lung Association, had been outflanked, but they moved quickly. They too called for an ad ban. Congressman Henry Waxman, chairman of the Health and Environment Subcommittee of the House Energy and Commerce Committee, scheduled hearings on cigarette advertising for the summer of 1986. Other congressmen and some senators took an interest in the issue. It suddenly seemed like an idea whose time had come.

There were, of course, many objections to the idea of an ad ban. Anguished warnings were uttered in the print media that an ad ban would be the first step on the road to totalitarianism. Even some commentators who said terrible things about cigarettes and the industry defended cigarette advertising. Michael Kinsley, writing in *The Wall Street Journal,* said, "The philosophy of the First Amendment is that it's better to let good and bad ideas do battle with confidence that the good ones will usually win out, than to put the government in the business of sorting the good from the bad." He then went on to say that he was no friend of tobacco. The freedom of expression of the tobacco companies ought to be protected just like "the American Nazis, pornographers, and others on a similar moral level."

An ad ban would be a clear and present danger to the American way of life, according to Joe Epley, of Epley Associates/Public Relations of North Carolina (whose client just happened to be Philip Morris U.S.A.). He wrote a memo to his fellow PR practitioners warning, "It may be tobacco today, but tomorrow it could be food, or hospitals, or typewriters. In short, free commerce as we know it could become a relic of the past.''

Professor Burt Neuborne, former legal director of the American Civil Liberties Union, denounced the ad ban as government-imposed censorship. He wrote that all censorship arises from "paternalistic zeal to shield others, presumably less enlightened Americans, from speech that one or another pressure group thinks isn't particularly good for them.'' Neuborne quit the ACLU on July 1, 1986, and wrote and delivered testimony against the ad ban idea on behalf of the Tobacco Institute the following month.

The American Medical Association took the constitutional concern seriously enough to commission a study of the issue by two eminent constitutional scholars, Professors Vincent Blasi and Henry Paul Monaghan of the Columbia University School of Law. Although they found it easy to decide that a ban would be constitutional, the debate was not stilled. Many people continued to assume that an ad ban was unconstitutional.

Philip Morris ran a series of ads in 1986 promoting an essay contest about the First Amendment and cigarette advertising. The text of the ad implied that advertising was fully covered by the First Amendment and had never been "infringed on" by the government. This is quite false. There have been a number of important efforts to regulate cigarette advertising. The Federal Trade Commission was given the authority to regulate false and misleading advertising in 1938 and stopped misleading cigarette claims twenty-five times between 1938 and 1968. Congress has passed three laws mandating warning labels since 1965, first on cigarette packages and then on advertising as well. The 1970 law banned cigarette advertising from radio and television. None of this regulatory activity is possible against expression that is protected by the First Amendment.

The biggest change for cigarette advertising came when the weed was drummed off the air. In 1969, the cigarette companies had spent four out of five of their advertising dollars on television. This medium is universally held by advertising professionals to be by far the most effective way to reach people, especially young people. But in the late 1960's the Federal Communications Commission, prodded by the legal action of antismoking activist John Banzahf, applied the Fairness Doctrine to cigarette promotion. Soon the air was filled with antismoking spots, which proved spectacularly successful. Indeed, the effect of the antismoking spots wasn't just to present a viewpoint contrasting with the cigarette ads; they seemed genuinely to counteract the advertising and change the public's perception of smoking. The percentage of people smoking began to decline for the first time since the health scare of the early 1950's.

By the time Congress seriously considered banning cigarette advertising from TV, the industry had already decided not to fight the ban. If there were no TV ads, there would be no counteradvertising. And, in any case, television advertising had probably reached the point of diminishing returns. Both the costs and the controversy made television of doubtful value. When the final vote came, the lobbyists for the broadcasting industry found themselves alone in the legislative trenches, abandoned by the cigarette manufacturers, who went along with the ban. The broadcasters by themselves could not stop it.

They did try to challenge it in court, claiming that the ban on cigarette advertising on TV was an unconstitutional infringement of free speech, a violation of the First Amendment. The courts had no trouble with this. Unlike the print media, the airwaves are public property, they said, and thus what is broadcast is subject to regulation in the public interest.

Like many other challenges to cigarettes, the TV ad ban was turned to great advantage by Philip Morris. This company was prepared. Then President Joseph Cullman told *Business Week* on January 27, 1973, that his company had been planning for an ad ban: "We knew a few years in advance that there was a strong possibility of a TV ban . . . and we knew that we would have to make some changes." The company's response began back in *1967*. Philip Morris did a computerized study of all its sales outlets to determine exactly how many cigarettes were sold by each one. To meet the demand quickly, the company acquired sixty-five new warehouses across the country and increased its sales force from 450 to 900. PM made up for the loss of television by convincing its retailers to push PM brands.

The conversion of cigarette advertising from television to print was a major challenge for advertising agencies. It opened up the competition between the companies in the same way that the health scare and resultant rush to filters had. The biggest beneficiary of the TV ad ban was Philip Morris's main brand, Marlboro. It just happened that the Marlboro Country campaign translated to print effortlessly. The images that had worked so well on television also worked in newspapers and magazines.

The same could not be said of the brand's biggest competitor, R. J. Reynold's Winston. The TV campaign of this brand was based on the slogan "Winston tastes good like a cigarette should." The advertising professionals agreed that the print campaign for Winston could not be based on the slogan; it had to be said out loud to work. Since that time, Winston has been a brand in search of a theme. It was the ability of Philip Morris to take advantage of the health scare of the fifties and the ban on television ads that eventually catapulted this company from last place among the six American cigarette manufacturers to first place.

In the two years after the broadcast ban took effect, 1971 and 1972, the industry spent far less on advertising than before. While antismoking activists savored their victory in getting cigarette ads off the airwaves, the companies saved hundreds of millions of dollars. They took advantage of the enforced savings to invest in other businesses, sparking a major round of corporate diversification.

By 1975, the industry had returned to big spending on advertising, but there were some problems. The first warnings, mandated by Congress in 1966, required labels only on cigarette packs. When the government imposed warning labels on cigarette ads in 1972, the creative people had to do some thinking. It didn't take Marlboro long to work out its strategy to minimize the warning. Earl Glass, a Leo Burnett art director, says, "We try to keep the warning label away from the packs. We don't want the warning label right under the pack. Some other brands put the warning at the top right where you first see them. We try to keep them at the bottom, and below the pack."

But the early worries about the warnings were later allayed. As Jim Oates, a Leo Burnett account executive, noted in 1986, "The warning has been a minor thing to deal with."

Although the TV ad ban inaugurated an era of expanded profits for the biggest of the cigarette makers, it also tore the fragile and important aura of legitimacy that had once blessed cigarettes with its presence. The ban probably hastened the growing awareness that smoking was harmful. Advertising became harder and harder, more of a challenge. As one public relations man said recently, defending cigarettes is now the Mount Everest of public relations. More money had to be spent, and it was. From 1974 to 1984, total advertising and promotional expenditures increased from 1 cent per pack sold to 3.3 cents per pack sold (in constant 1974 dollars).

By the late 1980's, cigarette advertising had become ubiquitous. The cigarette, the most dangerous product on the market, was the most heavily advertised.

The idea of banning all cigarette advertising and promotion in the United States did not occur to more than a handful of visionaries before the late 1970's (Norway banned cigarette ads in 1977). But when it finally did, it ran smack into contemporary Supreme Court decisions protecting advertising under the First Amendment. Even if it was politically possible, an ad ban would have to undergo rigorous constitutional scrutiny.

A ban on cigarette advertising could be challenged under the First Amendment to the Constitution, which states, "Congress shall make no law . . . abridging the freedom of speech." These ten words, part of a larger guarantee of religious liberty, freedom of the press, and the right of assembly, are the perennial subject of lawyerly debate.

Few theorists (the late Justice Hugo Black, however, was one) have believed that *all* speech must be free from regulation. Obscenity may be banned (once it's defined), and words that incite a mob to violence may be outlawed. The government may regulate within reason the time, place, and manner of speech. The citizen's right to speak out on political matters is inviolate, but one cannot speak in the middle of a busy street.

But all of these qualifications are exceptions to the general rule of free speech, a rule that historically applied only to expressions of political and social ideas. Commercial speech was not thought to be covered by the First Amendment.

148

When the Federal Trade Commission was given the right to deal with unfair and deceptive business practices in 1938, deceptive advertising became a prime target. In 1942, the Supreme Court mentioned in the case of *Valentine* v. *Chrestensen,* almost as an afterthought, that commercial speech was not protected by the First Amendment. This makes sense, since for government to regulate false advertising, it must first make the distinction between truth and falsity in statements made in advertising. It is precisely this inquiry that the government may *not* make in regard to expressions of social and political ideas.

Until 1976 there was not the slightest doubt that advertising had no First Amendment protection at all. Then the Supreme Court was presented with a case that cried out for a remedy. The Virginia legislature had passed a law forbidding pharmacists from advertising the price of prescription drugs. In the case of *Virginia Board of Pharmacy* v. *Virginia Citizens Consumer Council*, a Virginia resident who had to take prescription drugs on a daily basis and two nonprofit organizations sued the state of Virginia, claiming that the First Amendment entitled them to receive information regarding drug prices that the pharmacists wanted to communicate to them through advertising.

The Court began its analysis of the case by noting that this was *not* a question that involved information of "public interest," that is, information that might have some bearing on constitutional rights. The court had recently decided the landmark case of *Bigelow* v. *Virginia*, where it had overturned a Virginia ban on advertisements for out-of-state abortions. But the pharmacy case did not involve information regarding actions that were specifically protected by the Constitution, as had the abortion case. The ideas to be communicated in this case were purely commercial; the essence of the communication was, in the words of the Court, "I will sell you the X prescription drug at the Y price."

Justice Harry Blackmun, who became the Court's leader in pushing for "commercial free speech," wrote the opinion in this case and explained that the distinction between speech that is fully protected by the First Amendment and that which is not depends on the content of the speech, not the motive of the speaker. Even if the only purpose of the expression is financial gain, it may be protected. A corporation's expression of a political view intended to further its economic interests, for example, is fully protected (this is the legal niche into which R. J. Reynolds is attempting to put its controversy ads). But in the pharmacy case, the content of the speech was purely commercial; it did no more than propose a commercial transaction.

But there was another element to be considered, Justice Blackmun said. Ordinarily, freedom of speech is thought of as a right belonging to the person who is doing the speaking. But it also protects the right to receive information. For example, citizens have a First Amendment right to receive political publications from abroad. Justice Blackmun declared that "if there is a right to advertise, there is a reciprocal right to receive the advertising."

The Court leaned heavily on the value to the plaintiffs in the case of receiving the information that the druggists wanted to advertise. In Richmond, the price of one prescription drug varied from $2.59 to $6.00; in Newport News, tetracycline sold for $1.20 in some places and $9.00 in others. A law forbidding pharmacists to advertise their prices made comparison shopping very difficult, particularly for the elderly and infirm.

This was one of those cases that just cried out for a remedy. Justice Blackmun wrote, "Those whom the suppression of prescription drug price information hits the hardest are the poor, the sick, and particularly the aged. A disproportionate amount of their income tends to be spent on prescription drugs, yet they are the least able to learn, by shopping from pharmacist to pharmacist, where their scarce dollars are best spent." The opinion went on to say that advertising, even if it is tasteless and excessive, is nonetheless dissemination of useful information regarding "who is producing and selling what product for what reason and at what price." This is important information in our free-market economy, more important to some people than political and social ideas, and therefore should enjoy some First Amendment protection

In any First Amendment analysis of a challenged law, the Court must consider the state's interest in making that particular law. Here the state of Virginia claimed that the law was necessary to foster a high degree of professionalism among pharmacists by keeping the public ignorant of the advantages of low-cost and presumably less "professional" pharmacists. Blackmun found this approach "highly paternalistic." It is better, he wrote, to assume that price information is not in itself harmful, and that people will perceive their own best interest if only they are well informed.

Some governmental restrictions are permissible, even if this one wasn't, the Court ruled. Like "pure" free speech, which is fully protected by the First Amendment, commercial speech can be regulated as to time, place, and manner. But commercial speech may also be banned if it is false, misleading, or deceptive. The Court said, in one of those pronouncements that have been used in countless briefs since, "The First Amendment as we construe it today does not prohibit the state from insuring that the stream of commercial information flows cleanly as well as freely."

Justice Blackmun got carried away with the extremely appealing facts of this case and made a statement that was later to plague the Court in a series of commercial speech cases. He declared, "What is at issue is whether a state [and by analogy Congress] may completely suppress the dissemination of concededly truthful information about entirely lawful activity, fearful of that information's effect upon its disseminators and its recipients. Reserving other questions, we conclude that the answer to this one is in the negative."

William Rehnquist, then an associate justice, wrote a stinging dissent in this case. Sounding a theme that would become his constant refrain in similar cases, Justice Rehnquist said that the First Amendment was intended to protect speech related to public decision making. Only speech regarding political, social, and other public issues should be protected. The First Amendment did not, he wrote, protect the right to information that would help in deciding "whether to purchase one or another type of shampoo." He warned that the effect of the majority's ruling would be to overturn the ban on cigarette advertising in the broadcast media that the Congress had passed in 1971, unless the advertisements were specifically found to be deceptive.

Justice Rehnquist might have been right about this, but the cigarette companies had accepted the TV ad ban and were not about to initiate litigation with all its uncertainty in order to get restored to them the right to pay the networks vast sums of money. The broadcasters were not in a good position to sue. After several years of hard times, they had finally gotten free of their addiction to cigarette advertising dollars. As they had been burned by the cigarette companies once, they were unlikely to take any more risks.

Because of the strong language of the *Virginia Pharmacy* case, other commercial speech cases found their way to the U.S. Supreme Court in the late 1970's and early 1980's. Some of these cases were brought on behalf of speech that just seemed like it shouldn't be protected, and the Court had to pinch some of the bloom off *Virginia Pharmacy* in order to uphold laws that restricted commercial speech.

In *Ohralik* v. *Ohio Bar Association*, a 1978 case, the Court was presented with the question of whether the First Amendment protected an attorney whose speech consisted of a personal solicitation of clients. Albert Ohralik had approached the victims of an automobile accident, both young women, one while she was still in the hospital, and persuaded them to become his clients. Later both women fired Ohralik and filed a complaint against him with the bar association. The lawyer was put on indefinite suspension from the practice of law by the Ohio Supreme Court. He appealed to the U.S. Supreme Court, claiming that his solicitation of the two women was protected speech and was constutionally indistinguishable from the type of lawyer advertising that the Court had recently considered in the case of *Bates* v. *State Bar of Arizona*. In that case, the Court had held that truthful advertising of "routine" legal services was protected by the First Amendment.

Ohralik's cause was not very appealing to the Supreme Court. It just did not seem possible that the First Amendment was intended to protect a classic case of ambulance chasing. The Court, speaking through Justice Lewis Powell, declared, "We have not discarded the common-sense distinction between speech proposing a commercial transaction which occurs in an area traditionally subject to government regulation and other varieties of speech." The Court went on to cite laws that had been properly upheld restricting expression in the commercial context involving securities transactions, corporate proxy statements, and employers' threats of retaliation for the labor activities of employees.

The Court held in the *Ohralik* case that the government had the power to regulate Ohralik's conduct in solicitation of clients "in furtherance of important state interests." Maintaining standards among members of the licensed professions was held to be such an interest. The point was, the Court said, that the speech in question was merely a subordinate component of a business transaction. The idea here was that there could somehow be a distinction between "speech" and action.

A year after *Ohralik,* the Court considered a case, *Friedman* v. *Rogers,* that involved a Texas law forbidding optometrists to practice under a trade name. In upholding the power of the state to prohibit this type of commercial speech, the Court seemed to negate much of its holding in *Virginia Pharmacy.* Justice Blackmun, the author of that case, dissented from the majority opinion in this case. In his view, the Court wrongly allowed Texas to prohibit "the dissemination of truthful information about wholly legal commercial conduct."

Justice Powell, writing for the majority, attempted to distinguish optometrists' trade names from pharmacists' prices. He said that the type of advertising held to be protected by the First Amendment in *Virginia Pharmacy* had been "self-contained and self-explanatory" while optometrists' trade names had "no intrinsic meaning," no informational content, and it was the *information* transmitted by commercial speech that invoked the First Amendment. In any case, because trade names could be deceptive and because the state had an important interest in prohibiting deceptive advertising, it could ban the use of optometrists' trade names.

After the *Virginia Pharmacy* case, some legal commentators had agreed with Justice Rehnquist that the already existing ban on broadcast advertising of cigarettes was invalid. But the *Friedman* case, decided only three years later, changed all that. Professor Daniel A. Farber wrote in the *Northwestern Law Review* that "as a practical matter, cigarette advertising may be subject to almost complete suppression as a result of *Friedman.*"

By early 1980, the Court had managed to create massive confusion regarding its new doctrine of commercial free speech. It was impossible for anyone other than the Court itself to reconcile cases as disparate as *Virginia Pharmacy, Ohralik, Friedman*, and several others.

While the focus of the Court's concern was on the distinction between commercial and noncommercial speech, the real problem lay elsewhere. Characterizing a lawyer's statements as a "subordinate component," as the Court did in *Ohralik*, or a trade name as having "no intrinsic meaning," as in *Friedman*, demonstrated what Professor Archibald Cox said was "the futility of attempting to maintain a general constitutional distinction between commercial advertising and commercial activity." What was "speech" and what was "action"? Wasn't the question itself more appropriately addressed by philosophers, who could confine themselves to the realm of ideas, than by judges, who must deal with the nitty-gritty of real life?

Even more serious than the confusion the Court had generated was the specter of the Court substituting its judgment for the more democratic decisions of the legislative branch in economic matters. For the first thirty-eight years of this century, the Supreme Court had followed a theory called "economic due process," which resulted in the Court's invalidating on constitutional grounds many laws designed to better the conditions of working people. State laws prohibiting child labor, for example, were found to be an unconstitutional infringement on the rights of employers. Much of the early New Deal legislation was invalidated under this concept. "Economic due process" is universally discredited and no longer has any supporters. Liberals have always deferred to the legislative branch of government in economic matters, and conservative legal theorists of our era hate the idea of an activist judiciary (as a reaction to the liberal and activist Earl Warren Court).

The Warren Burger Court was extremely uncomfortable about being charged with undue judicial activism under the guise of extending First Amendment protections. But it was nevertheless determined to give commercial speech *some* protection. It finally found a systematic way to do it in a case arising in New York State. *Central Hudson Gas and Electric Company* v. *Public Service Commission of New York* involved a utilities company that had been ordered by the state agency that regulated it to stop sending out written notices promoting the use of electricity. This was at a time when the country was going through an oil shortage and the government was urging conservation.

Seven justices of the Supreme Court decided that the agency's ban was a violation of the First Amendment (only four could agree on an opinion; three filed concurring opinions in which they reached the same result by slightly different reasoning). Justice Rehnquist, as usual, dissented. He still had not bought the idea that any commercial speech was entitled to protection.

The *Central Hudson Gas* case finally brought together the disparate threads of reasoning about commercial free speech and will probably be the most important case in this field for many years to come. If there is a ban on cigarette advertising and it is challenged in court, it will have to pass muster under the reasoning of this case.

The Court rejected the "highly paternalistic" view that government had the "complete power" to suppress or regulate commercial speech (exactly what Justice Rehnquist thought the government did have the power to do). Quoting from its opinion in *Virginia Pharmacy*, the Court declared that "people will perceive their own best interests if only they are well enough informed, and the best means to that end is to open the channels of communication rather than to close them."

The "open channels" argument is a staple of ordinary First Amendment theory. But the Court finally realized that the issues involved in regulating advertising are different from other free-speech issues. Citing *Ohralik,* the Court stated that it had always recognized the commonsense distinction between speech merely proposing a commercial transaction, which occurs in an area traditionally subject to government regulation, and other varieties of speech.

Justice Powell, writing the Court's opinion, stated explicitly that the Constitution offers a lesser protection to commercial speech than to other, more traditionally guaranteed forms of expression. The degree of First Amendment protection of commercial speech turns on the nature of both the expression *and* the governmental interest served by its regulation.

The Court reiterated its holding in *Friedman* that the First Amendment's concern for commercial speech is based on the informational function of advertising. Messages that do not accurately inform the public of lawful activity are not protected. Also, "the government may ban forms of communication more likely to deceive the public than inform it."

If the advertising is not misleading, the government can restrict it only in order to promote a "substantial" interest. (Fully protected speech, by contrast, can be restricted only if there is a "compelling state interest," which has been intrepreted to be a very strict standard. Yelling "Fire!" in a crowded theater is a classic example of speech that can be banned.) Furthermore, the type of regulation that would restrict commercial free speech must be designed carefully to achieve the government's goal. If the law was too broad and there was another more limited way of getting to the desired result, the law would be found invalid.

In *Central Hudson Gas,* the Supreme Court finally tried to systematize its First Amendment analysis of commercial free speech with a "four-point analysis" that has been used in many cases since. This is the Court's analysis:

> At the outset we must determine whether the expression is protected by the First Amendment. For commercial speech to come within that provision, it at least must concern lawful activity and not be misleading. Next, we ask whether the asserted governmental interest is substantial. If both inquiries yield positive answers, we must determine whether the regulation directly advances the governmental interest asserted and whether it is not more extensive than is necessary to serve that interest.

Since *Central Hudson Gas* there have been a number of Supreme Court decisions involving commercial free speech, and they have all been decided on the basis of the four-point analysis. The most important for the cigarette industry was the case of *Posadas de Puerto Rico Association* v. *Tourism Company of Puerto Rico.* The Court's views on commercial free speech had changed so much that Justice Rehnquist finally got to write the opinion of the Court, while Justice Blackmun, the original exponent of commercial free speech, was one of three dissenters (the others were Justices Thurgood Marshall and John Paul Stevens).

The Court upheld a Puerto Rico law forbidding the advertising of gambling aimed at residents of Puerto Rico, while allowing it if aimed at nonresidents. The Puerto Rico legislators wanted "the tourists to flock to the casinos to gamble, but not our own people." The Court found this to be a "substantial government interest" and also held that the law that had been passed to implement it was not more extensive than necessary to achieve its goal.

The Court considered the argument often expressed by the cigarette industry that the government does not have the power to prohibit the advertising of a legal product even if the government does have the power to prohibit the product itself. According to this argument, the power to prohibit a product or activity is the lesser power; the power to prohibit its advertising is the greater power.

Justice Rehnquist specifically rejected this argument. If the government has the right to prohibit something, it necessarily follows that it has the "less intrusive" right to reduce demand for it by prohibiting advertising. In an unusual congruence of legal reasoning and common sense, Justice Rehnquist went on to say that "it would be a strange constitutional doctrine" that would concede to the legislature the authority to totally ban a product or activity, but deny to the legislature the authority to ban advertising for a product. As examples, the opinion cited "legislative regulation of products or activities deemed harmful such as *cigarettes*, alcoholic beverages, and prostitution [emphasis added]." These may be banned outright or authorized in some limited fashion; advertising for them can be banned. If the legislature has the power to ban something, the First Amendment does not prohibit "the intermediate step" of banning advertising for it.

Justice Rehnquist's mention of cigarettes was "dicta." It was not an essential part of the Court's opinion, but merely illustrative. Therefore it does not have the force of law carried by the "holding" of a case, which is the rule on which the case is decided. But Supreme Court dicta are often clues to what the Court is thinking. The *Posadas* decision came down on July 1, 1986, a little more than six months after the AMA had called for a ban on cigarette advertising. It heartened those who were in favor of the ban and brought forth much wringing of hands from the advertising industry (although little comment from the cigarette industry).

Writing about the advertising industry in *Advertising Age*, Steven W. Colford said that the reaction to *Posadas* was "gloom, doom, and uncertainty over how proposed bans on tobacco and alcohol advertising might be treated by the Court." Colford quoted noted First Amendment lawyer and advertising industry advocate Thomas McGrew, who said, "The Court may not have reversed itself by 180 degrees [from the *Virginia Pharmacy* decision], but it certainly did turn 179 degrees." David Versfelt, counsel to the American Association of Advertising Agencies, told *Ad Age,* "It's a dark day for Madison Avenue."

Nevertheless, an advertising ban on cigarettes would have to pass the four-point analysis of the *Central Hudson Gas* case. The discussion would probably go something like this:

The first argument on behalf of a ban is that cigarette advertising is misleading by its very nature. The very existence of cigarette advertising lends an aura of legitimacy to cigarettes. Citizens may, and do, conclude that if cigarette smoking were actually proven to be harmful, the government wouldn't allow it to be advertised. Images of young healthy people smoking cigarettes make it seem that smoking is not only acceptable but desirable and healthful. Furthermore, health warnings do not make the advertising *not* misleading.

Indeed, if cigarette advertising were not misleading about the health issue, the cigarette companies would not advertise. The truth about cigarettes is that they are addictive, cause a multiplicity of illnesses, and have no beneficial properties whatsoever. Ninety percent of those who smoke say they would quit if they could. Truthful ads would scare away potential customers who do not have a strong death wish.

Even under the most extreme view of First Amendment protection for commercial speech, the government has the power to ban misleading advertising, to ensure that "the stream of commercial information flows cleanly as well as freely."

The problem with this argument is that "deception" is usually thought of in terms of *statements*. Advertising for an oven that says it is self-cleaning, when in fact it is not, is a clear example of deception. A cigarette company ad that says that smoking has not been proven dangerous, if it is found to be commercial speech at all, can be banned as deceptive. But what about an ad that says no more than "Alive with pleasure" or "The experience you seek"? What about that Marlboro man with the chaps and spurs who is the strong silent type? He doesn't say anything at all, let alone anything deceptive.

Common sense tells us that the purpose of cigarette ads is to associate attractive images and cigarettes in the mind of the viewer. Many, if not most, judges will not find this "deceptive." In a case involving liquor advertising, a judge wrote that Americans were bombarded with advertising everywhere and it was not the business of the courts to protect citizens from the excesses of Madison Avenue.

If cigarette advertising is not found misleading by its very nature, the judges would have to look at the government's interest in banning cigarette promotion. This should present no problem. Reducing the demand for cigarettes would result in a decrease in smoking and its related toll of death and disease. This would also reduce the need for costly medical care, much of it supplied by the government through Medicare and Medicaid. These are certainly "substantial governmental interests."

The next two parts of the *Central Hudson Gas* test take a little more thought. Does the ban on cigarette advertising advance the asserted government interest? That depends on whether an ad ban would actually reduce the prevalence of smoking. This would be hotly debated. The cigarette companies maintain that advertising is solely for the purpose of convincing smokers to change brands, and it does not get people to begin to smoke.

Here the experience of foreign countries that have banned cigarette advertising is sure to be closely scrutinized. What evidence there is suggests that an ad ban does not affect adult smoking patterns, but does reduce smoking among young people. William McCarthy, a UCLA research psychologist, said many studies have shown that where ad bans are instituted, as in Norway, there is little effect on adult smokers already addicted to nicotine. "But you do see a decrease in the number of kids who start by about 50%. In other words, only one-half the kids you would expect to start will start," he told *Advertising Age* on August 8, 1986.

Courts have addressed the issue of the effectiveness of advertising in several cases involving state restrictions of liquor ads. The Tenth Circuit Court of Appeals remarked in the case of *Oklahoma Telecasters Association* v. *Crisp*, "The entire economy of the industries that bring these challenges is based on the belief that advertising increases sales." The Fifth Circuit Court of Appeals said in the case of *Dunagin* v. *City of Oxford, Mississippi*, "We simply do not believe that the liquor industry spends a billion dollars a year on advertising solely to acquire an added market share at the expense of competitors."

What makes people smoke is a very complex question, but most people, including most judges, would find it hard to dispute that advertising, at least in the United States, is a significant factor. Therefore, banning cigarette advertising would serve the asserted governmental interest.

But *Central Hudson Gas* requires that another point be considered. Is a ban on cigarette advertising more extensive than necessary to serve the asserted governmental interest (to reduce smoking)? The cigarette companies would argue that the present warning labels are sufficient and that the decline in rates of people smoking are proof of this. But the government could counter this by saying that the rate of smoking among young people is still too high and is not decreasing fast enough. The government could also argue that a total ban on cigarette promotion would remove the seal of legitimacy that advertising seems to convey about smoking. The late Senator Maurine Neuberger wrote in 1962, "The mere continuation of massive cigarette advertising campaigns acts as an implied assurance or warranty of the safety of cigarettes to a people who have learned to expect that what is advertised may not really be a bargain, but will, at least, not kill you."

Given the retreat from commercial speech protection since *Virginia Pharmacy* and the *Posadas* case, and the growing recognition about just how unhealthful cigarettes are, it is more than likely that a ban on cigarette advertising and promotion would be held constitutional. Several bills have already been introduced to do just that. The United States is not the only country considering such a ban. *Advertising Age* recently reported that the movement to restrict cigarette advertising has begun in the Netherlands, Argentina, Australia, South Korea, Singapore, Hong Kong, Brazil, New Zealand, and the United

Kingdom. The government of Canada announced in April of 1987 that it would introduce a bill in Parliament to ban cigarette advertising in that country.

Banning cigarette advertising is beginning to seem like the right thing to do—morally right. Even a conservative from a tobacco state finds the idea appealing. Senator Strom Thurmond has said that he would have no objections to a ban on cigarette advertising, at least if it was coupled with a ban on advertising for alcohol.

But beyond the moral correctness of an ad ban, there is a very important practical question. What would an ad ban do to or for the cigarette industry? The industry is already a kind of financial black hole, a whirlpool of cash, sucking more and more companies into its grasp. The first effect of an advertising ban would be to allow the cigarette makers to save between $1.5 billion and $2 billion each year. At the same time, their sales would be only marginally affected, at least at the beginning.

Against this has to be balanced the usefulness to the industry of advertising. Barbara Lippert of *Adweek* criticized the Kent campaign that had silhouettes of people against full-color backgrounds because the silhouettes looked like ghosts. Her magazine gave the Kent ghosts campaign an "award" as one of the worst ads of 1986 and said about it, "Scary visuals made the product seem as lethal as a nuclear blast."

Lorillard withdrew the ads and replaced them with pleasant, brightly colored scenes. I saw them looming over the entrance to Madison Square Garden when I took my children to the circus and, except for the fact that they were cigarette ads put in a place where thousands of children would see them, thought that they were very pretty.

But Lippert used the ads to make a larger point. She wrote in the February 9, 1987, issue of her magazine, "Basically there's a hollow part to all cigarette advertising. Because of the reality of the Surgeon General's warnings, changes in health awareness and ad restrictions the cigarette industry must observe there's little left to say. . . . Whether we have one more couple windsurfing or yukking it up on a gorgeous beach, there is no *there* there. It doesn't jibe with what we know about smoking."

Lippert articulated something very perceptive about cigarette advertising: "All ads can do is try to give a good feeling about 'the experience you seek.' And if most smokers could choose, and effortlessly be relieved of the habit, they'd spend those special moments on the beach, at a bar or wherever—without a cigarette."

When cigarettes were banned from the broadcast media in 1971, it was because the companies agreed to the ban. The reason they agreed to it was because the antismoking ads that were aired as a result of the Fairness Doctrine appeared to be working. How could a relatively small number of public service messages, produced on budgets not comparable with cigarette ad budgets, overwhelm the effect of a billion dollars' worth of cigarette ads?

To answer this question we have look at the work of media guru Tony Schwartz, who also happens to hate cigarettes. In 1961, ten years before the TV ad ban, Schwartz produced the first antismoking TV spot the American Cancer Society ever sponsored. The message, which later won many prizes, simply showed two small children trying on grown-ups' clothes, playing. The voice-over said, "Children imitate their parents. Children learn by imitating their parents. Do you smoke cigarettes?" The girl then looked at the camera and giggled while on the screen came the words "American Cancer Society."

Joyce Jones, in 1961 a New Jersey housewife and mother, recalls seeing the spot while smoking a cigarette in front of her two children. "I remember the exact moment when I saw the spot," she told me. "It really scared me. I thought of my kids; I wanted to be with them, to see them grow up." She quit smoking within days.

Schwartz has written a book called *The Responsive Chord* in which he argues that the goal of advertising is not to transmit information from a sender to a receiver, but rather to awaken a thought that is already in the viewer's mind. Schwartz does not know Joyce Jones, but he did get right into her mind and awaken her latent fear of smoking-related death.

By now most Americans know that smoking is harmful. Most people don't know just how harmful it really is, but they have a negative feeling about it. It is relatively easy to awaken this latent feeling with antismoking spots. But advertising for cigarettes, on the other hand, goes against the grain. When Lippert says there is no *there* there, she is saying that there is no positive chord about smoking in viewers' minds that can be struck by cigarette ads.

The cigarette companies still try, but they recognize the problem. In 1981, a Brown and Williamson senior vice president for marketing, Scott Wallace, explained that the advertisements for the new Barclay brand were meant to recall a time when people did not have negative thoughts about smoking. He said then, "The idea was to harken back to when smoking was really a pleasure; to the day when the person at the next table wasn't complaining to the maître d'. . . ." By 1984, the *U.S. Tobacco and Candy Journal,* the trade magazine of tobacco distributors, lamented, "There is no question that the cigarette manufacturers are losing the all-important battle for the social acceptability of their product." It was clear, the editorial said, that the "antismoking forces" were winning the battle for the consumer's mind. Joseph Kolodny, dean of tobacco distributors, warned in 1984, "The sharp diminution of the status of cigarettes as a fashion symbol [is] an acutely challenging industry problem."

The belief that smoking is harmful has penetrated Marlboro Country itself and embarrassed the real Marlboro man. Former adman Norman Muse reported an incident in a bar in Sheridan, Wyoming, when he and some cowboys were taking a break from shooting Marlboro ads (the Leo Burnett agency uses real ranch hands, not models, for the ads). A man Muse dismisses as "a drunk" came up to the cowboys and said, "Don't you feel guilty about prostituting yourselves to sell cigarettes?"

The industry has responded to this rising tide of negativity by aiming at those segments of the population who are least likely to have made up their minds about smoking—the young and the uneducated. As Dr. Blum of the anticigarette organization DOC notes, smoking is rapidly becoming a blue-collar phenomenon. At Harvard, only 2 percent of entering students smoke cigarettes. Advertising dollars are following this shift and upscale magazines like *Vogue* and *Newsweek* are being abandoned by the cigarette companies in favor of *Field and Stream* and *Popular Mechanics.*

The cycle of cigarette usage is thus coming full circle. Before the big national brands were taken up by the middle classes starting around

World War I, cigarettes, often hand rolled, were the poor man's smoke. By the late 1980's, cigarette smoking is once again becoming associated with the least glamorous elements of society. Advertising seems powerless to change this trend.

Not only has advertising been unable to stop the erosion of cigarettes' image, but it has also proved ineffective in changing brand preferences. By 1985, industry watchers were reporting that less than 10 percent of all smokers switch each year. Nearly $2 billion seems a high price to pay for this.

The cigarette companies cannot voluntarily forgo advertising. They still compete with each other and no one can afford to give the others an edge. But they have undoubtedly been preparing for the possibility of an ad ban, as Philip Morris did for three years before TV was closed to cigarettes. There are some aspects to an ad ban that would suit the companies very well.

Most important, if cigarette advertising were totally banned, it would be extremely difficult to introduce a new brand. An ad ban would be an almost insurmountable barrier to entry into the cigarette market. At the same time, it would be almost impossible for an existing brand to take away market share from another existing brand. The current brands would be frozen into their market shares for the foreseeable future. To paraphrase Governor George Wallace, Marlboros today, Marlboros tomorrow, Marlboros forever.

Of course, much would depend on the specific law that got passed. Congressman Michael Synar's aim now is a total ban on all promotion, but it is likely that some kind of compromise will be reached that would allow some types of promotion. What these might be was suggested in an article in the business magazine *Media and Marketing Decisions*. The author, Rebecca Fannin, asked knowledgeable marketing people what strategies the cigarette companies might follow if their ads were banned. There were some imaginative suggestions. Hire the novelists Judith Krantz and Danielle Steel to write about jet-setters who would show the glamour of smoking, one expert suggested, or pay production companies to introduce brands on TV shows and movies (this has already been done in *Superman II*, which featured a Marlboro truck).

Buy a mountain, one marketer suggested, build a luxurious ranch, and promote visits to the Marlboro Mountain through direct mail. Even the smaller companies could do this kind of thing. A mountain would cost much less than the $43 million Brown and Williamson spends to advertise Kools each year.

Other suggestions included greatly expanding coupon promotions, offering coupons redeemable for two dollars off the next carton purchased and so on. Young people smoke more if cigarettes are cheaper, so these promotions would help boost sales to them. The industry could go back to premiums that would be redeemable for anything from stainless steel flatware to vacations in the Bahamas.

One marketer warns that "point-of-sale space would become very precious." Retailers' decisions about displaying brands would be extremely important. Philip Morris and R. J. Reynolds would of course have a great deal of clout with the retailers since these companies own General Foods and Nabisco.

The package that is put at the point of sale could be a selling device itself. RJR/Nabisco began marketing tests in April of 1987 for a new cigarette in a package that showed a glittering chrome logo with the brand name MAGNA spelled out in bold script against a cherry-red background. *The Wall Street Journal* reported that the "macho design looks more like the nameplate on a flashy sports car or motorcycle than a cigarette pack." Philip Morris tried out a menthol brand it called PM Blues in a royal blue pack with green stripes and a reflective brand of silver foil encircling the brand name. The *Journal* quoted New York packaging consultant Jonathan Prinz, who said, "Packages are looking younger because the companies want to attract younger smokers."

A direct-mail marketer named Dan Ginsberg said that it would be possible for a brand to gain market share even if advertising were banned, but it would take a highly sophisticated direct-mail campaign. "It might require as many as five or six mailings. You might drop a postcard alerting them of news of a new brand. Then, for instance, if it were Marlboro, you might mail them a statue of a cowboy. A follow-up mailing could be another statue, maybe of the horse. Then perhaps a replica of the cigarette pack followed by the product itself. Finally you could deliver a coupon good for two more packs and then a questionnaire to get their consumers' insights into the product.'' It could well be that the real purpose of the expensive *Philip Morris Magazine* is to compile a mailing list of smokers against the day when ads are banned.

There are in Washington today a range of proposals regarding new laws to restrict cigarette advertising. The Synar bill would simply ban all cigarette advertising and promotion, period. Senator Bill Bradley of New Jersey and Congressman Pete Stark of California have introduced a bill that would not ban advertising, but would prevent the cigarette companies from deducting advertising expenses from their income tax.

There is another legislative option that may become viable. In the 1965 law requiring the mild warnings on cigarette packages, the industry managed to get a major concession. A clause was inserted forbidding the states to regulate cigarette advertising (the federal preemption clause). This provision was originally temporary but was made permanent in the next warning label act, of 1971. The effect of the clause is twofold. It takes almost all power away from the states when it comes to cigarette promotion (the exception is billboard regulation, for constitutional reasons) and it also has been used to stop product liability lawsuits. This clause could be repealed, leaving cigarette advertising to the mercy of the fifty state legislatures.

Ironically, what seems like the most severe and far-reaching measure, a total ad ban, is really the mildest alternative for the industry. What's important to the managements of the cigarette companies is growth and profits. An ad ban would immediately add hefty chunks to the bottom line and provide the wherewithal to acquire new businesses, which would allow for future growth. The savings would also allow more capital to be put into expansion of foreign markets. It is evident that the only immediate hope for expansion of cigarette sales is abroad, particularly in the Third World where there is little or no public awareness of the hazards of smoking, no government regulation of advertising, and no warnings.

The Bradley-Stark proposal would genuinely hurt the industry. Because of competitive pressure, the cigarette companies would have to continue to advertise, but it would cost them far more than it does now. The disadvantage of the proposal is that it would allow them to continue to advertise, and some part of the population, the most vulnerable part, would be lulled into thinking smoking is OK.

The most drastic action against the industry would be the simplest legislatively and constitutionally. It would be to repeal the preemption clause. If it were repealed, the movement for restriction on advertising would be shifted to the states. Some would surely do nothing, but some would pass restrictive laws. Inevitably, the restrictions would vary. Some states would ban advertising outright (California almost did this in 1969, but was preempted by the renewal of the federal law), while other states would impose warning requirements more stringent than the federal requirements. It would be very difficult for the industry to comply with a patchwork of state laws, and this would make it much more costly to market cigarettes in the United States. The result would be less money for acquisition of other businesses and foreign expansion. The downside of this approach is that it would take several years for the states to act and in the meantime cigarettes would continue to be advertised. Some states would never restrict cigarette advertising.

An argument that has been used in favor of an ad ban is that the media would be much more likely to report on the hazards of smoking if it did not feel under pressure to please cigarette advertisers. But cigarette companies now control advertising budgets for Ritz crackers and Life Savers, Del Monte pineapple and Miller beer. Oreos are owned by RJR/Nabisco, Hydrox by American Brands (American Tobacco), and Jell-O by Phillip Morris. When Tony Schwartz tried to get an East Coast radio station to air one of his antismoking spots in 1985, the station manager, who was a friend, turned him down, saying that he got a lot of 7-Up advertising and didn't want to jeopardize it (at the time 7-Up was owned by Philip Morris).

Antismoking activist Dr. Elizabeth Whelan wrote an op-ed piece in *The Wall Street Journal* asking, "Should we ban cigarette advertising?" The answer was in the "two cheers for" genre. "Probably, yes, if only on the ground that it is unethical to promote as glamorous, healthy and sophisticated a product that is inherently dangerous when used as intended.'' She went on to suggest that the ban be only one part of a regulatory scheme reflecting society's general disapproval of smoking. But, she warned, an ad ban is not the magic bullet that will slay the cigarette monster. It will take a lot more to do that.

# 8

# HIDING
# BEHIND THE FIRST
# AMENDMENT

The tobacco industry faces unique problems, but it has unique resources. No other legal product is virtually condemned by the U.S.
government. But at the same time, no other toxic product is allowed
to be promoted and sold with only the slightest regulation. More and
more people are becoming aware that cigarettes are harmful, but they
still are among the most profitable products on the market. And the
industry continues to lavish more money on advertising than any other
business.

When the American Medical Association called for a total ban
on cigarette advertising and promotion in 1985, there was much surprise and even alarm expressed in the media. The tobacco industry
spends more than $1.5 billion per year on cigarette advertising and the
nation's print media are the major beneficiaries of this largess.

But the tobacco industry was not caught unaware. There had been rumblings among health advocates for years about the need for an ad ban. It seemed one of the most understandable ways to fight smoking. The industry had been anticipating this fight and developing responses both to counterattack on the ad-ban issue and to plan for what the manufacturers would do if ads were banned.

R. J. Reynolds responded to the challenge by developing a series of advertisements that did not look like ads. Instead they looked like corporate opinion advertising. If they could escape being classified as "commercial speech" (ads meant to promote the company's products), they could not be banned because they would be protected by the First Amendment. Philip Morris sponsored an essay contest offering prizes to those who defended the right to advertise cigarettes, using the First Amendment as a justification.

Both the R. J. Reynolds and the Philip Morris campaigns are harbingers of the future of cigarette promotion. Advertising the indefensible requires new approaches and these are interesting pilot projects. The companies have attempted to blend cigarette promotion into a more respectable format, to look like the kind of expression that should be protected by the First Amendment. The campaigns represent a leap forward in advertising innovation. Like some new technology, they present serious difficulties for laws that were written with more straightforward commercial communications in mind.

But the R. J. Reynolds controversy ads and the Philip Morris essay contest show the cigarette companies at their most devious and most dangerous. They are attempting to use the First Amendment as a license to lie in order to sell products that can no longer be successfully promoted if they tell the truth. In the process it is not only the health of millions of Americans that may be adversely affected, it is also the prestige of the First Amendment.

American cigarette companies are constantly doing market research and they know very well that people do not trust them. They are acutely aware that the image of smoking continues to deteriorate. People know that cigarettes are unhealthful and the status of the cigarette companies in public esteem has fallen lower than that of a used car salesman with a lot full of Edsels. The only news about smoking is bad news.

R. J. Reynolds decided to attack this situation head on with a series of ads that began to run in 1984. The series opened with an ad that asked the question "Can we have an open debate about smoking?" (An earlier version had the term *healthy debate*, but market researchers found that people didn't like it because they felt that it implied that cigarettes were healthy—which was probably the too-clever intent of the copywriter.)

The "open debate," like most of the controversy ads that followed, looked like a hybrid. It had the large headline of an advertisement, but was all text and had no pictures or graphics. The message was found in a few phrases of the ad: "You may assume the case against smoking is closed. But this is far from the truth. Studies which conclude that smoking causes disease have regularly ignored significant evidence to the contrary. These scientific findings come from research completely independent of the tobacco industry. . . . Like any controversy, this one has more than one side. We hope the debate will be an open one."

When staff attorneys of the Federal Trade Commission saw this ad, they were very disturbed. The ad did not carry the warning label that is mandatory on all cigarette advertising. There was no doubt that the ad was false and misleading. After all, fifty thousand published studies have proven beyond a reasonable doubt that smoking causes a variety of diseases. This is no longer an open question.

But government agencies in the Reagan era were not noted for their regulatory zeal and the staff, mindful that the final word would be had by commissioners who were political appointees, had to proceed cautiously. After a year of investigation, including meetings with R. J. Reynolds officials, the attorneys decided not to proceed against the cigarette maker.

The ads came out over a period of a year and half and they provoked much comment in the advertising community. Some attempted to be cute, like the one that began with "What not to do in bed." Readers were advised of all things that they *could* do in bed—"and yes, you can snuggle"—but "don't ever light up a cigarette when you're in bed." Having fought legislation that would mandate fire-safe cigarettes, Reynolds surely knew the dangers of cigarette-caused fires. Of course, nothing was said about all that.

Other ads had a tough tone, like the one about smoking in public that said, "Smokers and non-smokers have to talk to one another. Not yell, preach, threaten, badger, or bully. Talk."

Several of the ads were about passive smoking. They gave smokers arguments to use against those who would restrict their smoking. One ad said, falsely, "There is little evidence—and certainly nothing which proves scientifically—that cigarette smoke causes disease in non-smokers."

The most amusing ad was the one that modestly proposed that the solution to the problem of smoking in public was not "segregation or confrontation" as "others" proposed (all those antismoking kooks, presumably, starting with the surgeon general). The RJR solution was "more daring": It was "common courtesy." In an excess of copywriter's enthusiasm, the ad goes on to say, "For these outlandish views we might be called dreamers and cockeyed optimists. But we continue to believe in the power of politeness to change the world." This little nugget of hypocrisy was on behalf of a company whose products regularly kill perhaps a hundred thousand Americans each year.

The ads displayed an amazing level of arrogance. In a direct challenge to health advocates, RJR quoted an American Cancer Society official, Lawrence Garfinkel, to prove that passive smoking is not an important health-policy issue. The quote was out of context, of course, and Garfinkel's protests were seen by those who read the letters to the editor of *The New York Times*. The ad went on to say that passive smoking is not a governmental problem or a medical problem. "It's a people problem."

Finally, RJR clearly stepped over the fine line it had been walking with these ads. *The New York Times,* and other newspapers around the country, ran an ad on March 19, 1985, headed "Of cigarettes and science." This ad was a total distortion of an extremely important study of the relationship between a number of risk factors and heart disease.

The Multiple Risk Factor Intervention Trial (MR FIT, pronounced "Mr. Fit") followed twelve thousand men who were considered to be at high risk because they had high blood pressure and high cholesterol levels, and smoked cigarettes. This government-funded study cost $115 million and took ten years, ending in 1982. Half of the men were given normal medical care. The others received a special diet, treatment for hypertension, and counseling to stop smoking.

The RJR ad explained, "After 10 years there was no statistically significant difference between the two groups in the number of heart disease deaths."

RJR failed to mention that men in *both* groups had quit smoking and that the death rate for these was 50 percent lower than the death rate for the smokers. Indeed, one of the main conclusions of the authors of the MR FIT study was that "those who quit smoking had significantly lower rates of CHD [coronary heart disease] and, for the most part, total mortality."

So the ad reported that the conclusion of the study regarding smoking was the opposite of what it really was. The ad went on to state, coyly, "We at R. J. Reynolds do not claim this study proves that smoking doesn't cause disease. Despite the results of MR FIT and other experiments like it, many scientists have not abandoned or modified their original theory [that smoking causes disease] or re-examined its assumptions. They continue to believe these factors cause heart disease. But it is important to label their belief accurately. It is an *opinion. A judgment. But not scientific fact* [emphasis added]."

There was nothing equivocal about this ad. It was an out-and-out lie. The Federal Trade Commission finally acted, filing a formal complaint against the company on June 16, 1986. This was the commission's first action against a cigarette company in nearly ten years. The complaint alleged that the cigarette company had made the following false representations:

a. The MR FIT study was designed and performed to test whether cigarette smoking causes heart disease.
b. This major government study provides evidence that smoking is not as hazardous as the public has been led to believe.
c. MR FIT tends to refute the theory that smoking causes coronary heart disease.

\* \* \*

Deception consists not only of telling lies, but of selectively not telling the truth. The FTC complaint charged that R. J. Reynolds had failed to disclose:

a. that men in the study who quit smoking had a significantly lower rate of coronary heart disease death than men who continued to smoke; or

b. that the MR FIT study results are consistent with previous studies showing that those who quit smoking enjoy a substantial decrease in coronary heart disease mortality.

Four of the five commissioners voted to issue the complaint. The chairman, Daniel Oliver, issued a statement concurrently with the complaint dissenting from it. He said, "I am concerned about taking any action that may inhibit free expression of views that might not be popular to government regulators." This was an odd turn of phrase from someone who is supposed to be one of the chief government regulators. The dissent, as it was styled, did not mention the First Amendment, but it said that the ad "engages an issue that is a subject of public concern."

R. J. Reynolds responded to the complaint with a motion to dismiss the proceedings. "Of cigarettes and science" was an expression of opinion on an issue of social and political importance, and was therefore protected by the First Amendment, the cigarette maker asserted. Therefore, the Federal Trade Commission had no jurisdiction to regulate the ad and the complaint should be dismissed. The cigarette company also demanded that the FTC stop its investigation.

The only defense for RJR was the constitutional one. The ad was obviously and purposely misleading, but if it was found to be non-commercial speech, fully protected by the First Amendment, it could not be regulated. There could be no inquiry into whether it was false, deceptive, or misleading.

In developing a case against RJR, the FTC managed to subpoena some company documents that shed light on the "controversy ad" campaign, if not on the specific ad itself. Marked SECRET/RJR, these were reports on four focus groups. These were groups of consumers, mainly smokers, who had been shown the controversy ad series. Marketing specialists had talked with them about the ads and recorded their responses.

The focus group research was done under the aegis of a relatively new department of RJR. The Social Responsibility Department, according to one of the documents, "was founded in April of 1983 as a response to the growing negative attitude toward smoking. The mission of this area is to minimize the impact of the various controversies surrounding smoking on the Company's ability to meet its business objectives and to do so in a manner consistent with socially responsible corporate action."

This is another example of doublespeak: a "social responsibility" department in a corporation whose main product is both deadly and addictive! In the anti-utopia of Orwell's *1984*, the government's agencies were the opposite of what they were called. The Ministry of Peace waged war; the Ministry of Love operated the torture chambers; the Ministry of Truth's mission was to lie. The job of the Department of Social Responsibility is presumably to find ways to allow R. J. Reynolds to continue to pursue the most socially irresponsible conduct ever seen in corporate America.

A central purpose of the ads was clearly stated in the summary. "Most smokers reacted positively to the executions [ads]. It appeared smokers need support in the current negative smoking environment and this effort provides support. It shows smokers someone (RJR) cares about them."

Certain key points about the ad series became clear to RJR's researchers through the focus group discussions. These were ideas "we may want to stress . . . in future smoking and health executions." People did not trust the use of statistics, which "can be manipulated to say almost anything." However, "the constitutional hypothesis," the idea of a genetic link that makes smoking dangerous only to some individuals, "reinforces something people tend to believe."

The focus group respondents were very impressed that RJR was sponsoring "independent" research on smoking and health. "This sponsoring seemed to demonstrate that we care about the safety and well-being of smokers. In addition, it communicated that we are a socially responsible company."

175

The Federal Trade Commission sent the focus group reports and the ads to a marketing expert for his analysis and opinion. Dr. Dennis L. McNeill, a professor at the University of Denver and former FTC marketing specialist, sent the commission an affidavit stating that "Of cigarettes and science" was clearly targeted at smokers. "Since the health issues discussed in the ad are critical to a smoker's decision to quit or continue smoking it is obviously an effort to promote the sale of cigarettes. . . . The ad attempts to convince smokers not to quit their habit."

Dr. McNeill's analysis of the ad is worth considering; it should be required reading for newspaper editors who have to decide whether to run the piece.

The ad is premised on a recognition that smokers are aware that smoking is harmful to their health [thus the ad is intended for the prized customers, the well-educated upscale smokers, not the young or poor]. The ad states: 'You probably know about research that links smoking to certain diseases. Coronary heart disease is one of them.' Reynolds obviously knows smokers must continually attempt to reconcile their habit with their knowledge of its hazards. To assist them, the ad does not purport to present evidence developed by Reynolds on smoking and health; rather, it presents, in an apparently balanced fashion, evidence from a credible, impartial outside source, the MR FIT study. Moreover, to heighten the believability of the importance of the study, Reynolds relies on the *Wall Street Journal*'s characterization of the MR FIT study [which said merely that it was one of the largest medical experiments ever attempted] and further points out that it was a lengthy, very expensive Government funded study. The balanced content and the use of independent (i.e., not generated by Reynolds) information lends credibility to the ad's overall message. Finally, the ad implies that the study results were not widely publicized, apparently because those results were not consistent with scientists' long-held opinions. The last point is buttressed in the final portion of the ad, wherein Reynolds impliedly criticizes scientists for their unwillingness to change their view or, at the very least, for not being open-minded. Taken as a whole, the ad is a powerful attempt to convince smokers that they do not need to quit their habit.

Furthermore, Dr. McNeill maintained, the ad was effective.

Indeed, if I had been asked to design an ad whose purpose was to convince smokers of reduced health risk of their smoking, I would have selected a format and persuasive techniques much like those employed by R. J. Reynolds.

Unfortunately, the focus group reports and Dr. McNeill's affidavit could not even be considered until the issue of whether the First Amendment applied to the ad was decided. If it was protected as free speech, no one could stop it, however full of prevarication, however many smokers it lured to abandon the effort to quit smoking.

The hearing, which was limited to the constitutional issue, was held at the FTC headquarters in Washington on July 22, 1986. Administrative law judge Montgomery Hyun opened with a shocker. He disclosed that his wife owned "a number of shares" of Philip Morris stock. The FTC lawyers were flabbergasted. They knew that his wife was a cancer researcher. But the FTC attorneys did not challenge him. They might have charged bias, but they chose not to. One of them told me in a resigned tone, "We didn't think we'd get anyone better."

Since the only issue to be decided at the hearing was the constitutional one, whether the FTC had jurisdiction over the ad, the focus reports were not considered. There was a glimpse, however, of the nature of the R. J. Reynolds position. Sometimes in the heat of oral argument a lawyer will slip up and reveal the basis of an argument that his client would just as soon not have on the record.

Judge Hyun asked RJR's lawyer, First Amendment expert Floyd Abrams, what his response was to the FTC lawyers' charge that the ad was a promotional message meant to keep people from quitting smoking. "Does it make any difference?" Judge Hyun asked. Abrams replied that only the words of the advertisement count. "What does not make a difference is whether people who will read what we said . . . will therefore think well then it is all right, maybe I should not quit smoking cigarettes." Abrams added, with perhaps too much careless disregard, "We take the risk as a society that Reynolds will be wrong and *maybe even deliberately wrong* [emphasis added]."

Three hundred fifty thousand smoking-related deaths each year certainly ought to make a difference, at least to the Federal Trade Commission, if not to R. J. Reynolds.

The FTC attorneys argued that this proceeding resembled a recent Supreme Court case where an ad had been found to be subject to FTC jurisdiction because, although the ad did not refer to a specific brand, the manufacturer had sufficient market control to promote its product without mentioning its brand names. The FTC argued that the purpose of the ad was commercial and it should be considered "commercial speech" and therefore subject to regulation.

FTC attorney Judith Wilkenfeld emphasized that a hearing on the merits of the case was needed. If the case was allowed to proceed to a full-blown administrative trial, the Federal Trade Commission would be able to subpoena all the relevant documents, of which the focus group reports were a small sample. The record would show, Wilkenfeld believed, that RJR's motivation in running the controversy ads was strictly commercial—a new and imaginative way to sell cigarettes.

Judge Hyun ruled in favor of R. J. Reynolds, dismissing the complaint and holding that "Of cigarettes and science" was noncommercial speech and not subject to Federal Trade Commission regulation. The question of whether something is commercial or noncommercial speech is a novel and difficult issue; there are few court decisions on this point to provide guidance.

Still, it is surprising that Judge Hyun managed to contradict himself on the key point. In one place he wrote, " 'Of cigarettes and science' is clearly an editorial; it is not commercial speech by any stretch of the imagination." But five pages later in his opinion he wrote, with somewhat more modesty, "Admittedly, proper classification of Reynolds's ad is not an easy task. The thought that it may be possible to craft promotional messages in the guise of an editorial gives us pause."

After the decision, the FTC attorneys appealed to the full commission. In a highly unusual move, William MacLeod, the director of the Bureau of Consumer Protection, the attorneys' supervisor, filed an opinion with the commission favoring RJR and opposing his own subordinates. The full commission ordered MacLeod either to withraw his opinion or to instruct the staff attorneys to withdraw their appeal. The bureau had to speak with one voice; it could not be allowed to express opposing views to the commission.

For purposes of appeal to the full commission on the constitutional issue, the predictable allies joined the fray. The FTC attorneys were supported by amicus curiae briefs from Action on Smoking and Health (ASH) and the Coalition on Smoking OR Health, a joint effort of the American Cancer Society, the American Lung Association, and the American Heart Association.

The R. J. Reynolds side was supported by briefs from the American Newspaper Publishers Association and the American Civil Liberties Union. The newspaper publishers admitted that they had no position "on the merits of the underlying debate," which presumably meant whether or not the ad was a misrepresentation of the MR FIT study. Their only interest was "in preserving the free flow of information to the public on all matters of public concern." A more honest statement would have to read, "Our real concern is to continue to earn advertising dollars for publishing cigarette ads."

Newspapers have less interest in their constitutional right to publish ads that are not so lucrative. They routinely refuse ads for everything from "happy hours" at bars to X-rated movies. Some newspapers will not print antismoking ads lest their cigarette company advertisers be offended.

The American Civil Liberties Union was not embarrassed to lend its underdog image to one of the world's largest corporations. Reynolds's interests, the ACLU said, were the public's interests. It was very important to allow corporations unfettered expression because they were very "well suited to contribute to social dialogue on matters of public concern." Corporations could contribute something unique. RJR for example, "is one of the few speakers in society interested in, and capable of, putting forth its views and challenging the prevailing opinion on the dangers of cigarette smoking." Indubitably.

If the FTC were to prevail, the ACLU said, corporations would be discouraged from speaking on matters of public concern affecting their business or products. This view is an adaptation of the traditional First Amendment argument that government must be prevented from undertaking not just out-and-out censorship, but any action that would have a "chilling effect" on the expression of opinion. This is a realistic recognition that free speech is a delicate flower that must be carefully tended. But commercial speech has never been seen in this light, and for good reason. Expression promoting business is hardy as the weeds and thistles and does not need a hothouse atmosphere.

Of course, the legal issue is only part of the story. Practical concerns are critical. Free speech means one thing to an individual of no means or to a small organization, but something quite different to a megabucks corporation for which free speech allows nearly unlimited amplification of whatever it wants to say. "Of cigarettes and science" created a major stir because R. J. Reynolds had the money to have it published in hundreds of newspapers around the country. Some refused the ad, but most accepted it. Included in this inglorious assemblage was the nation's premier newspaper, *The New York Times*.

When "Of cigarettes and science" appeared in the *Times* on March 19, 1985, health advocates around the country went crazy. Many of them had been very disturbed about the RJR controversy ads (the American Cancer Society's feathers had certainly been ruffled when their man Lawrence Garfinkel was quoted out of context), but this ad was different. It was a calculated thumbing of the nose at the antismoking community; it seemed purposely meant to add insult to injury. It also seemed unbelievable that the good gray *Times* would publish something so misleading.

Scott Balin, an attorney for the American Heart Association, wrote to the paper objecting to the ad and pointing out that it was false. He also submitted a counter-ad, which he requested the *Times* publish as a public service. The ad was refused and Balin's letter wasn't answered.

Dr. Elizabeth Whelan wrote three times to A. M. Rosenthal, then executive editor of the *Times*. She pointed out the "inequitable situation wherein the manufacturers of a product which is now the leading cause of premature death in this country, can purchase space in the nation's most prestigious newspaper to present a distorted view of a major cause of heart disease. Yet those of us in the scientific community, who do not have access to the type of advertising budgets that the tobacco companies do, cannot communicate the truth.''

Finally, Dr. Whelan wrote, ''I believe, and I hope that you agree with me, that a newspaper has an obligation not to print information that it knows to be false, whether as news or as advertising.'' In reply, Sydney Gruson, vice chairman of the *Times* organization, wrote tersely that the ad had been published in accordance with the newspaper's advertising acceptance policy.

The *Times* policy makes a distinction between ordinary advertising and opinion advertising. There is a flat prohibition against fradulent, deceptive, or misleading statements for ads that are obviously designed to sell a product or service. But with opinion ads, the policy states that the *Times* ''expects opinion advertisers to avoid inaccurate or misleading statements of purported facts.'' The paper does not take any responsibility for the accuracy of the facts stated in opinion ads.

Two months later, after the Federal Trade Commission had filed its complaint against RJR, the *Times* ran an editorial about ''Of cigarettes and science.'' The paper took issue with the ad's assertion that the ''controversy over smoking and health remains an open one.'' Fortunately, according to the editorial, the issue to be decided was *factual,* not constitutional. And although advertisers should be allowed wide latitude, ''in law and decency scientific findings should have to be rendered scrupulously, particularly in matters of life and death.'' There was an acknowledgment that the *Times* had published the ad, but no apology, explanation, or offer to correct the record.

Less than two months later, the *Times* commented on the case again. Soon after Judge Hyun's decision, the paper ran an editorial that did not mention the previous editorial, but contradicted its main point. The issue, the *Times* editors now claimed, was strictly a *constitutional* matter. They agreed with Judge Hyun that the RJR ad was fully protected noncommercial speech. And if the ad was misleading the public and encouraging people not to quit smoking? Why then, the *Times* said majestically, ''the remedy is that anyone who regards the arguments as false, *as we do,* remains equally free to say so [emphasis added].''

The *Times* allowed itself, to its own profit, to be taken in by RJR's clever new advertising strategy. The paper put "Of cigarettes and science" into the same classification as Mobil Oil's comments on the new tax bill or the commentary of the head of the American Federation of Teachers on school board policies.

RJR was not the only cigarette company to wrap itself in the First Amendment. The clever public relations people at the nation's largest cigarette manufacturer, Philip Morris, flooded the nation's newspapers and magazines in the fall of 1986 with notices of an essay contest. The company announced that it would give away a total of $150,000 to fifty-four people from around the country who would defend the right to advertise cigarettes. The ad asked, "Is Liberty Worth Writing For? Our Founders Thought So. And We Think So Too."

At the top of the ad was a reproduction of an original of the First Amendment: "Congress shall make no law respecting an establishment of religion, or prohibiting the free exercise thereof; or abridging the freedom of speech, or of the press; or the right of the people peaceably to assemble, and to petition the Government for a redress of grievances."

Philip Morris, manufacturer of Marlboros and Virginia Slims, among others, has the slickest public relations operation in the business. Cultural institutions around the country are deeply in its debt. Indeed, the lobby of its headquarters building on Park Avenue is a branch of the Whitney Museum, complete with an espresso bar. So it was not surprising that the First Amendment ad looked classy, not at all like a cigarette advertisement. Even the patrician *New Yorker* magazine was fooled; it published the ad although it has long refused cigarette advertising.

The purpose of this public relations campaign was to associate the image of the First Amendment, and its connotations of liberty and tradition, with the cigarette industry. Since the industry was under attack, it would adopt the image of the underdog, the champion of freedom against the tyrants who would ban cigarette advertising. Please forget that Philip Morris is one of the world's largest corporations with gross revenues of $25 billion per year, that it has the largest advertising budget of any company in the country (over $1 billion per year) and does not look kindly on publications or individuals that report the facts about smoking and health.

The scientifically established dangers of smoking amount to one of the most underreported health stories of the century (how many people know that smoking can cause cervical cancer, for instance?). Editors and publishers fear, with reason, the wrath of Philip Morris, R. J. Reynolds, and the other companies if they dare to print the truth about smoking. For the cigarette companies to wrap themselves in the First Amendment and proclaim their belief in the free flow of information is an exercise in unabashed hypocrisy.

Thomas Jefferson would have been astonished to see the First Amendment being used as a shield by the modern-day merchants of death. It was meant to apply to the expression of political and social ideas. It would never have occurred to him that freedom of speech meant the freedom to say anything, no matter how deceptive, in order to sell goods.

The Supreme Court extended limited First Amendment protection to advertising for the first time in 1976. The issue involved a Virginia law that forbade pharmacists to advertise the prices of their drugs. The Court could not resist striking down this anticonsumer law, and thus began a line of cases that resulted in much confusion among judges and legal commentators and not a little muddle in the Court itself.

Finally, in 1980, the Supreme Court brought some order out of what was becoming chaos. The Court made it clear that commercial speech enjoyed a kind of second-class protection. Any false or misleading commercial speech could be banned, since the Constitution does not prevent the government from "insuring that the stream of commercial information flows cleanly as well as freely." From a practical point of view, even more important was the Court's ruling that some commercial speech could be banned though it concerned entirely lawful conduct and was not misleading.

An ad that had merely a picture of, for example, two attractive young people falling over each other on ice skates, and the name of a cigarette brand, would fall into this category. While it is psychologically misleading in the extreme, it could not be considered legally misleading. (Where are the false or misleading statements? In the viewer's mind, of course.)

According to the 1980 ruling, if the government can show an important reason to regulate a particular type of commercial speech, and if the regulation in question actually advances the asserted governmental interest, and if the regulation is not more extensive than necessary, the government's power will not be limited by the First Amendment.

The Supreme Court further limited the First Amendment rights of advertising in 1986. About six months after the AMA's call for an ad ban, the Court said in a case arising in Puerto Rico that if the government can outlaw a business entirely, it can take the lesser step of outlawing advertising for the business. Judge Rehnquist, writing for the majority, cited by way of example cigarettes, alcohol, and prostitution.

But readers of the Philip Morris First Amendment writing-contest ad who didn't know this legal history would have been totally misled. The ad said:

> The First Amendment has been a preoccupation of writers and scholars, journalists and politicians for the last 200 years. It has also drawn the grateful attention of business leaders because it promised that the free flow of information about legally sold goods and services would not be infringed upon by government.
>
> The men and women of Philip Morris believe in the principles set forth in the First Amendment and rise to defend its longstanding application to American business. . . .

The ad is based on a lie. The First Amendment did not apply to commercial speech until 1976, and then only in a very limited way. And there has never been a promise that information about goods and services would not be "infringed upon" by the government. The government has a right, most would say an obligation, to clamp down on false and deceptive advertising.

It should not be too surprising that cigarette makers misrepresent issues like this. After all, they continue to deny that cigarettes have been proven to be harmful, which is the biggest lie of all.

Both the RJR controversy ads and the Philip Morris ad represent the new frontier in cigarette advertising. Ads that look like editorials, ads that hide behind political values, are indications that the companies know that traditional advertising no longer works and that new and innovative techniques must be tried.

Nevertheless, the new strategies have to be taken seriously. The cigarette makers have shown that they have no compunctions about lying. And, if *The New York Times* is representative, the print media are willing to allow them to hide behind the First Amendment to carry on this new type of advertising.

The ads are filled with misrepresentations and distortions simply because nothing positive can honestly be said about cigarettes and their promotion. The credibility of the industry is at a low ebb. Cigarettes are the most advertised product in America but more and more people are quitting smoking. These ads are a way to try to establish the industry's legitimacy and to stem the defection of the upscale smokers whom the manufacturers need so badly. If the Federal Trade Commission is rebuffed and Congress does not act effectively, we will likely see more of these kinds of ads. And they just might work.

# 9

**DIVERSIFICATION —THE CANCER SPREADS**

In 1986 I was asked to debate Walker Merryman, vice president of the Tobacco Institute, on a radio talk show. This kind of thing is done on the telephone. I was sitting at my desk at home in New York, Merryman was in his office in Washington, and the host was at a Miami station. The host was unduly solicitous, I thought, of Merryman and rather harsh with me. The topic was cigarette advertising. It was one of those shows where people call in. A man who sounded to me like he was probably middle-aged or older had a question for Merryman: "How can you sleep at night knowing that the products you're selling are killing innocent people?"

When there was no quick answer from Merryman (I imagined he was sputtering *sotto voce*), the host, whose name I have forgotten, broke in and said that we should stick to the issues and avoid personal attacks. But I wouldn't let it go at that. I said that people involved in selling cigarettes do have a moral responsibility and that the question was a good one—their personal role in the business ought to be questioned.

Like the caller, I used to wonder how the cigarette executives lived with themselves. Orwell's idea of doublethink, after all, cannot be fully realized in a nontotalitarian society. Within the company it may be possible to talk about smoking as no more harmful than a T-bone steak, but step outside and just about everyone who has graduated from high school knows that smoking is bad for you.

Then I ran across the notion of "cognitive dissonance," which is the psychological conflict resulting from incongruous beliefs and attitudes held simultaneously. To be a normal law-abiding business-person and to know that what you produce is the number one preventable cause of death in your country has got to produce cognitive dissonance. A characteristic sign of cognitive dissonance is seen when people faced with overwhelming evidence say that the case against them is not proved, that more evidence, more and more evidence, is needed. An industry-funded report expressed the favored attitude in 1968: "It is evident that we have a long road to travel and that this will be done slowly. Many years may be required to gather sufficient experimental facts and data to clear what is at best a muddied picture."

A classic study of the overcoming of cognitive dissonance was done by psychologists Festinger and Carlsmith in 1959. They took a group of volunteer subjects and asked them to perform a task that they all agreed was exceedingly dull. Then the subjects were told that another group was going to do the same task, and "as a favor to the experimenters" would they please tell the next group that the task was interesting and fun.

Some of the first group were given one dollar each to tell the lie; others were given twenty dollars. Those who were given one dollar experienced conflicting feelings. Some felt guilty about lying; others made themselves believe that the task really was fun after all, not dull. But the people who had been given twenty dollars did not experience conflict. They did not change their opinion about the dullness of the task—and they did not feel guilty about telling the lie. The larger amount of money acted as an "external justification" for their behavior and removed the experience of cognitive dissonance.

Perhaps this explains how tobacco executives live with the ethical dilemma—"external justification" in many large-denomination bank notes. The handsome rewards are the reason why the cigarette companies are able to continue to attract bright young executives (although many business school graduates refuse to work for a tobacco company), despite society's disapproval. Industry polls show that only 37 percent of the country has a favorable impression of the tobacco industry.

It's rare to get a statement from a tobacco executive that recognizes ethical issues, and the ones that do are hedged with qualifications. Gerald H. Long, president of R. J. Reynolds Tobacco Company, said to the *Washington Times* on May 19, 1986, when asked about the health consequences of his product, "If I saw or thought that there were any evidence whatsoever that conclusively proved that, in some way, tobacco was harmful to people, and I believed it in my heart and my soul, then I would get out of the business and I wouldn't be involved in it. Honestly, I have not seen one piece of medical evidence that has been presented by anybody, anywhere that absolutely, totally said that smoking caused the disease or created it. I believe this. I'm sitting here talking to you with an extremely clear conscience."

It's clear that Long has dealt with the cognitive dissonance created by his job, but less clear just how. Is he lying to the public only, or to himself as well?

Outside of the South it is no longer quite respectable to make your money from tobacco (although money per se is not without cachet). When Laurence Tisch bought $780 million worth of CBS stock (a 24.9 percent interest) and then became its president, there were many newspaper and magazine stories about him. Tisch is one of those rich and powerful New Yorkers who has a personal image not necessarily identified with any particular business. He is the chairman of New York University's board of trustees, and a board member of the Metropolitan Museum of Art. *The New York Times* characterized him as "a driving force behind the Jewish Federation of Charities." Society reporters probably find it distasteful to discuss where the money needed to indulge in so many good works comes from.

But the CBS takeover raised this very question. Tisch and his brother Preston owned a controlling interest in the Loews Corporation, but this was a conglomerate with no clear image of its own. What was Loews?

*Newsweek*, in a profile of Tisch that was part of a long section entitled "Civil War at CBS," said, "Loews consists of four major units: Lorillard [manufacturer of Newport and Kent cigarettes], CNA [an insurance company], Loews Hotels, and Bulova watches." *New York* magazine, in profiling Tisch, went into a little more detail. "In 1985, CNA made $4.8 billion for Loews, 71% of the company's total revenues. Over the next several years, as the percentage of Loews business represented by tobacco inevitably continues to decrease in a health-conscious America, CNA is expected to keep generating lots of cash."

Busy reporters had only to open the Loews annual report to see near the front two pie charts, one showing cigarettes and the other insurance as a percentage of the corporation's business. Insurance was 66.5 percent, cigarettes a mere 25.5 percent.

But the charts, and the reporting, could not have been more misleading. The numbers and percentages were *revenues*, not income. Most revenues of insurance companies must be banked for future claims. The billions taken in are essentially held in a kind of escrow, never really belonging to the insurance company. Indeed the major source of insurance industry profits is the interest on this money. Comparing revenues of an insurance company with those of a manufacturing operation is like comparing apples and oranges. The important figure in the Loews annual report was called "income contribution," which was the accurate measure of the importance of a subsidiary.

If *Newsweek* and *New York* had turned a few more pages in the Loews annual report and studied a detailed chart, they would have come up with a very different picture of the company. A look at the income contribution category showed that in 1985 insurance earned $17.6 million, while hotels earned $35.0 million, and watches earned $34.0 million. Cigarette sales in the same year made an income contribution of *$325.6 million* to the Loews Corporation. The Lorillard tail wags the Loews dog.

Laurence Tisch was not known as a cigarette baron and he did nothing to remind people that his great fortune derived from that dirty business. But the fact remains that it was cigarette money that bought control of CBS. Ironically, it was a Lorillard brand, Newport, that, at the time Tisch was being portrayed as the ultimate philanthropist, was carrying on one of the most blatant youth-oriented advertising campaigns ever. Young people were pictured climbing trees, standing on their heads, in a pie-eating contest—images that could only have been meant to appeal to teenagers, if not preteens. And Newport has been successful, thus contributing to Tisch's ability to make his charitable contributions and seize control of one of the nation's vital resources, a television network.

There are six American companies that manufacture cigarettes, and Lorillard is not one of the largest. The table below shows 1986 *cigarette* revenues and profits for the six companies.

## CIGARETTE SALES AND EARNINGS, 1986

| COMPANY | SALES (IN MILLIONS) | EARNINGS (IN MILLIONS) |
|---|---|---|
| PHILIP MORRIS<br>Marlboro, Merit,<br>Virginia Slims, Benson<br>and Hedges, Parliament | $12,661 | $2,870 |
| R.J. REYNOLDS<br>(RJR/NABISCO)<br>Winston, Camel, Salem,<br>Vantage, Now | 5,866 | 1,659 |
| BROWN AND WILLIAMSON<br>(British American Tobacco<br>Company—BATUS)<br>Kool, Viceroy, Richland,<br>Raleigh, Barclay | 2,305 | 536 |

| COMPANY | SALES (IN MILLIONS) | EARNINGS (IN MILLIONS) |
|---|---|---|
| AMERICAN TOBACCO (American Brands) Lucky Strike, Pall Mall, Carlton, Tareyton | 5,169 | 498 |
| LORILLARD (Loews Corporation) Newport, Kent, True, Old Gold, Satin | 1,568 | 433 |
| LIGGETT GROUP Eve, L&M, Lark, Chesterfield, generics | 552 | 188 |

The central fact about cigarette manufacturing is that it is splendidly profitable. *Forbes* magazine said on January 13, 1986 (almost exactly twenty-two years after the first surgeon general's report on smoking), "Only the mint makes money more easily [than cigarettes]." John Maxwell, a financial analyst who is the accepted authority on cigarette sales, has said, "I can't think of anything more lucrative than those little white tubes."

There are a number of reasons why cigarettes remain so profitable, but the most important is the fact that cigarettes kill. The ultimate irony of the cigarette business (and now also the smokeless tobacco industry) is that health concerns about smoking have kept out competitors for the past thirty years, a period when cigarette profits climbed into the stratosphere. Any normal industry that proved so lucrative would be quickly inundated with competition. Not so the cigarette business.

Other large companies do not covet cigarette profits or lay plans to horn in. If they did, even Philip Morris, a giant by any standards, would feel the heat. But there is absolutely nothing for the cigarette makers to worry about. James Bowling, former senior vice president of Philip Morris, says, "The Procter and Gambles don't dare come in. Their shareholders would revolt." No company that is not presently in the tobacco business would be foolhardy enough to enter it now. Besides the normal barriers to entry, including lack of expertise and access to tobacco, which could be surmounted by a determined newcomer, there are the really formidable barriers that are unique to the cigarette business. Product liability lawsuits, congressional committees, antismoking groups, proliferating smoking restrictions, the surgeon general—who would choose to face all this, unless already committed to the business?

Perhaps the most important reason other companies do not enter the tobacco field is the stock market. Tobacco companies, although extremely profitable, are not stock market favorites. Any company big enough to enter the cigarette market would soon find its stock dropping in price, thus reducing the company's value. The established six have it all to themselves, forming a classic case of oligopoly (control by a few competing sellers of the amount and price of a product or service to a large number of buyers).

The six cigarette makers do compete with each other, but except at times of stress (such as in the early 1950's), the competition is rather genteel. A 1987 Winston ad puts down its chief competition with the slogan "Real People Want a Real Cigarette," thus implying that the Marlboro man is less than a real person. This is about as tough as cigarette ads get. There is virtually no price competition among branded cigarettes. An established pecking order has emerged that leaves Philip Morris and R. J. Reynolds at the top, with almost 70 percent of the domestic market between them, and three of the other four with small but profitable percentages (Brown and Williamson has about 10 percent, American Tobacco and Lorillard about 8 percent each; Liggett has about 4 percent. "Small" for members of the cigarette oligopoly is still beautiful; 8 percent of the American market means earnings of close to half a *billion* dollars per year.

What little price-cutting competition exists is among the lowest-priced 5 percent of the market, occupied by generic (unbranded) cigarettes. Philip Morris, Lorillard, and American Tobacco do not deign to compete in this relatively unprofitable arena. Liggett was the pioneer in the generic market in the early 1980's and its sales cut into the R. J. Reynolds and Brown and Williamson brands. The two larger companies fought back by cutting prices on certain brands and selling them as "branded generics."

Liggett could not compete. It became the only weak American cigarette company. Liggett and Myers had diversified heavily in the 1970's and taken over Alpo Pet Food, which became very profitable. The Liggett Group, as it became known, was then taken over by a British conglomerate called Grand Metropolitan in 1980, but was sold to investors Robert E. Gillis and Bennett S. LeBow in 1986. Grandmet kept Alpo. Liggett, manufacturer of Chesterfield, had tried to innovate with generic cigarettes. But, although generics' share of the market grew, the profits were very low, much lower than for branded cigarettes. Liggett's profits declined precipitously, from $66.7 million in 1984 to about $6.4 million in 1985.

The future for generics looks very poor compared with branded cigarettes. In 1984 a 1 percent share of the market for a nondiscounted brand represented about $180 million per year in sales and $40 million in operating income. A 1 percent share consisting entirely of generics represented about $153 million in sales but only $4 million in operating profit.

Cigarettes are part of the "packaged consumer goods" business, the lucrative world of name brands that are not subject to the vagaries of the market, as are commodities. And in this group, cigarettes occupy the most privileged position.

Demand for cigarettes is fundamentally unlike demand for other products. Since cigarette consumption is based on addictive behavior, there are none of the cyclical patterns of buying, the ups and downs, that plague other businesses. Smokers buy cigarettes in the winter and in the summer, on Christmas and on Sundays, rain or shine. While there might be some brand switching (below 10 percent of smokers now switch each year), smokers do not quit cigarettes to go to another product, the way people might go from, say, cottage cheese to yogurt.

And smokers do not usually reduce the quantity of cigarettes they buy. "Cutting down" as a way of reducing dependence on cigarettes simply does not work. Research on cigarette addiction shows clearly that smokers will take in the amount of nicotine to which they are habituated, one way or another.

Cigarettes, unlike most other packaged consumer goods, are not "price sensitive," except for young beginning smokers. Smokers have to have their cigarettes and have shown over and over again that a small increase in price will not deter most of them from smoking just as much as before. The cigarette companies have taken advantage of this factor by raising the price of cigarettes by 36 percent over the general inflation rate between 1981 and 1986. When excise taxes were raised in 1983 from eight to sixteen cents per pack (the first raise in federal cigarette taxes since 1951), the companies sneaked in a seventeen-cent wholesale price increase about the same time.

There was a great deal of bitterness among tobacco distributors at that time, since the companies had pushed them to make an all-out fight against the tax increase by using the argument that increased cigarette prices hurt the low-income people who could afford them the least. One wholesaler wrote to the *U.S. Tobacco and Candy Journal* and called the companies "profiteers." The wholesalers knew better than anyone that more than half the total price increase between 1981 and 1986 went to the manufacturers, and less than one quarter of the increase went to the higher federal excise tax. The companies could raise prices with impunity because they are an oligopoly. Stock analyst Diana Temple of Salomon Brothers told the *U.S. Tobacco and Candy Journal* in 1982, "The cigarette industry *because of its peaceful competitive structure* is able to achieve much stronger price increases than many other consumer product fields [emphasis added]."

Professor Jeffrey E. Harris of MIT wrote in *The New York Times* (March 15, 1987), "As prices rose, so too did tobacco profits. For Philip Morris USA, the domestic tobacco subsidiary of the largest manufacturer, pretax operating profits increased from $910 million (or 9.1 cents per pack) in 1981 to $2.05 billion (or 19.1 cents per pack) in 1985."

Every company raised its cigarette prices seventeen cents in one five-year period. But again, cigarette profits are protected by the health issue. The purpose of normal antitrust action is to prevent manufacturers from artifically inflating the price of goods through illicit agreements. But in the unique case of cigarettes, higher prices (although not higher profits) are more in the public interest than lower prices, since fewer young people smoke when cigarettes are more expensive. Thus, there is no incentive to enforce the antitrust laws against the cigarette companies, even if anyone in the laissez-faire 1980's were inclined to do so

Another reason cigarettes are so profitable is that state and federal excise taxes have been held down by the political might of the cigarette lobby. Although there is almost constant skirmishing in Congress about these levies, the protax people have been losing the battle. As long as excise taxes are kept at a relatively low rate, the companies are able to minimize their effect on profits by increasing prices. Despite the complaints of the Tobacco Institute about taxes, the percentage of the price of a pack of cigarettes that goes to taxes has *decreased* from 48.7 percent in 1955 to 30.8 percent in 1986.

The fact that cigarettes kill has resulted in higher profits not only because it keeps competition out, but because the primary (and ineffectual) industry response to the threat was to promote filtered cigarettes. The switch that began in the early 1950's from standard cigarettes (like Camels) to filters and then to low-tar cigarettes was a great boon to the companies' bottom lines. Filter cigarettes use less tobacco than nonfilters, and the filter material is cheaper than tobacco. Filter cigarettes are cheaper to make than standards.

Even more important, since smokers must take in a relatively constant amount of nicotine in order to satisfy their habit, and since most filters have less nicotine than nonfilters, smokers must smoke more cigarettes. This is particularly true of ultralow-tar cigarettes. Thus, although the total number of smokers in the United States has declined from about 63 million in 1951 to about 53 million in 1987, the total number of cigarettes sold has *increased* in that same period from about 450 billion to about 600 billion. Almost 95 percent of all cigarettes now sold in the United States are filtered. Fewer people now smoke more cigarettes—and the companies are richer than ever.

The cigarette companies have been able to increase profits also because they have finally beaten back the tobacco farmers. Since the introduction of the tobacco price support program in the New Deal years of the 1930's, the companies were forced to pay a government-established price for tobacco. Since the government restricted the amount of tobacco grown, the price could be kept fairly high, thus guaranteeing tobacco farmers a good return. At the same time, there was no real foreign competition for the growers; American smokers liked American tobacco. But in the 1970's, the cigarette companies began developing sources of high-quality tobacco in Brazil and Zimbabwe.

When the tobacco price support program was attacked legislatively, the cigarette companies sat silently on the sidelines awaiting their moment. This came in 1985 when Senator Jesse Helms, who had been elected by the growers, took the companies' side and pushed through a bill that effectively transferred power over the program from the government to the cigarette companies. The amount of tobacco grown would now be dictated by the manufacturers. The farmers had to accept a lower support level and, perhaps even more important, the principle that they had to compete with tobacco grown by extremely low wage labor in the Third World. Lower tobacco prices mean higher profits for the companies.

Cigarette manufacture is a relatively inexpensive business. It is not capital-intensive because cigarettes are relatively simple to make, and now because of large-scale automation it is not labor-intensive. RJR/Nabisco's vast new plant at Tobaccoville, North Carolina, is equipped to produce 110 *billion* cigarettes per year with a work force of only twenty-three hundred. State-of-the-art machines now spit out eight thousand cigarettes per minute.

The industry is continuing to develop new strategies to increase profitability. Some brands now come in packs of twenty-five instead of twenty. Smokers pay for the extra five cigarettes, although the per-cigarette price is the same. But because of economies of scale, the per-cigarette cost of a twenty-five-cigarette pack is less than the per-cigarette cost of a twenty-cigarette pack. Of course, this strategy increases profits only if people smoke more cigarettes. Respected cigarette-industry analyst John Maxwell has been quoted as saying that Philip Morris is following up on the discovery in the soft-drink market that people will drink more if they can be persuaded to buy big two-liter bottles. "Consumption goes up with availability," he says.

Smoking-related disease is also correlated with consumption, so the extra five cigarettes per day will cause more cancers, heart attacks, and cases of emphysema, as well as more profits.

## DIVERSIFICATION

Since the late 1950's, the cigarette companies have embarked on a major program of diversification. Once confined solely to tobacco products, some to only one or two brands of cigarettes, they began to branch out and buy up businesses of all types. The corporations that depend on cigarettes no longer have the word *tobacco* in their names. The American Tobacco Company became American Brands in 1969; Liggett and Myers Tobacco Company became the Liggett Group in 1973; Brown and Williamson Tobacco Corporation became Brown and Williamson Industries in 1974; R. J. Reynolds Tobacco Company became R. J. Reynolds Industries and then RJR/Nabisco in 1987. Philip Morris and Lorillard never had the forbidden word *tobacco* in their names.

Different motives have been attributed to tobacco industry diversification. Probably the most common one currently is that the cigarette companies are afraid of product liability suits and are hoping by diversifying to protect as many of their assets as possible. The most benign interpretation is that the cigarette companies have finally seen the handwriting on the wall, cigarettes are finished, and they are slowly trying to evolve into totally nontobacco companies.

This is wishful thinking; cigarettes are just too lucrative to give up. When RJR took over Nabisco, it changed its name to RJR/Nabisco, made the Nabisco CEO, F. Ross Johnson, president of the combined company, and allowed Johnson to move corporate headquarters out of Winston-Salem, North Carolina, where they had been since 1875, to Atlanta. All of this makes it look like the company is backing away from tobacco. But the numbers show otherwise. Total sales of the diversified company by product line contrast starkly with earnings, as shown in the table below.

## RJR/NABISCO, 1986

| PRODUCT LINE | SALES (IN MILLIONS) | PROPORTION OF TOTAL |
|---|---|---|
| Tobacco | $5,866 | 36% |
| Nontobacco* | 10,112 | 64 |
| PRODUCT LINE | EARNINGS (IN MILLIONS) | PROPORTION OF TOTAL |
| Tobacco | $1,659 | 64% |
| Nontobacco* | 958 | 35 |

*Includes Nabisco and all other nontobacco operations

A similar relationship between tobacco and nontobacco profits ("operating income") is seen in the other tobacco behemoth, according to the table below.

## PHILIP MORRIS, 1986

| PRODUCT LINE | "OPERATING REVENUES" (IN MILLIONS) | PROPORTION OF TOTAL |
|---|---|---|
| Tobacco | $12,661 | 50% |
| Nontobacco* | 12,718 | 50 |
| PRODUCT LINE | "OPERATING INCOME" (IN MILLIONS) | PROPORTION OF TOTAL |
| Tobacco | $2,870 | 75% |
| Nontobacco* | 971 | 25 |

*Includes General Foods and all other nontobacco operations.

The stark reality is that cigarettes pay far better than cookies. Indeed, it is the vast cigarette profits that drive the move toward diversification. The cash generated by cigarettes cannot be effectively plowed back into the cigarette business. The companies have built all the new facilities they can possibly use. Their consumer market in the United States is shrinking due to forces beyond the cigarette makers' control. Cigarette advertising already saturates the print media—and is so lacking in credibility that it may have become counterproductive for the companies.

The great profits also cannot be safely turned back to the shareholders. Many investors are reluctant to put their money into cigarette stocks because of the perceived risk due to liability suits, as well as the growing social disapproval of smoking. Yet the companies are among the most profitable imaginable. The result is an unrealistic price/earnings ratio or multiple. (*Price* refers to the price of the stock and *earnings* to the earnings per share. If the price is twenty dollars and the earnings per share are one dollar, the ratio is twenty. If the price is twenty dollars and the earnings per share are two dollars, the ratio is ten.) A very low ratio makes a company vulnerable to being taken over by another firm. This is exactly what happened to Lorillard, which was seriously undervalued by the stock market and was taken over by the Tisch brothers' Loews Corporation. While a takeover may benefit the stockholders, it makes managers nervous—they could all be thrown out by the new owners.

Cash can be used for overseas expansion, but even this has limited possibilities. The European market is saturated and the competition from foreign companies fierce. Japan, a highly attractive market for cigarette makers, with a rate of smoking among males around 70 percent, remains protectionist. Although Philip Morris in particular would like to crack the Japanese market, it has been thwarted by a discriminatory distribution system that makes American cigarettes much harder to market than domestic Japanese ones (which, however, are made with American tobacco; many U.S. tobacco growers suspect that the cigarettes PM sells in Japan contain more Brazilian tobacco than American). In the spring of 1987, in a desperate move to increase its market share in Japan, Philip Morris cut the prices of its cigarettes so that they would be competitive with Japanese brands.

Expansion into the Third World is the best hope for the American companies' growth. Some developing countries' governments are delighted at the new source of revenue generated by cigarette excise taxes, and there is little or no consciousness of the health risks of smoking. But business prospects in Africa, Asia, and South America are not as glittering as they were years ago in the developed countries. Third World consumers don't buy cigarettes by the carton, and political and social instability makes for a chancy business environment.

One of the stranger pairs of business partners got together in Xiamen, People's Republic of China, where RJR and the Chinese government have gone into a joint venture to produce RJR-brand cigarettes as well as a new jointly named brand. As a company spokesman said to me, "The PRC is the largest cigarette market in the world." The RJR/PRC cigarettes will also be marketed throughout Southeast Asia.

The safest way to use cigarette cash is to invest it by taking over new businesses—i.e., diversification. But this does *not* mean a lessening of commitment to tobacco. On this point the cigarette companies themselves are emphatic. Jim Thompson, Philip Morris's vice president for media, said in 1984, "The energy behind the diversification and growth of this corporation has been generated by our cigarette profits." Whatever other businesses the tobacco companies own, it is cigarettes that will continue to provide the bedrock of profits.

When I asked William Kloepfer, Tobacco Institute vice president, if the companies were planning to get out of cigarettes eventually because of the controversy they generate, he answered, "A smile doesn't show on your tape, but I am smiling. I've heard what you've just said since my first day with the TI twenty years ago. Business profits have increased steadily during that time." The people who talk of the companies abandoning tobacco are not themselves involved in the business and don't know much about it, Kloepfer said.

It is easy to dismiss everything the tobacco companies say, since they deny what everybody knows is true, that cigarettes have been proven to be harmful. But on the question of their commitment to cigarettes, they are in earnest. Those who profit from the industry (wholesalers and retailers, manufacturers' employees, suppliers), and want it to endure, need to be reassured that the companies will continue business as usual.

There are economic reasons why the tobacco companies have

diversified, were almost forced to diversify, but there were political reasons as well. Business school theorists have recognized diversification as an accepted response to pressures brought to bear on an industry not from customary market forces, but from outside political problems. The cigarette companies diversified as a way of investing their great profits, but an even more important reason was to blunt the health-motivated attacks on the industry.

Professor Robert H. Miles, author of *Coffin Nails and Corporate Strategies,* says that companies have four goals: legitimacy, efficiency, growth, and security. Under normal circumstances the primary goal is efficiency; legitimacy is usually the least important of the four. Many observers assume that the purpose of diversification is to further the primary goal of efficiency (i.e., to increase the ability to make money). But for the cigarette companies, the primary, overriding goal is *legitimacy*. Viewed from this perspective, the purpose of diversification is not primarily to make more money, but to plant high hedges of glittering brand names (Oreos, Jell-O, Ritz crackers) around the sinister cigarette business.

If any company was in need of legitimacy it was American Tobacco, the remnant of the American Tobacco Trust, which had monopolized the American cigarette business until it was broken up by a trust-busting Supreme Court in 1911. American Tobacco, which was for many years after that the largest tobacco company in the United States, began a trend toward diversification that was to leave it with a new name and a new image. In a move that the two industry giants were later to copy, American Tobacco created a corporate superstructure with a nontobacco name and made its tobacco business a division of the corporation. American Tobacco became embedded in a company with the sanitized name American Brands.

This company now represents itself as a broadly based conglomerate. It manufactures staplers and staples (Swingline), employs an army of security guards (Pinkerton), helps Southern tobacco farmers forget their declining fortunes (Jim Beam bourbon), and insures people's lives (nonsmokers get lower rates at Franklin Life Insurance). American Brands makes my favorite mass-production cookie, Chip-A-Roos. The company also makes Jergens lotion, pots and pans, and golf balls.

American Brands' share of the tobacco market, with its Carltons, Lucky Strikes, and other less well-known brands, is down to about 8 percent. Yet even with this relatively small percentage, and even with all the other well-known products and services it offers, cigarettes are still central to American Brands. *Forbes* magazine wrote on August 12, 1985, about the company's former CEO, Ed Whittemore, "For all his company's careful diversification, he cannot afford to get rid of a business that generates half his revenues and half a billion dollars a year in operating profits. Not yet."

Although it is now more important as a way of protecting cigarette companies' profits, diversification was originally thought of as a way of hedging their bets. One RJR offical told business professor Robert Miles about the beginning of diversification of his company, "It was felt at the time that all of R. J. Reynolds's eggs . . . were in the tobacco basket. Cigarettes constituted 95% of Reynolds volume, and the company had 28% of the total U.S. cigarette market." The official also said, "A health issue in smoking had been raised. It had to be considered that it might slow down growth or possibly produce a decline in cigarette volume. Even assuming this issue would be overcome, a single-product business was open to unforeseen challenges."

R. J. Reynolds's first move toward diversification was cautious. It allowed its Archer Aluminum division, which had simply made foils and packaging for RJR cigarettes, to market consumer packaging and wrapping in the late 1950's. Then RJR began to acquire outside companies. The cigarette maker turned toward packaged food and drink products very early. It acquired Hawaiian Punch in 1963, and Chun King in 1966. The following year RJR bought Patio Foods, and picked up Filmco, a maker of plastic wrappings for groceries.

In a relatively daring departure, RJR moved into the transportation industry with the purchase of McLean Industries, the owner of Sea-Land, the largest container sea-freight service in the world at the time (the booming economy of Alaska could not exist without Sea-Land). The purchase price was a bargain $115 million, but RJR spent another $172 million to expand the fleet of freighters and modernize equipment. Then, in order to ensure there would be fuel for the Reynolds fleet, the company bought the American Independent Oil Company (Aminoil) for $55 million.

RJR never had much credibility as an industrial company. It was used to the easy money of the cigarette world and didn't seem suited to the rough and tumble of heavy industry. The board of directors was troubled by the poor showing of the new acquistions and questioned the judgment of the company's top management. RJR stock sank into the doldrums, fetching far less than it should have been worth. In a desperate bid to get the stock market to see the company's potential as an oil/transportation giant, it chartered a jet used formerly by the Rolling Stones and flew a group of financial analysts to the West Coast to see the industrial operations at work and admire their efficiency. The reviews of the experts were mixed (although they surely like being wined and dined), and the buying public was not impressed.

By the late 1970's, RJR executives realized that they had to make a commitment to the food business to make their continued participation in that field worthwhile. RJR Chairman J. Tylee Wilson wrote in the *Planning Review* in July of 1985, "The choice was simple: Expand our presence in foods, or retire from the field. Actually, we'd already made that choice when we decided that RJR's future lay in consumer products." The solution was to buy Del Monte Corporation, the California fruit and vegetable canner, for $617 million in 1979. This purchase was criticized, Wilson says, because Del Monte was known as a somewhat stodgy company with a low return on assets. "But we knew that the Del Monte name was synonymous with quality and recognized and respected all over the world."

Finally, RJR got out of oil and transportation. It sold Sea-Land and, soon after, Aminoil to Phillips Petroleum in October 1983 for a total of $1.7 billion in cash.

In 1982, RJR bought Heublein, which besides its leading brands, such as Smirnoff vodka and Inglenook wines, owned Kentucky Fried Chicken, which looked like a trendsetter in the fast-food business. RJR attacked fiercely on the fried-chicken front—the sun was not to set on Colonel Sanders. In 1984, RJR announced that a new chicken outlet would open somewhere in the world an average of once a day by 1987. The total number of stores was to be seventy-five hundred, of which one third were to be in foreign countries. But in July of 1986, RJR flew the white flag over its poultry empire. It sold Kentucky Fried Chicken to PepsiCo for $850 million. Reynolds Chairman Wilson said the company could best achieve its goals "by concentrating our resources and efforts in the packaged goods business."

While RJR was experimenting in diversification, it was also building a vast new cigarette factory at Tobaccoville, North Carolina. This was part of a $2 billion program of plant expansion and modernization.

In 1985, RJR made a really major move into diversification. It bought Nabisco for a whopping $4.6 billion. There was no fight. RJR paid a premium price for the food company's stock and guaranteed its top eleven executives double their annual salaries and bonuses for three years if they were fired. The takeover immediately made RJR the nation's largest consumer-goods company, with sales of over $19 billion, compared to the former industry leader, Procter and Gamble, with sales of about $13 billion. The diversification paid off in a big way. RJR's multiple increased from a six at the time it was trying to impress stock analysts in the mid-1970's to a respectable, if not spectacular, twelve.

Nabisco was the name that had been chosen by the former National Biscuit Company in 1971 to add zip to its image. Ten years later the company merged with Standard Brands. Its gold-plated brand names include Ritz crackers, Planters peanuts, Triscuit wafers, and one of the nation's commercial classics, Oreos. The origin of the name Oreo is shrouded in the mists of time (around 1912), but it carries with it instant good feelings. Over 100 billion Oreos have been sold since they first came on the market. When it was bought by RJR, Nabisco had 40 percent of the American cookie market.

After the giant merger, RJR went through a major restructuring, changing its name to RJR/Nabisco. J. Tylee Wilson was dismissed by the board of directors and F. Ross Johnson, former head of Nabisco, was made CEO of RJR/Nabisco. Johnson casually sold the company's wine and spirit business, Heublein, and then stunned North Carolinians when he announced that corporate headquarters were to be moved from Winston-Salem, where they had been for nearly one hundred years, to Atlanta. Then the talk of "divesting" tobacco began.

There was speculation from some quarters that the new company wanted to be free of the tobacco taint, to unload the controversy and acrimony associated with cigarettes. How this could be done with cigarettes representing more than 60 percent of the corporation's profits was not clear.

Proposals for "divesting" tobacco were floated as trial balloons in the spring of 1987. Although they were quietly shelved soon thereafter, they were important because they may rise again. The outlines of the tobacco "divestment" idea showed that the purpose of the plan was was not to jettison tobacco, but merely to put it at arm's length; to insulate the rest of the company from tobacco's problems while continuing to reap tobacco's profits.

Probably the first concern was the stock market. Tobacco stocks were chronically undervalued, but Nabisco had an excellent public image and ought not to be pulled down by cigarettes. So the plan was floated to "spin off" RJR's tobacco operations to a limited partnership, of which RJR/Nabisco would be a 95 percent owner. The other 5 percent would be sold as limited partnerships. It was hoped that this would insulate the company's stock from the negative effect of tobacco.

Another advantage of the plan had to do with cigarette liability suits. If plaintiffs ever succeeded, they would damage a discrete part of the corporation, not the whole. Whether the courts would allow the corporation to protect its nontobacco assets at the expense of successful litigants, one can only speculate. But certainly there would be substantial damage to the value of tobacco stocks—unless the parent company was believed to be somehow independent of tobacco.

R. J. Reynolds has been one of the preeminent cigarette companies throughout the twentieth century. Philip Morris is pretty much an upstart. Until the late 1950's it was the smallest of the six American cigarette companies, and therefore its need to diversify lagged behind RJR's. PM's hold on its cigarette identity is not quite as absolute as it once was, but unlike the older companies, such as RJR/Nabisco and American Brands, it still identifies itself primarily as a cigarette company. But PM nevertheless has begun to diversify in a way commensurate with its giant size.

Diversification proceeded slowly at Philip Morris. Although it was actually the first of the six cigarette companies to diversify by acquiring an outside company (Milprint, a packaging products firm), it was cautious about allocating its resources to nontobacco businesses.

Trying out another area, PM bought American Safety Razor, and then bought Polymer Chemicals, which made specialty products for the textile and chemical industries. In 1962, PM bought Nicolet Paper Company. In the same year PM added shaving cream to its razors with the purchase of Burma Vita, whose Burma Shave signs were "a contributor to three generations of Americans through its famous roadside signs" (according to the PM 1963 annual report).

In 1969 PM went into the land business and, as befit the emerging cigarette giant, bought a whole town, Mission Viejo in California. The same year, PM took a major plunge into the beer business, buying Miller Brewing Company of Milwaukee for what finally amounted to $227 million. Soon after that, it acquired 7-Up. The company has struggled with Miller since then, letting the beer company lose money for a few years while it gained market share. Advertising for the brand changed from the lackluster slogan "The champagne of bottled beers" to the more compelling "Welcome to Miller Time," whose theme was supposed to be "work reward."

Although Miller was the first brewer to make a big splash with "lite" (i.e., low-calorie) beer, the company has not made much money for its parent. It may be that PM was not used to operating in a really competitive environment. Anheuser-Busch, manufacturer of Miller's archrival Budweiser, picked up on the work-reward theme and did it even better with the slogan "For all you do, this Bud's for you." As the magazine *Marketing and Media Decisions* pointed out, "Philip Morris learned that beer drinkers are a lot less loyal to brand names than smokers." When PM raised the price of Miller, a tactic that usually does not affect brand choice in cigarettes, Miller drinkers deserted to Bud in droves. Sales of Miller High Life declined from about 23.5 million barrels in 1980, when the price went up, to 14.2 million in 1984.

An analyst for the securities firm of Bear Stearns figures that Miller's operating profits have been so meager that they cover only the interest on the approximately $1 billion that Philip Morris borrowed to build breweries and bottling plants in the seventies. Ominously, Miller High Life slipped in market share from 14 percent in 1979 to 8 percent in 1984.

Nor was 7-Up an altogether happy experience for Philip Morris.

PM bought the nation's third-ranking soft drink in 1978 for $520 million. Recognizing the nation's growing health-consciousness, the company began advertising 7-Up as caffeine free (ironically, the cigarette makers have never been loath to play up health concerns about other products, even when they are actually inconsequential). Nevertheless, 7-Up's share of the soft-drink market continued to decline. Pepsi-Cola and Coca-Cola were simply too strong. Finally, PM cut its losses and sold the soft-drink company in 1986.

The watershed year for PM diversification was 1985. The company then restructed itself into a new holding company, Philip Morris Companies, Inc. The company also sold off most of its industrial operations, explaining its rationale: "We divested these profitable operations because they were no longer significantly integrated with our major businesses and were removed from the branded consumer products industries."

That year PM took the biggest step into diversification of any tobacco company yet. In a merger that was the largest ever outside of the oil industry, PM bought General Foods for about $5.8 billion. This was not one of those corporate takeovers fought out by investment bankers and Wall Street wheeler-dealers. There was no attempt to save a billion dollars here or there. PM simply made an offer GF could not refuse. The cigarette company paid 3.5 times book value for the food company's stock, in what amounted to more than twice what the stock had been trading for in the previous year. General Foods was so big that some commentators felt it was unclear who would become predominant in the new conglomerate, the cigarette people or the food people. A glance at subsequent PM annual reports dispels any illusions; the cigarette executives predominate as usual, and General Foods is just another subsidiary of the cigarette maker, Philip Morris.

General Foods was a stable company with unspectacular but steady profits. Its brands are as established as could be: Kool-Aid, Log Cabin syrup, Oscar Mayer hot dogs, Maxwell House coffee, Post Grape-Nuts, Entenmann's cakes. Business analysts had criticized the company, however, for slow growth in its net income.

PM and RJR appear to be following closely the received wisdom in business circles that mere addition of companies, no matter how profitable, is not wise. The goal of diversification should be "synergy.'' The acquired companies should interact with their new parent as a unified organism. One for all and all for one. This should make all the conglomerate's businesses stronger and especially bolster the main product, cigarettes.

The tobacco products contribute their profits to bolster the development of the nontobacco products, and the latter contribute their image, legitimacy, and constituency to bolster cigarettes against the unsympathetic (to cigarettes) outside world.

The really important synergistic effect for cigarettes has little to do with making more money from nontobacco products. If that were the purpose of diversification, the cigarette companies would have taken over companies with weak management but strong basic resources and prospects. The classic example of this was the Loews Corporation's takeover of Lorillard in the late 1960's. In this kind of situation, the acquiring company replaces the old management with fresh blood and attempts to increase the acquired company's market share and eventually its profits.

But companies like General Foods and Nabisco had strong, effective management. Indeed, the fact that RJR replaced its CEO with Nabisco's is a strong indication that the normal diversification theory does not apply to this acquisition.

In any case, there is no legal business that makes more money than cigarettes. Cigarettes are in need, more than anything, of defenses against attacks from outside the business world. In their comfortable oligopoly, it is not competitors that cigarette manufacturers have to worry about, but rather outside meddlers who want to reduce or eliminate smoking. The dangers to the cigarette industry are political, not economic. Surgeon General Koop expressed the cigarette companies' worst fears when he called for a ''smoke-free society by the year 2000.''

Companies totally identified with tobacco would not have the credibility to fight this effectively. Diversified companies can. The synergistic effect of diversification is seen in four areas: advertising, marketing, the legal arena, and politics. Each of these is crucial if the companies are to flourish and continue to profit from their deadly wares. And then there is a kind of fog of goodwill that is generated by diversification. . . .

Even before the latest megamergers, the tobacco companies loomed large on Madison Avenue. More money is spent to promote cigarettes than any other product, close to $2 billion per year. But the new acquisitions have catapulted the tobacco companies from mere preeminence to virtual sovereignty over the ad world. The two largest corporate advertising budgets now belong to Philip Morris and RJR/Nabisco.

What will the effect of all this ad clout be on the reporting of the story of smoking and health? If experience is a guide, it will have a very significant effect. There is plenty of evidence that magazines and newspapers do not report newsworthy stories on the health hazards of cigarettes because they fear the loss of advertising revenue from the tobacco companies. The acquisitions increase their reach considerably. Television and radio stations and networks, which have not been vulnerable to tobacco industry pressure before, now have to look over their shoulders.

Even those agencies or ad executives who do not, for ethical reasons, work on cigarette ads will have to be sensitive to the cigarette industry. It's not that these people will become *pro*cigarette. It's just that they will not be able to be *anti*cigarette.


In 1986 the *Reader's Digest* advertising department was contacted by the American Heart Association about doing an advertising supplement on heart disease and life style. Since smoking is the number one cause of heart attack, the AHA proposed to devote at least one third of the text to the dangers of cigarettes. The *Reader's Digest* has a long history of publishing articles opposing smoking, has always refused cigarette ads, and has been unfraid of attacking the industry for many years, so it seemed a perfect fit.

The *Digest* advertising department turned down the idea. A significant portion of the magazine's advertising comes from food companies that are now owned by cigarette companies. The advertising people feared that they would not be able to sell the supplement to the food companies.

\* \* \*

Media wizard Tony Schwartz called the station manager of an East Coast radio station to ask him why he wouldn't accept an anti-smoking ad Tony had produced. With the manager's permission, Tony tape-recorded the response:

> My concern in carrying any of these spots is that we do considerable business with Miller beer and other companies . . . with Philip Morris directly, also . . . not with the cigarette side of it, but companies that they're affiliated with. And we have some kind of concern as to, would there be a backlash? Uh, no matter how covert it might be . . . we do a lot of business with 7-Up [then owned by PM], Miller beer, and General Foods. . . . There's a real concern there as to how . . . what would happen. We probably do in excess of three hundred thousand dollars a year on Miller beer. Uh, that's a considerable amount of money, which we certainly wouldn't want to jeopardize. That is the only concern I have on carrying any of these from a business perspective. [Other voice in background: ". . . retaliation from the agencies."] Uh, we may not get anything directly from Philip Morris, but the agencies that handle these accounts, uh, can certainly buy around a radio station . . . whether it's directly on direction from Philip Morris or someone else, or from their own concerns about it, not wanting to piss off a client.

Marketing was also an important factor in the new mergers. RJR's former chairman J. Tylee Wilson said that one of the attractions of Nabisco was its established global market. RJR, whose foreign tobacco sales accounted for only nine percent of its earnings in 1986, is eager to expand its overseas operations.

But when RJR gets to Main Street, Third World, it will have to face down its nemesis, Philip Morris's Marlboro man. He *is* American cigarettes to a good part of the world. PM did not need to look for a company with an extensive foreign network—it already had one of its own. General Foods' markets are primarily domestic, which is just fine with PM.

Owning the largest food companies means even more clout than before with both wholesalers and retailers. From small convenience stores to supermarkets, retailers are aware that cookies and cigarettes are made by the same company. It certainly would not make business sense to stop selling Camels, or to avoid giving them prime shelf space, if the retailer wanted to continue selling Oreos.

Diversification also will help the cigarette companies weather the storm of product liability lawsuits that has broken over them. First, diversification changes their image. Distinguised broadcaster Eric Sevareid contributed an article to *The Philip Morris Magazine* in part because he thought that PM had gone far beyond cigarettes. When the manufacturers go into court it is no longer simply as tobacco companies, but as diversified corporations. If the public thinks of them as trying to phase out tobacco, so much the better. More important, diversification surrounds the vulnerable tobacco operations with thick layers of corporate muscle.

If the worst (from the industry's point of view) happens and the plaintiffs start to prevail, the companies' stock will be severely affected. Successful lawsuits would further drive down the prices of cigarette stocks, which are already subject to artificially low multiples, and perhaps seriously weaken the companies' financial bases. But a diversified company that is not popularly thought of as depending on cigarettes has a better chance of keeping the price of its stock at a reasonable level. Thus, even if the large majority of profits comes from tobacco, if the company is *perceived* to be extremely diversified, it has a better chance of surviving the product liability lawsuits.

With economic might comes political clout. Diversification spreads the clout. In the past, the tobacco companies have not hesitated to use their food subsidiaries to promote the interests of cigarettes against health-motivated assaults on smoking.

- When Nabisco was taken over by R. J. Reynolds, its workplace nonsmoking policy was quickly shelved. General Foods was forced to drop smoking cessation efforts from its wellness program when it was taken over by Phillip Morris.

- When San Francisco Supervisor Wendy Nelder introduced an ordinance regulating smoking in the workplace, she was approached by Del Monte executives, who told her that their parent company, R. J. Reynolds, was very unhappy about the law and wanted her to drop it. She refused.

- In another incident, Del Monte was ordered by RJR to retract its offer of funding for a nutrition program produced by Dallas public television station KERA because the station had produced several shows about the hazards of smoking.

Diversification also greatly adds to clout on the federal level. The Tobacco Institute used to be a Southern club, but no more. Now it courts members of Congress from all over. After all, the economic power of the cigarette giants is now felt in almost every state.

The effect of diversification is to spread the influence of the tobacco industry, tainting unexpected corners of society. Take the case of the American Heart Association and Fleischmann's margarine. The voluntary health organization and the margarine company have a lot in common. The AHA has gone on record with the warning that saturated fat is a known cause of heart disease, and recommending margarine, which is made of unsaturated fat, as a substitute for butter. This is such a strong selling point that Fleischmann's ran a series of television ads in 1986 (after being acquired by R. J. Reynolds) featuring a young man who had had a heart attack, warning of the dangers of saturated fats. There was no mention in the ad, of course, that smoking is the number one cause of heart disease in the United States.

Fleischmann's was a subsidiary of Nabisco. Before that company was acquired by RJR, Fleischmann's had agreed to help fund a film to be made by the AHA on the dangers of smoking. When Nabisco was taken over by RJR, the money had not yet been sent to the organization but the commitment had been made. Larry Joyce, vice president of the American Heart Association, told me that Fleischmann's then agreed to send the money, but on one condition—that its name not be associated in any way with the film.

After this incident, the AHA sent the company a letter saying that it could no longer accept anything from Fleischmann's because it was now owned by a company whose products are the number one cause of preventable death in the country.

According to Joyce, two Fleischmann's executives flew to the organization's headquarters in Dallas to try to convince the health group of the company's good intentions. The executives told the AHA leaders that Fleischmann's would be run independently of RJR and that they had just as much freedom as before. Joyce responded by asking them if they would participate in a project he had in mind—the *Reader's Digest* advertising supplement that featured the major risk factors of heart attack, including smoking. Joyce says that the attitude of the Fleischmann's people changed dramatically. They snapped closed their attaché cases and beat a hasty retreat.

One business consultant, who did not want his name revealed because so many potential clients were owned by the tobacco industry, told me that the most effective strategy for government action against the cigarette companies would be to forbid them to buy other businesses. They should be singled out, he said, and subjected to special regulations that would prevent them from infecting other firms. This would make it possible to "stop the cancer from spreading."

But it's already too late. The cigarette interests have burrowed deeply into the consumer products industry and threaten to go much further. There is talk of another major purchase soon. The target may be another huge food company, or even Coca-Cola, or perhaps other companies with deeply familiar brand names. And this will not be a contested, fought-out takeover with much public comment. The cash generated by cigarettes makes it possible for RJR or PM to purchase other companies with the ease of an Arab sheik buying a Rolls-Royce.

# 10

THE CORRUPTING
TOUCH

The tobacco companies say that they are like any other legitimate business, but they are not. What other business has to defend itself by arguing that its products are ''legal''? Like the Soviet government, the cigarette companies suffer from a lack of legitimacy. And like the Soviets, they do everything within their power to stifle criticism. The cigarette companies have a siege mentality and will go to great lengths to defend their deadly products. Everyone within their growing economic empire must follow the procigarette line or suffer the consequences. Fancy talk about the glory of the First Amendment is strictly for outside consumption.

Take the case of Olympic diver Greg Louganis. He trained for the 1984 Olympics (where he was to win two gold medals) at the Mission Viejo training center in southern California. Mission Viejo had been the home of the top American swimmers and divers, including Mark Spitz, who won seven gold medals at the 1972 Olympics.

The swimming club, and the town in which it is located, is owned by a subsidiary of Philip Morris called the Mission Viejo Realty Group.

Greg Louganis was born in 1960. By the time he was eight years old he had started to smoke. He said to a congressional committee studying cigarette advertising, "Smoking was more of a way of rebelling than something I enjoyed. I thought I was cool and that it would make me more grown up—like my parents who both smoked. I thought that my neighborhood pals would accept me if I joined the guys every day outside school to sneak a smoke. By the time I was in junior high, I was hooked on these deadly products, and I was willing to risk whatever future I might have had as a diver and an athlete, all to get my daily fix of those little tobacco sticks. I know now from reading the statistics on nicotine addiction and smoking habits that 85 to 90 percent of smokers start before or during their teenage years. As a diver I kept rationalizing that I didn't need a great amount of wind to succeed, just power and strength."

Louganis continued to smoke until he was twenty-three, even though he had to do it surreptitiously: "My diving coach at the time, Dr. Sammy Lee, would never coach me again if he ever found out that I had even contemplated the idea of smoking cigarettes." But then one day he had a personal epiphany that enabled him to quit smoking: "I had been practicing at the Mission Viejo facility one day and on the way out I noticed this twelve-year-old kid smoking. When I asked him why, he said that he wanted to be just like me! He knew I smoked and he figured that it did not seem to affect my diving performance, so he thought it must be all right to smoke. At that point I began to question what I was doing, and I quit smoking. I realized that in a way *I* was a 'Marlboro Man' of sorts. . . ."

Louganis later told me, "After I quit I wanted to tell every twelve-year-old that I had quit." So he started doing volunteer work for the American Cancer Society. According to his manager, Jim Babbitt, the Mission Viejo executives were not very happy about this: "They grimaced when the ACS was mentioned."

And they warned Louganis to "keep a low profile." "I was very disappointed,'' he says. ''Number one, I was acting as an individual and I don't feel that it was right for the company to have the power to say, 'Don't say this, it's against what our company is selling.' Maybe they could say that I was biting the hand that fed me, but I believe that there is a higher value.''

Louganis's activities that the Mission Viejo executives and their masters at Philip Morris on Park Avenue found so displeasing reached a crescendo in January of 1984. In that Olympic year, Louganis was asked by the American Cancer Society to be national chairman of its annual Great American Smokeout. Babbitt was very enthusiastic. He told me, ''I was pushing for it heavily. I thought this would have made Greg a hero in other areas than diving. It would have been a real coup for him, a great move for Greg and his career. And, after all, he's told me that he considers quitting smoking the greatest accomplishment of his life.'' An athlete of his stature in that position would have a major effect on the image of smoking among young people.

But it was not to be. Babbitt got the message from the public relations department of Mission Viejo. If Greg were to accept the honorary position from the American Cancer Society, he would be barred from training at Mission Viejo. ''It was done very subtly, very polished. But also very definite.'' Louganis's coach, Ron O'Brien, was the best in the world. The diver could not contemplate competing in the Olympics without his guidance. But O'Brien worked for Mission Viejo.

Babbitt says the threat of Louganis's being sent away from Mission Viejo, away from his coach, was the sports world's equivalent of saying, ''I'll kill your mother.'' And it didn't stop there. Two of the public relations people told Babbitt that if Louganis accepted the Cancer Society invitation, they too would be fired. ''Heads would roll,'' Babbitt says.

Both Louganis and Babbitt agreed that there was really no cnoice. The diver declined the honorary position so that he could go to the Olympics. Of course, he could not explain why, at the time, since even this would have been considered a hostile act.

The most ironic footnote to this story is that after his great success in Los Angeles in the 1984 Olympics, his first offers for endorsement contracts came from tobacco companies, and a PM subsidiary. Louganis rejected them without discussion.

Philip Morris's clout extends from the pools of southern California to the stodgy enclaves of New York's business world (and far beyond, of course). The United States Chamber of Commerce planned a conference on "Critical Health Issues in the Workplace" for corporate leaders, to be held in New York on June 19, 1986. The topics to be covered were smoking, alcohol, drug abuse, and AIDS. Smoking would be the major drawing card for the conference, since many corporate leaders are under pressure to ensure a smoke-free workplace for their employees, but are often unsure about how to do it without creating dissension.

But then the cigarette interests stepped in. The conference chairman, Michael Berne, an attorney who specializes in health issues, said that Philip Morris threatened to withdraw from the chamber of commerce if smoking was not dropped from the agenda. Under pressure from one of its largest members, the chamber gave in and the conference went ahead—without smoking on the agenda.

Berne was intensely angry when he told me at the conference about the Philip Morris pressure, but he refused to talk to me later, despite repeated telephone calls. His public relations consultant, George Zeppenfeldt, explained his reluctance to cooperate further: "If they [Philip Morris] want to, they can break anybody."

Indeed, the cigarette companies have managed to generate a miasma of fear that gives pause to most of those who would speak out against them. But there are still some people who will attack the business. One company tried to make an example of Chicago television anchor Walter Jacobson, after he said on his news show on WBBM-TV in 1981 that Brown and Williamson tried to lure children to smoke. He was slapped with a multimillion-dollar libel suit.

Jacobson had dared to challenge the cigarette makers head on, by saying that they purposely market to young people. In his broadcast he reported on a public relations strategy that had been developed for Brown and Williamson and revealed in a Federal Trade Commission report. Jacobson quoted the report with his own commentary: "For the young smoker—a cigarette falls into the same category with wine, beer, shaving, or wearing a bra, says the Viceroy strategy, a declaration of independence and striving for self-identity. Therefore, an attempt should be made, says Viceroy, to present the cigarette as an initiation into the adult world, to present the cigarette as an illicit pleasure, a basic symbol of the growing-up, maturity process. An attempt should be made, say the Viceroy slicksters, to relate the cigarette to pot, wine, beer, sex. Do not communicate health or health-related points.''

The newsman was not as cautious as he could have been in attacking cigarettes. He failed to report that Brown and Williamson said it had never used this strategy and that it had dismissed the advertising agency that suggested it. But Jacobson's case was fatally weakened by the judge in the case, who refused to admit the testimony of the author of the report, a Federal Trade Commission employee, who was not allowed to say to the jury what he said to reporters outside the courtroom—that he thought Jacobson's commentary fairly reflected the FTC's report about cigarette advertising.

The controversy over the televised report emphasized the lurid aspects of cigarette promotion, but at the risk of minimizing the chronic ongoing patterns of appealing to young people. There is little evidence that the cigarette companies equate their products with pot, or indeed with anything illegal. That would be too controversial—and unnecessary. It's just that they do their best to glamorize cigarettes to make them as appealing as possible to young people.

It's obvious that sex is used to make cigarette ads entice the young. A 1986 Lucky Strike campaign featured beautiful young models with lots of flesh showing and faces sullen, steamy, and rebellious. The slogan was "Light My Lucky." And the more the cigarette companies and the Tobacco Institute proclaim that smoking is an adult custom, "like drinking, driving, joining the army, marrying" (as the Tobacco Institute said in a booklet it wrote called "Helping Youth Decide"), the more appealing they make smoking to young people. Tony Schwartz asks rhetorically in one of his antismoking spots, "Do you think they know that? Hmmm?"

When the jury awarded Brown and Williamson $3 million in general damages and $2 million in punitive damages, a message was sent to the media—cover the tobacco industry at your peril. The jury's award was affirmed by the circuit court of appeals in September, 1987.

If the industry knows how to deal with its enemies, it also knows how to make use of its friends. The cigarette companies don't mind spending money to try to put cigarettes in a good light. It isn't so much a matter of praising cigarettes as one of just lumping them in with other products. This is about the most they can expect from reputable sources. The companies' core strategy is, as it has been since 1954, to make it seem like there is a *controversy* about cigarettes.

For example, there is a book called *Consuming Fears*, edited by MIT Professor Harvey Sapolsky. This is a collection of essays published by the prestigious Basic Books. It is a study of "product-risk controversies." Included are chapters about diet, salt, artificial sweeteners, tampons, formaldehyde insulation—and cigarettes. For cigarettes, this is pretty good company. It's like putting Adolf Hitler together with Donald Trump and T. Boone Pickens and saying they're all pretty much the same, all "controversial." The book was done under a $250,000 grant from Philip Morris, which, however, according to Dr. Sapolsky, "has not had nor sought a role in the conduct, management, or publication of the study."

There are a few academics who are willing to exonerate cigarettes. For example, there is a book entitled *Smoking and Society: Toward a More Balanced Assessment,* edited by Robert D. Tollison, a professor at George Mason University in Virginia. This book sets out to prove that cigarettes don't cause cancer (in an essay written by a psychologist, not a medical doctor) and that the real threat about tobacco arises from those who would like to restrict it one way or another. "Overzealous Crusaders Endanger a Free Society," proclaims a representative subheading in one chapter.

In the one-paragraph preface of this book, Professor Tollison writes that the book is "an outgrowth of a workshop on smoking and society held in New York City in the summer of 1984. The purpose of the workshop was to bring together a group of concerned scholars to address the conventional wisdom about smoking from various perspectives—economic, social, health and so on." The preface concludes with "We acknowledge the assistance and support of representatives of a number of tobacco companies in our efforts."

When I talked to him, Professor Tollison told me that the "conference" had been a meeting only of authors of the articles in the book, along with tobacco industry representatives. He refused to tell me the names of the tobacco people present and referred me instead to a lawyer at the law firm of Jacob, Medinger, and Finnegan—the same firm that defended United States Tobacco in the *Marsee* case in Oklahoma City. Professor Tollison, who is a consultant to the cigarette industry, did tell me that one of the firm's lawyers had helped him find authors for the book.

Philip Morris often operates at a much classier level of public relations. Former Federal Trade Commission chairman Michael Pertschuk, a highly respected opponent of smoking, got a letter one day in late January, 1987, from Professor James C. Thomson, Jr., of Boston University, inviting him to participate in "an important national forum this April on commercial speech and the First Amendment sponsored by Boston University's Institute for Democratic Communication and funded by Philip Morris."

The letter went on to say, "The forum, titled 'Free Speech and Advertising—Who Draws the Line?' will focus on two conflicting views of advertising and promotion: one calling for restriction of commercial speech for the public good; and the other calling for the continued protection, also for the public good, of commercial speech under the First Amendment."

This was to be one of those seminars presided over by Charles Nesson, "the noted Harvard Law Professor," with the best and the brightest in the nation debating several sides of the same question. Professor Thomson's letter assured Pertschuk that "comfortable hotel accommodations" would be provided and that there would be a reception hosted by Boston University the night before so that the forum participants could meet each other "in a relaxed setting."

Pertschuk declined the invitation, which he told me was a very "troublesome" one. There clearly are significant questions regarding a ban on cigarette advertising, he said, but the cigarette maker would gain legitimacy just by being associated with the distinguished panel. There was something wrong about the whole business, he thought: "It's as if the Mafia had sponsored a colloquium on RICO [the Racketeer Influenced and Corrupt Organizations law]."

The idea for the seminar had actually originated at Boston University, Professor Thomson told me, and Philip Morris was later brought in as a funding source. Once involved in the project, the firm showed "suaveness, smoothness, and even-handedness," according to Thomson. "They spent a lot of money and heard terrible things being said about them." But "they were fortunate to have in bed with them some eloquent First Amendment folks, like Ira Glasser of the ACLU and Mike Gardiner of the American Newspaper Publishers Association." Unfortunately, Greg Louganis did not have the help of these same eloquent speakers when his rights to speak out against smoking were suppressed by Philip Morris.

A number of Philip Morris executives flew to Boston to watch the seminar being taped, although PM did not join the debate directly; "they preferred not to be on the panel lest it seem too much their show."

Officials of the American Medical Association, which had begun the momentum for an ad ban, agonized about whether to participate. Finally, they agreed, to Professor Thomson's relief. "That was the ball game for me. If the AMA had refused to participate, the panel would have been distorted."

The Philip Morris executives were highly pleased with the show, even though, as Professor Thomson says, "there was a lot of wincing at what they heard." The project cost them a mere hundred thousand dollars. Though tape-recorded, the proceedings probably won't be broadcast, but instead will be distributed free to colleges and universities around the country. Professor Thomson sent a letter announcing the availability of the tape to thirty thousand professors of journalism, law, business, political science, and health sciences. Philip Morris will pay for the distribution. The net gain in legitimacy for cigarettes is great.

The hardest group for the cigarette people to co-opt are scientists. These, after all, are the people who best understand the effects of smoking. But, like social climbers with no sense of shame, the cigarette companies keep trying to buy acceptance. Once in a while their boldness leads them into a major faux pas.

Instead of increasing its legitimacy, the industry suffered a public relations black eye in June of 1986. R. J. Reynolds and Philip Morris (along with some other organizations) were planning to sponsor a conference on the health effects of tobacco smoke on nonsmokers, to be held at Georgetown University School of Medicine. The conference was organized by a professor of pharmacology, Sorell L. Schwartz, who had received research funding from the tobacco industry.

Many of the scientists who were invited were not told of the cigarette industry involvement. On June 12, 1986, *The Washington Post* reported that Dr. Alfred Munzer of the American Lung Association had said that when he called the Office of Continuing Education at Georgetown and asked who the sponsors were, "I was told that legal counsel had advised them that they could not disclose the names of the sponsors." But Dr. Munzer persisted, and when he found out that the hosts of this conference on passive smoking were cigarette companies, other scientists who were independent of the industry were alerted. At the last minute some of the most prestigious scientists refused to attend.

The program was canceled because, according to Dr. Thomas Stair, Georgetown's assistant dean for continuing medical education, "the people who were going to present the best evidence that there are long-term hazards from passive smoking were the ones most easily scared away. The ones who are unabashed apologists for tobacco . . . were the ones hanging in there."

Georgetown University officials probably had no thought of helping the tobacco industry, any more than Boston University officials or Professor Thomson did. They just did not understand that simply to allow the industry and its minions to appear in the same forum as legitimate scientists and other experts is a victory of sorts for smoking.

The cigarette companies and the Tobacco Institute like to take the long view of their troubles. When asked about the decline in the number of Americans who smoke, William Kloepfer of the Tobacco Institute told me, "Whatever the trend is, I don't necessarily see it as permanent. We've had fluctuations in the past. I guess one of the things one learns in developing a longer view as distinguished from a snapshot is about the relative standing of tobacco in society over the past five hundred years. It's had its ups and downs—ups higher than now, and downs lower than now in certain ways.''

A cigarette company midlevel manager, who did not want his identity revealed, told me that the important thing for the industry is to keep the issue going, to keep doubt alive, to make sure people don't make up their minds. ''What [the cigarette companies] are afraid of is cutting off debate. When you do that, you cut off communication and the companies can't get their message across.''

In this manager's view, all the companies have to do to soothe smokers is keep alive a kernel of doubt about the relationship between smoking and disease. ''There are so many studies thrown at us every day about all the things that are bad for us. But people want choices; they don't want to be told what to do.'' The doubt that the industry casts on the evidence about smoking also gives smokers hope—it feeds the denial syndrome that is already a strong part of their addiction.

The real fear of the cigarette makers, according to this manager, is the grass roots antismoking movement among nonsmokers. The growing body of evidence linking environmental tobacco smoke (passive smoking) with diseases, including lung cancer, is the biggest threat to the industry thus far. The cigarette companies can count on addiction to keep a large number of smokers on their side, but with nonsmokers, only pure political power counts.

When legislation comes up in Congress, the industry has been able to muster its resources effectively to defend itself. But at the state and particularly the local level, it has not been very effective. The current round of nonsmoking laws and ordinances began in Minnesota in the mid-1970's and soon spread to other states. In California, in particular, they became very popular. When San Francisco passed a workplace nonsmoking ordinance in 1983, and successfully defended it against a tobacco industry referendum, the movement really took off. Los Angeles passed a similar law in 1985. Dozens of localities across the country followed suit.

In the past it's been impossible for the cigarette companies to keep up with local events, but that will probably change. Philip Morris has begun to compile a computerized data base with profiles of thousands of local and state officials across the country. With the vast resources at its command, PM will then have a better chance of being able to head off nonsmoking ordinances from Maine to California.

Philip Morris has also been compiling a huge mailing list of smokers. In 1986, Philip Morris wrote to all its employees and asked them to send in the names of at least two friends who were smokers. The company also put inserts into packs of Benson and Hedges cigarettes, urging smokers to write to the company for more information on subjects such as taxes.

The nation's largest cigarette company may already have developed the technical capability of getting the smokers on one mailing list to put pressure on the officials on the other list. Subscribers to *The Philip Morris Magazine* got an alarming letter in the mail from the company one day in September of 1986. "Your right to choose is being threatened!" warned K. Michael Irish, PM's director of government affairs. A proposed New York City ordinance would "treat ALL smokers in New York like social outcasts. . . ." PM said that fines for smoking in a restricted area would be as high as one thousand dollars for the third offense—"A THOUSAND DOLLARS FOR SMOKING A CIGARETTE!" What to do? "Within the next few days, we will be calling you to ask for your help in opposing this restrictive anti-smoking measure."

It is ironic that the cigarette companies are able to count as their allies the people who are most hurt by their product—smokers. We didn't see the women who had been injured by Dalkon Shields defending A. H. Robins; asbestos victims didn't write letters supporting Johns-Manville. But, while cigarettes are, like these other dangers, potentially lethal, they are addictive.

The New York City measure has been kept bottled up in committee. The New York State Public Health Council passed regulations that would have imposed one of the nation's strictest smoking limitations on public places throughout the state. But at the very last minute, the regulations were suspended by court order. There is little chance that the New York legislature, which is notoriously subject to outside influence (that is, outside influence with a lot of money) would pass a no-smoking law.

Wherever the cigarette makers have some leverage, they will use it to defeat such proposals. In Rancho Mirage, California, the city council considered a law banning all smoking in restaurants. R. J. Reynolds was persuasive in making the council reconsider its plan. The cigarette company threatened to pull the Nabisco–Dinah Shore Golf Tournament out of town. The tournament brings about 80,000 people to the city and generates up to $13 million. The council saw the error of its ways and passed a milder ordinance.

But the health effects of cigarette smoke on nonsmokers (as well as the annoyance factor) are also being tried in the court of public opinion—a forum where the cigarette companies do not do so well. Their attempts to counter the growing distaste for cigarettes and smoking range from the angry to the absurd. Raymond J. Pritchard, chairman and CEO of Brown and Williamson, told the Tobacco Merchants Association, "The smoking restriction movement should be viewed for what it is—a disreputable effort on the part of the anti-smokers to achieve indirectly what they have failed to achieve directly. . . . The anti-smokers have apparently decided to put a hobnail boot on every smoker in America. . . ."

The perfect nonsmoker, in the industry's view, would be the author of a piece published in *The Philip Morris Magazine*'s spring 1987 issue. Entitled "I'm Too Understanding to Mind," it purports to tell the intimate feelings about cigarettes of the author, Roberta Sandler, who says that she used to smoke, but doesn't anymore. "No reason," she writes. But she just loves those cigarettes anyway. Does it worry her that her husband is a smoker who is as "devoted to them as deeply and sincerely as he's committed to me"? Absolutely not. Why is that? Because Sandler finds cigarettes so sexy! "Confidentially, I think it's a turn on."

Does other people's smoking bother her? No way. She tells smokers, "It would bother me if you *didn't*." And when she dines at a restaurant, where does she suggest they sit? That's right—in the *smoking* section. Sandler just loves to have people smoke in her car and she is quite proud of never asking them to open the window. While Sandler's understanding extends to loving the smell of smoke on her husband's clothes and their bed linens, what she simply cannot understand is the attitude of some puritanical ex-smokers. "I continue to be amazed and amused that I offend *other* ex-smokers when I lean toward smokers, inhale deeply, and say with a broad smile, 'Could you blow it in my face?' ''

Aside from the editorial glitches—shouldn't she be inhaling *after* she smiles broadly and makes her disgusting request (or perhaps she inhales *first* so that she can hold her breath while being assaulted by cigarette smoke; if so, she better not tell Philip Morris), and isn't saying something "confidentially" to 5 million readers a contradiction in terms?—this article is astonishingly out of touch with popular attitudes. Of course, it's meant to be read by smokers, not nonsmokers, but even so, it totally misses the mark. Most smokers are somewhat ashamed of their addiction and would like to quit. And studies have shown that even smokers do not like to be around other people's cigarette smoke.

The decline in the percentage of people smoking has led to a less tolerant attitude about cigarette smoke. It is only when you're around cigarette smoke often that you learn to tolerate it. If you're rarely exposed, it's hard to tolerate when you *are* exposed. Perhaps there will come a time—perhaps it has come already—when a critical mass of nonsmokers is reached and smoking is just not socially acceptable.

The U.S. Public Health Service has set the stage for protection of nonsmokers from ambient cigarette smoke through its 1986 report. This report focused on passive smoking and determined that non-smokers could get diseases from simply being exposed to others' cigarette smoke. The danger is particularly acute, Surgeon General Koop said about smoking in the workplace. "The right of a smoker to smoke stops at the point where his or her smoking increases the disease risk in those occupying the same environment."

The 1986 surgeon general's report was as significant for non-smokers as the 1964 report had been for smokers. It reached three major conclusions. In Dr. Koop's words:

> FIRST: Involuntary smoking is a cause of disease, including lung cancer, in healthy nonsmokers.
>
> SECOND: The children of parents who smoke compared to children of nonsmoking parents have an increased frequency of

respiratory infections, increased respiratory symptoms and slightly smaller rates of increase in lung function as the lung matures.

THIRD: Simple separation of smokers and nonsmokers within the same airspace may reduce, but does not eliminate, exposure of nonsmokers to environmental tobacco smoke.

The surgeon general could not determine the exact number of lung cancer deaths in nonsmokers due to passive smoking, but estimated that it was between several hundred and several thousand annually. He cited the National Academy of Sciences estimate of about twenty-four hundred lung cancer deaths each year from this source, and contrasted the number with the thirteen hundred to seventeen hundred new cancer cases (all sites) resulting from toxic air pollutants in the general environment.

As for smoking on airplanes, the surgeon general said, "The only way I know to eliminate the hazard on airplanes is to eliminate smoking."

Predictably, the Tobacco Institute attacked the report. Its president, Samuel Chilcote, even called for an investigation of the surgeon general for allegedly suppressing pro-cigarette-smoke evidence. Chilcote's letter to the secretary of health and human services, Dr. Otis Bowen, went unheeded, however.

The New York State regulations probably would not have been passed, at least in the tough form they took, without the 1986 surgeon general's report. But it may not be enough to overcome the political clout of the industry in state legislatures and city councils.

But changing public attitudes are leading to changes in the private sector. America's mania for fitness and good health is having a large impact. The business community is beginning to recognize the wishes of nonsmokers for clean air. Surgeon General Koop says about nonsmokers, "They're becoming more militant and that's a powerful weapon." The recognition of the pleasure of a tobacco-free environment is spreading into the most unlikely places. When I went to Raleigh, North Carolina, to interview tobacco farmers, the hotel I stayed in proudly offered nonsmoking rooms.

A great deal of society's attention is now deservedly drawn toward the scourge of AIDS. The solution to this terrible disease, the cure, the vaccine, the treatment, waits only on scientific discovery. Fortunately, there is no AIDS lobby, no AIDS Institute trying to keep us from saving lives. There is no industry making billions of dollars from the perpetuation of the human misery of AIDS. And, terrible as it is, the toll of AIDS is far less than the toll of cigarette smoking. Three hundred fifty thousand Americans die, and an uncounted number suffer, each year from the effects of the nation's most advertised product.

Despite the declining numbers of smokers, we can have no confidence that cigarettes will go away. The cigarette companies themselves do not believe this will happen and they will do everything within their power to make sure it doesn't. When they affirm their commitment to tobacco, they should be taken seriously. They have not given up hope for a resurgence of smoking. It will not happen this year or next, but they hope that smoking will once again be a growth industry in the United States. The example of the 1950's shows that cigarettes can take a lot of pummeling and yet rebound to become more prevalent than ever. The power of addiction ought not to be underestimated.

Cigarettes are just too profitable to give up. Like the Ring in Tolkien's fantasy, cigarette profits corrupt all who touch them. R. J. Reynolds is now run by a man who had nothing to do with cigarettes until his company, Nabisco, was acquired in 1985. Now F. Ross Johnson's mission in life is to defend cigarettes.

Those fighting cigarettes in the name of public health have not often chosen the right battleground. Unfortunately, the antitobacco forces usually make little or no effort to understand the industry or to consider the effect of their actions on the tobacco business. They have often fallen prey to the temptation of making a moral statement with little regard for the consequences. For example, the AMA has long complained about the tobacco price support program as an unwarranted example of government support for tobacco, without considering the serious health consequences of abolition of the program. The AMA's call for a ban on cigarette advertising also played directly into the industry's hands. It allowed the cigarette companies to occupy the public relations high ground and portray themselves as victims of a

Carry Nation–type raid on their civil liberties. The health lobby, by supporting the ban, has projected a negative image of itself.

This moralistic approach has often been counterproductive. The American cigarette industry has grown richer than it ever was, while under fiercer attack than any other type of business, perhaps in our nation's history. The richer it gets, the more powerful it becomes. It has already taken over a television network and a major part of the food industry. What is to prevent it from buying up more and more of the economy, and all to protect the most profitable product yet—cigarettes?

Most of the anticigarette organizations are all too timid about the central issue of profitability; they implicitly concede the right of cigarette manufacturers to make money on their deadly products. But as a policy matter, cigarettes ought *not* to be profitable. Just as they make people addicted, their profits make corporations addicted. The solution is aversion therapy. If cigarettes were not so profitable, companies would not devote so much effort to defending them. Congress and the states clearly have the power to ban cigarettes altogether, so they also have the power to make them unprofitable.

But how to do it? First, by starting with the principle that cigarettes smokers should pay their own way. The cost to society of smoking-related diseases is staggering. The price of a pack of cigarettes should reflect this cost. Both cigarette companies and adults who continue to smoke should be made responsible for it. This could be done by raising the excise tax on cigarettes and earmarking it to pay the health costs of smoking. It has been estimated that a pack of cigarettes that accurately reflected these costs would be about three dollars. This would also reduce consumption.

The cigarette companies should not be allowed the free ride of an advertising ban. While it is desirable to eliminate cigarette advertising, it is more important to make sure that the companies do not reap a giant windfall that would allow them to further extend and consolidate their power. An advertising ban would virtually eliminate brand competition and lock the companies into their current market shares forever, while having only a modest depressing effect on overall consumption. This is a recipe for increased profitability.

An excellent alternative to the ad ban proposal was put forward by Senator Bradley and Congressman Stark. This would take away the tax-deductible status of cigarette advertising, making it far more expensive than it is now. The real government subsidy to tobacco doesn't go to the farmers; it goes to the cigarette companies in the form of this tax deduction for advertising.

Scott Balin, vice president of the American Heart Association, told me that the ad-ban proposal that the Coalition on Smoking OR Health was pushing was in fact the moderate alternative. The Bradley-Stark proposal was much tougher.

The most far-reaching proposal of all regarding advertising is the simplest legislatively. Congress could simply repeal the provision it passed in 1965 that preempted state legislation regulating cigarette advertising. The federally mandated warning labels would continue, but states that wanted to could require the cigarette companies to include much tougher warnings. For example, the taboo words *death* and *addiction* could be required by states that want them. States could also ban cigarette advertising, if they chose to do so. The California legislature almost did this, but was stopped by the passage of the federal preemption law. Repeal ought to be popular across the board, from prohealth liberals to states' rights conservatives.

The cigarette companies have argued that allowing the states to regulate advertising would make it very difficult and expensive for them to do business. They are right.

If cigarette advertising continues to be allowed, it should be much more tightly regulated by the Federal Trade Commission. Advertising that appeals to young people should be banned.

Surgeon General Koop touched a nerve when he called for a "smoke-free society by the year 2000." If it were not for the cigarette industry's efforts, this would be an easily attainable goal. Even with industry opposition, it is not impossible. The federal government ought to embark on a major antismoking educational campaign. This could be financed by part of the increased cigarette excise tax. The experience of the antismoking advertisements that were broadcast before the TV ad ban shows that these can be extremely effective. How much more effective they would be now, without cigarette ads on the air!

Tobacco state representatives in Congress have been the most effective defenders of the cigarette companies, but they need not be. Unlike the cigarette company people, the tobacco growers and their ·representatives freely admit that smoking is dangerous. But as long as the tobacco price support program is under attack from the health lobby, they have no choice but to turn to the cigarette companies for protection. Yet this program restricts the amount of tobacco that can be grown and ensures a higher price for the weed than it would have if it were grown on an unrestricted basis. The only winners from the abolition of the program would be the cigarette companies.

The tobacco price support program should be continued for the present, but efforts should be made to help growers find a way of making a living with some other crop. Fruits and vegetables offer a possible alternative, but tobacco growers do not know how to market them. In fact, there are few marketing networks in their areas for them to plug into. The U.S. Department of Agriculture should develop programs to help tobacco farmers learn how to grow and market new crops.

If the tobacco state representatives did not support cigarettes, many positive changes would be possible. Proposals for an increase in cigarette excise taxes in 1986 failed in the House Ways and Means Committee because of the opposition of Congressman Charles B. Rangel, a Manhattan Democrat. The ostensible reason was because excise taxes are regressive and fall most heavily on the poor. The real reason was that the North Carolina Democratic congressional delegation had cultivated Rangel and given him their votes on issues affecting his constituency in exchange for his support on tobacco.

Product liability lawsuits are a major threat to the industry, but have been severely hampered by appeals courts decisions that have construed the law preempting state actions regarding cigarette advertising as affecting private lawsuits. Repeal of the same preemption clause that keeps states from regulating cigarette advertising would allow these suits to proceed unhampered.

Plaintiffs need not be limited to private individuals. States and the federal government, which directly pay billions of dollars for cigarette-related health costs in the Medicare and Medicaid programs, ought to bring suits of their own against the cigarette companies to recoup some of these costs.

Other areas of product liability should be explored. One fruitful area might be on behalf of nonsmokers who have contracted diseases as a result of long exposure to others' smoke. Although the scientific evidence for the dangers of passive smoking is not nearly as strong as for direct smoking, it is building. In Sweden a nonsmoking woman was awarded workmen's compensation for her case of lung cancer, which the court found to be caused by years of working in a smoky office. Of course, the issue of the plaintiff assuming the risk voluntarily, which is a major question in the minds of juries in cases involving smokers, does not apply in these cases.

Another area of litigation that has already begun, but very slowly, has to do not with diseases, but with fires. The majority of household fires are caused by cigarettes, and there is plenty of evidence that the industry could, if it wanted to, make cigarettes that would extinguish themselves, instead of burning long enough to set furniture on fire. The plaintiffs in these suits could also be nonsmokers.

Prophecies of the doom of the cigarette industry have always tended to be premature. It is currently in the interest of the industry to let speculation continue on this track. The belief that cigarettes and tobacco use will just die out naturally disarms the opposition. But it is not enough just to let things happen. The industry has been fighting a war against the public ever since smoking was found to be dangerous. The manufacturers have learned very well not just how to survive, but how to prosper. There must be a concerted national effort, led by the federal and state governments, to teach young people about the dangers of smoking and to single out the tobacco industry and make it pay its own way.

Like a cancer that has metastasized, the cigarette companies have spread throughout the American economy. Until now they have managed to escape the consequences of selling products that cause disease and kill. The time of reckoning has got to come. We know too much to let this man-made plague continue unabated.

# INDEX

Abrams, Floyd, 177–178
Ackerly, Barry, 141
Ackerman, Harold, 79
addiction, 16, 38, 51, 141–142, 224, 230
  advertising and, 118–119
  lawsuits and, 74, 83, 85
  nicotine and, 41, 91, 92, 194, 195, 215
  theory of, 118
additives, cigarette, 19, 29n, 59
advertising, 220–221
  antismoking, 139–140, 146, 162, 167,
    179, 209–210, 212
  deceptive, 158–159, 171–181, 183–185
  First Amendment and, 23, 144–146, 148–
    158, 169–185
  purposes of, 122
  R. J. Reynolds controversy, 23, 39,
    150, 170–183, 185
  of snuff, 91, 105, 108, 111, 114–115,
    124

  of Tobacco Industry Research
    Committee, 31, 32
advertising, cigarette, 26, 49, 54, 116–
  169, 199
  bans on, 23, 84, 120, 124, 130, 143–
    169, 228–230
  blacks and, 129–130
  diversification and, 208–210
  expenditures for, 22, 120, 130–131,
    145, 147, 148, 169
  Federal Trade Commission and, 37, 39,
    40, 42–43, 123, 145–146, 218
  fifties strategies for, 30–31, 37–44
  filter cigarettes and, 31, 35, 39, 41, 42
  health claims of, 31, 37–38, 41–42, 86,
    119, 121–122
  Hispanics and, 130–131
  lawsuits and, 84, 86
  media smoking coverage and, 133–141
  morality of, 117–118

advertising, cigarette (*cont.*)
  positive image in, 31, 39, 122, 161–
    162, 183, 218
  teenagers and, 40, 122–125
  women and, 22–23, 123, 125–129
*Advertising Age*, 158–161
Agricultural Adjustment Act (AAA; 1933),
    51–52
Agriculture Department, U.S., 52, 231
Allen, Larry, 104–105
allotments, 52, 67–68
American Brands, 19, 24, 29–30, 50, 82,
    120, 126, 167, 192, 196, 201–202,
    205
American Cancer Society, 33–34, 141,
    144, 162, 172, 179, 180, 215, 216
American Civil Liberties Union (ACLU),
    145, 179–180
American Council on Science and Health
    (ACSH), 128, 134–137
American Heart Association (AHA), 138,
    141, 179, 180, 209, 212
American Lung Association, 144, 179, 222
American Medical Association (AMA), 54,
    87, 140–141, 221
  cigarette advertising ban and, 23, 144,
    145, 157, 169, 228–229
American Tobacco, *see* American Brands
Ames test, 100–101, 103, 106
antismoking movement, 223–229
antitrust laws, 31, 50, 195, 201
asbestos, 37, 75–78, 80
Atkinson, Holly, 139
*Atlantic*, 138
Atomic Energy Commission, 34

Babbitt, Jim, 215, 216
Balin, Scott, 180, 230
Bantle, Louis, 111–112
Banzahf, John, 146
Barbour, Beverly, 45
*Barron's*, 40
*Bates* v. *State Bar of Arizona*, 152
BATUS, 19, 58, 120, 190
Becker, Bob, 105–106
Belli, Melvin, 85, 86
Benson, John, 122, 124, 127
Benson and Hedges, 34–35, 224
Berne, Michael, 217
*Bigelow* v. *Virginia*, 149
billboards, 129–130
Blackmun, Harry, 149–151, 153, 156
blacks, tobacco and, 20, 127, 129–130
Blaylock, Carlton, 64, 66
Blount, William P., 43

Blum, Allan, 37, 130, 163
Bonsack, James Albert, 49
Bowling, James, 191–192
Bradley, Bill, 166–167, 230
Braly, Dania, 94–98, 100–102, 110, 112–
    114
Braly, George, 79, 94–104, 106–109,
    112, 113
Brazil, 59–60, 70, 196
breast cancer, 20, 127, 135, 140
British American Tobacco Company, 19,
    190
Brown, Helen Gurley, 137
Brown and Williamson, 18–19, 24, 64,
    130, 190, 192, 193, 196
  advertising and promotions of, 120, 132,
    163, 165
  filter cigarettes of, 34, 35, 41, 42, 43
  media vs., 217–218
Buoniconti, Nicholas, 112
Burrell Advertising, 130
*Business Week*, 35, 38, 146

Caldwell, Robert, 66–67
California, 20, 36, 167, 205, 214–217,
    230
  antismoking movement in, 223, 225
Camel cigarettes, 30, 31, 59, 119, 121,
    125, 131
Camel Scoreboard, 125
cancer, 23–24, 27, 33, 41, 138
  health care costs of, 20–21
  nitrosamines and, 98–100
  *see also specific cancers*
cardiovascular disease, 16, 29, 133
  *see also* heart disease
Carlsmith, 187–188
CBS, 18, 134, 188–190
*Central Hudson Gas and Electric Company*
    v. *Public Service Commission of New
    York*, 154–156, 158–160
cervical cancer, 22, 29n, 183
*Chemical Week*, 31–32, 40
chewing tobacco, 46, 49, 89–91, 138
Chilcote, Samuel, 227
children, 217
  advertising and, 161, 162
  snuff and, 102, 105, 109–110, 112
  *see also* teenagers
China, People's Republic of, 49, 200
*Christian Century*, 32–33
cigarette industry, U.S.:
  antismoking movement and, 223–229
  defensive tactics of, 214–222
  fifties cancer studies and, 29–31, 33, 34

litigation and, *see* lawsuits
oligopoly in, 18–19, 192
price supports and, 61–71
public relations strategy of, 31–33
research activities of, 31–34, 36; *see also* Tobacco Industry Research Committee
sales and earnings of, 190–191
as tobacco family, 48, 53–54, 62, 63, 71
cigarettes:
   additives to, 19, 29*n*, 59
   advertising of, *see* advertising, cigarette
   demand for, 193
   filter-tipped, *see* filter cigarettes
   foreign, 14–15, 34, 199
   generic, 19, 193
   hand-rolled, 49, 164
   history of mass marketing of, 49–50
   image problem of, 53, 118, 161–164
   introduction costs of, 120–121, 164
   king-size, 34
   manufacture of, 195
   media's kid-gloves treatment of, 133–142
   price of, 55, 62, 63, 192, 194, 195, 199
   profitability of, 193–200, 229–230
   promotion of, 23, 124–125, 126, 128–129, 131–132, 164–166
   sales of, 30, 35, 36, 39, 166
   spending for, 19
   standards, 30, 36, 41
   stock in, 30, 88, 192, 199, 205
   taste of, 118
   taxes on, 54, 62–63, 64, 67, 194, 229, 231
   unfiltered, 14
   warnings about, *see* warnings, cigarette
Cipollone, Antonio, 73, 80
Cipollone, Rose, 72–73, 78, 80–82
Coastal Plains Farmer Show, 46–47
Coats, Andy, 97, 99, 104
cognitive dissonance, 187–188
Colford, Steven W., 158
Commodity Credit Corporation, 52, 53, 58, 61
comparative negligence, 74
competition, 31, 164
   advertising and, 122–125
   cigarette industry's lack of, 18–19, 191–194
   foreign, 53, 59–62, 70, 71, 196
   among lawyers, 78
Congress, U.S., 17, 19, 48, 51, 145, 185, 195, 223, 229, 231

cigarette advertising and, 145, 146, 148, 151, 230
lawsuits and, 80, 81
price supports and, 54–58, 61–70
snuff and, 114–115
tobacco farm crisis and, 62–70
*see also* House of Representatives, U.S.; Senate, U.S.
Connolly, Gregory N., 137–138
*Consuming Fears* (Sapolsky, ed.), 219
contributory negligence, 74
Copenhagen snuff, 46, 89, 90, 102, 103, 107, 113, 124
*Cosmopolitan*, 135, 137, 140
Council for Tobacco Research, 33, 121
coupon promotions, 165
Cox, Archibald, 154
"Critical Health Issues in the Workplace," 217
Cullman, Joseph, III, 21, 146

Darr, E. A., 30
Davis, Ronald M., 122–123, 129–130
deaths, 17, 21, 76, 82, 87, 122, 173, 230
   advertising and, 116–117
   from lung cancer, 16, 20, 28, 73, 133, 227
   from oral cancer, 90, 94, 113
Del Monte Corporation, 203, 211–212
DeVita, Vincent, 20, 91–92
Dewey, Thomas E., 32
Dichter, Ernest, 38
disease, smoking and, 17–18, 20–22, 87, 122, 171–179, 183, 188, 223
   fifties studies of, 14, 26–31, 33, 34
   health care costs of, 20–21, 62, 229, 231–232
   number of cigarettes and, 28–29
diversification, 147, 186–213
   advertising and, 208–210
   marketing and, 208, 210
   motives for, 197–201, 207–208
   politics and, 208, 211–213, 217
   product liability suits and, 208, 210–211
doctors, 31, 34, 35, 40
Dodds, Bruce, 85, 86
Dole, Robert, 68
Doll, Richard, 28
Duke, James Buchanan, 49–50
Duke of Durham cigarettes, 41
*Dunagin* v. *City of Oxford, Mississippi*, 160
Dunlop, George, 63, 64

Ebony Fashion Fair, 128
economic due process, 154

Edell, Marc Z., 78, 79, 81–82, 85, 86
emotions, addiction and, 118
emphysema, 16, 20–21, 29n, 135
endometrial cancer, 135
epidemiological studies, 17, 25, 113
Epley, Joe, 144–145
excise taxes, 54, 62–63, 64, 67, 194, 195,
    229, 231

Fairness Doctrine, 146, 162
Fallows, James, 138
Fannin, Rebecca, 164
Farber, Daniel A., 153
farmers, tobacco, 17, 46–71
    allotments of, 52, 67–68
    crisis of, 59, 61–71
    Duke trust vs., 49–50
    foreign, 60–61, 70, 196
    heritage of, 48–49
    political power of, 51–52, 56–58, 67
    see also price supports
Federal Trade Commission (FTC), 21,
    133, 149, 185, 217, 230
    cigarette advertising and, 37, 39, 40,
        42–43, 123, 145–146, 218
    1955 "guides" of, 39, 40, 43
    1960 ruling of, 42–43
    R. J. Reynolds vs., 23, 171–181
Festinger, 187–188
50 Plus, 138
filter cigarettes, 30, 31, 34–43, 59
    advertising of, 31, 35, 39, 41, 42
    cost of, 36, 195
    health and, 31, 35–37, 39–42, 121
    sales of, 30, 35, 36
Finnegan, Timothy, 87, 97, 104–108
First Amendment, 24, 105–106, 144–146,
    148–158, 169–185
    Philip Morris contest and, 23, 145, 170,
        182–185
    R. J. Reynolds and, 23, 170–183
    speech vs. action and, 154
Flack, Richard, 117, 123
Fleischmann's margarine, 212–213
Forbes, 121, 191, 202
Fowler, Kevin, 111
Friedman v. Rogers, 153–156
Froelich, Win, 83

Galbraith, Elayne, 83–85
Galbraith, John, 83–86
Gant, Harry, 111, 115
Garfinkel, Lawrence, 172, 180
Garrison, Walt, 91, 97, 101, 111
General Foods, 207, 208, 210, 211

Gillis, Robert E., 193
Glass, Earl, 147
Glasser, Ira, 221
Graham, Evarts A., 27–28, 39–40
Great Britain, cancer studies in, 28
Gruson, Sydney, 181

Hahn, Paul, 29–30
Happy Days, 102, 107
Harris, Jeffrey E., 194
Hatfield, Mark, 54, 57
health:
    Americans' interest in, 23, 53, 227
    cigarette advertising claims about, 31,
        37–38, 41–42, 86, 119, 121–122
    filter cigarettes and, 31, 35–37, 39–42,
        121
    magazine coverage of, 134–139
    occupational, 75, 232
    price supports and, 54, 55
    public, 17, 54, 62, 226–227
    see also disease, smoking and; specific
        diseases
health warnings, see warnings, cigarette
heart disease, 20–21, 26, 29n, 133, 135,
    136, 138, 140, 213
    MR FIT and, 172–179
Helms, Jesse, 56–57, 62–65, 67–69, 195
Hill, A. Bradford, 28
Hill, George Washington, 126
Hispanics, advertising and, 130–131
Hook, Carl, 92–94
Horrigan, Edward, 48
House of Representatives, U.S., 54, 57–
    58, 67, 144, 231
Huddleston, Walter (Dee), 55–56, 57
Hunt, James, 57, 69
Hunter, James, III, 82
Hunter, Saundra, 109–110
Hyun, Montgomery, 177–178, 181

Irish, K. Michael, 224
Israel, cigarettes in, 14–15

Jacob, Edwin, 105
Jacob, Medinger, and Finnegan, 97, 220
Jacobson, Walter, 217–218
Jenkins, Robert, 64–65, 66, 69
Jenks, Richard, 48, 55, 56, 65, 66, 68–69
Jennings, Alston, 97, 99–100, 109–110
Johns-Manville, 75–78, 80
Johnson, F. Ross, 197, 204, 228
Johnston, James W., 120
Journal of the American Medical
    Association (JAMA), 27–28

Joyce, Larry, 212–213
Judge, Curtis, 21–22

Kennedy, John F., 43
Kent, 18, 35–38, 41, 117, 161
Kent, Herbert A., 35
Kinsley, Michael, 144
Kintner, Earl, 42, 43
Kloepfer, William, 18, 200, 222–223
Kolodny, Joseph, 163
Kool, 18, 120, 130, 165
Koop, C. Everett, 17, 112, 208, 226–227,
    230
Kornegay, Horace, 62
Krantz, Judith, 164

Landry, John, 124
lawsuits, 72–115
    asbestos, 75–78, 80
    defenses in, 74
    depositions and, 84, 101–109, 111–112,
        114
    federal law and, 80–83
    in 1950's and 1960's, 73–74
    *see also specific lawsuits*
lawyers, personal injury lawsuits and,
    77–79
leaf dealers, 58, 68
leaf-processing plants, 60
LeBow, Bennett S., 193
Leo Burnett agency, 118, 122, 124, 127,
    147, 163
Life cigarettes, 41, 42
Liggett and Myers, 19, 24, 41, 80, 196
    diversification of, 192–193, 197
Liggett Group, 19, 80, 191, 193, 197
Lijinsky, William, 98–101
Lindquist, Per Eric, 106–109, 111
Lippert, Barbara, 117, 161–163
Loews Corporation, 18, 80, 120, 134, 189,
    191, 199, 208
Long, Gerald H., 128, 188
Lorillard, 18, 21, 24, 30, 64, 80, 117,
    134, 189–190, 192
    advertising of, 120, 161
    diversification and, 197, 199, 208
    *see also* Kent; Newport
Lotus Project, 107–108
Louganis, Greg, 214–217, 221
Lucky Strike, 19, 121, 126, 218
lung cancer, 14, 19, 26, 112, 116, 121,
    223, 232
    asbestos and, 37, 75, 76
    blacks and, 127
    deaths from, 16, 20, 28, 73, 133, 227

litigation and, 73, 83–85
statistics on, 20
studies of, 17, 25, 27–31, 34
women and, 127, 135, 136, 140–141

MacLeod, William, 178–179
McNeill, Dennis L., 176–177
Manning, Richard, 102–106, 109, 114
*Marketing and Media Decisions*, 206
Marlboro, 18, 36, 41, 119, 120, 121, 122,
    124, 127, 147, 163–166, 192
Marlboro Country, 119, 121, 124, 147,
    163
Marlboro Country Music Festival, 132
Marlboro Sports Calendar, 125
Marsee, Betty, 79, 88–90, 92–94, 96–98,
    101, 106, l09, 110, 113–114
Marsee, Sean, 46, 79, 89–94, 108, 113,
    115
*Marsee* v. *United States Tobacco
    Company*, 87–115, 220
    defense delaying tactics in, 95
    defense preparations in, 96
    jury in, 98, 99, 104, 106–109, 112–
        114
    publicity in, 89, 114
    punitive damages in, 94–95
Marshall, Thurgood, 156
Maxwell, John, 191, 196–197
*Media and Marketing Decisions*, 164
Merryman, Walker, 186, 187
Miles, Robert H., 201, 202
Miller Brewing Company, 206, 210
Millhiser, Ross B., 121
Mirabella, Grace, 139
Mission Viejo, Calif., 206, 214–216
More, 127, 128
More Light, 128
*Ms.*, 135–136
Multiple Risk Factor Intervention Trial
    (MR FIT), 172–179
Mulvoy, Mark, 137–138
Munzer, Alfred, 222
Murrow, Edward R., 13–14, 15, 23
Muse, Norman, 117–118, 163
mutagenicity, 100–101, 103, 106

NASCAR (National Association for Stock
    Car Racing), 125, 132
National Cancer Institute, 20, 91–92
National Center for Health Statistics, 129
National Public Radio, 60–61
Nelder, Wendy, 211
Nesson, Charles, 220
Neuberger, Maurine, 160

Neuborne, Burt, 145
New Deal, 51–52, 154, 196
*New England Journal of Medicine*, 122–123, 140
New Jersey, product liability law in, 80–82
Newport cigarettes, 18, 116–117, 123, 130, 131, 190
*Newsweek*, 136, 139, 140–141, 163, 189
New York, antismoking movement in, 224
New York State Public Health Council, 224
*New York Times*, 27, 34, 117, 172, 180–182, 185, 188, 194
nicotine, 39–43, 121
   addiction and, 41, 91, 92, 194, 195, 215
   filter cigarettes and, 35, 36, 37, 40–42
   1960 ruling on, 42–43
   in snuff, 91, 102, 107
nitrosamines, 98–100, 103
no-net-cost program, 58–59, 61, 67, 68, 69
North Carolina Farm Bureau, 52, 64–65
North Carolina Grange, 64, 66–67
Norway, cigarette advertising ban in, 143, 148, 159

Ohralik, Albert, 152–153
*Ohralik* v. *Ohio Bar Association*, 152–155
*Oklahoma Telecasters Association* v. *Crisp*, 160
Old Gold, 41
Oliver, James, 64, 66, 67
oral cancer, 46, 79, 90–94, 99, 112–113, 138, 140–141
Orwell, George, 21, 22, 175, 187

Pall Mall, 13, 19, 30, 34
Parker, John, 138
Parliament cigarettes, 34–35
Pearl, Raymond, 27
Pender, Heidi, 58, 60, 69, 70
Pennzoil, 95
personal injury lawsuits, 77–79
   *see also* product liability litigation
Pertschuk, Michael, 220
Petri, Thomas, 54, 68
Philip Morris (brand), 121
Philip Morris Companies Inc. (PM), 18, 24, 32, 34, 36, 60, 63, 64, 80, 144–147, 191–192, 197, 217, 220–222
   advertising and promotions of, 37, 119–122, 128–132, 145–147, 165–166, 167, 182, 208–210
   antismoking movement and, 223–224

   diversification and, 197, 199, 200, 205–207, 211, 213, 215–217
   First Amendment essay contest of, 23, 145, 170, 182–185
   profits of, 190, 193
   *see also* Marlboro; Virginia Slims
*Philip Morris Magazine*, 38–39, 131–132, 166, 211, 224, 225
Players, 120
PM Blues, 165
Poplin, J. H., 66
*Posadas de Puerto Rico Association* v. *Tourism Company of Puerto Rico*, 156–158, 160
Powell, Lewis, 152, 153, 155
pregnancy, smoking and, 21, 135, 137
price supports, 47, 48, 51–59, 61–71, 194–195, 231
   1985 amendments to, 68–70
   no-net-cost program and, 58–59, 61, 67, 68, 69
Prinz, Jonathan, 165
Pritchard, Raymond J., 225
product liability litigation, 24, 37, 43, 77–115, 192, 197, 231–232
   diversification and, 208, 211
   *see also* Marsee v. *United States Tobacco Company*
promotions, cigarette, 23, 124–125, 126, 128–129, 131–132, 164–166
*Psychology Today*, 140
public health, smoking and, 17, 54, 62, 226–227
Public Health Service, U.S., 226–227

Rangel, Charles B., 231
Ravdin, I. S., 29
*Reader's Digest*, 34, 37, 41, 122, 135, 209, 213
Reagan, Ronald, 56
Rehnquist, William, 151, 153, 155, 156, 157, 184
*Responsive Chord, The* (Schwartz), 162
Reynolds, R. J., 49
Rice, Dorothy P., 20–21
Richards, John, Jr., 141
R. J. Reynolds Tobacco Company (RJR), 18, 24, 30, 60, 63, 64, 165, 192, 193, 197, 199, 221–222, 228
   China market of, 200
   cigarette advertising and promotion of, 119, 120, 123, 124–125, 128, 130
   at Coastal Plains Farmer Show, 46–47
   controversy ads of, 23, 39, 150, 170–183

diversification of, 202–205, 207, 208, 211, 212, 213
FTC vs., 23, 171–181
Pride in Tobacco program of, 46–47, 54
Social Responsibility Department of, 175
*see also* Camel; Salem; Winston
RJR/Nabisco, 18, 48, 120, 124–125, 165, 167, 190, 196
diversification and, 197–198, 204–205, 208, 211, 212
Rolfe, John, 48
Rose, Charlie, 57–58, 62–71
Rosenthal, A. M., 180–181
Russell, David, 95, 97–98, 103–108, 112, 113–114
Ruth, Babe, 138

Salem cigarettes, 18, 117, 123, 130, 131
Sammons, James, 141
Sandler, Roberta, 225–226
Sarokin, Lee, 80, 81
Satin cigarettes, 120, 127, 128
Schwartz, Sorell L., 222
Schwartz, Tony, 162, 167, 210, 218
*See It Now* (television show), 14
Senate, U.S., 43, 54, 56, 64–65, 67, 68
Senior Service, 14
Sevareid, Eric, 131–132, 211
Sharp, James, 55–56
Silva Thins, 127
skin cancer, 28
Skoal, 89, 102, 107, 111, 124, 132
Skoal Bandits, 105, 107–108, 111, 112
Smokeless Tobacco Council, 115
smoking, smokers:
    asbestos and, 37, 76
    author's history of, 13–17, 23, 26
    concentration and, 16
    decline in, 53, 126, 138, 146, 160, 195, 222–223, 226, 228
    demographics of, 20, 126–127
    disease and, *see* disease, smoking and; *specific diseases*
    in fifties, 13–14, 26–44
    habituated, problems of, 118
    motivation for, 118
    passive, 172, 223, 226–227, 232
    as pleasure, 16, 30, 31, 43, 116, 119
    quitting, 15–16, 29n, 119
    *see also* cigarettes
*Smoking and Society* (Tollison, ed.), 219–220
snuff, 46, 49, 76, 77, 79, 87–115
    advertising of, 91, 105, 108, 111, 114–115, 124

as alternative to cigarettes, 89, 114
Ames test and, 100–101, 103
litigation and, *see Marsee* v. *United States Tobacco Company*
loose, 107
nicotine in, 91, 102, 107
oral cancer and, 46, 79, 90–94, 99, 112–113, 140–141
sales of, 89
warnings on, 91, 109, 114
Sobel, Robert, 35
Sondik, Edward, 20
sports, 90, 137–138, 225
    advertising and, 91, 111, 124–125
*Sports Illustrated*, 124, 137–138
Stair, Thomas, 222
Stark, Pete, 166–167, 230
State Department, U.S., 133
Stevens, John Paul, 156
stock, 30, 88, 192, 199, 203, 205, 211
Stockman, David, 56–57
Strauss, Lewis L., 34
strict liability, 74
Supreme Court, U.S., 50, 52, 73, 81, 82, 86, 106
    First Amendment issues and, 148–158, 178, 183–184
    four-point analysis used by, 156, 158
    *see also specific cases*
Sweden, 109, 232
Synar, Michael, 164, 166

tars, 39–43, 59, 121, 195
    filter cigarettes and, 35, 36, 37, 40–42
    1960 ruling on, 42–43
taxes:
    corporate income, 166–167, 230
    excise, 54, 62–63, 64, 67, 194, 195, 229, 231
teenagers, 72, 111–112, 140–141, 215
    cigarette advertising and, 40, 122–125
Temple, Diana, 193
Texaco, 95
*They Satisfy* (Sobel), 35
Thomson, James C., Jr., 220–221, 222
Thurmond, Strom, 161
*Time* magazine, 27, 137
Tisch, Laurence, 18, 21, 134, 188–190
Tisch, Preston, 189
tobacco, 45–71
    chewing, 46, 49, 89–91, 138
    farmers, *see* farmers, tobacco
    as filter, 34
    in filter cigarettes, 36, 59

INDEX

tobacco (*cont.*)
foreign, 59–62, 70, 71
inhalation of, 49
precigarette use of, 49
price of, 50, 51, 55, 56, 59, 60, 69–70, 196
smokeless, 85, 137; *see also* snuff
surplus of, 61, 62, 69
types of, 14, 59
Tobacco Action Network (TAN), 63
tobacco companies:
Big Lie tactic of, 17–18, 21–22, 32
charitable contributions of, 129–133
growers' ties with, 47–48, 53–54, 62–63
litigation and, *see* lawsuits; *Marsee* v. *United States Tobacco Company*
moral obligation of, 29, 186–188
sales of, 18, 19, 24, 30, 193, 197–199
*see also* cigarette industry, U.S.; *specific companies*
*Tobacco Grower*, 66–67
Tobacco Growers Association (TGA), 64–67
Tobacco Heritage Committee, 132–133
Tobacco Industry Research Committee (TIRC), 31–34, 40, 42, 44
*see also* Council for Tobacco Research
Tobacco Institute, 18, 19, 31, 44, 67, 70–71, 121, 132–133, 145, 200, 218, 222–223, 227
diversification and, 212
*Tobacco Observer*, 132–133
"Tobacco Smoking as a Possible Etiologic Factor in Bronchogenic Carcinoma" (Graham and Wynder), 27–28
Tollison, Robert D., 219–220
tongue cancer, *see* oral cancer
tuberculosis, 89–90

United States Tobacco, 46, 77, 79, 89
advertising of, 105, 108, 124
*see also Marsee* v. *United States Tobacco Company*
Universal Leaf, 60
*U.S. Tobacco and Candy Journal*, 63, 132, 163, 194

*Valentine* v. *Chrestensen*, 149
Vanderlip, Mrs. Frank, 126
Viceroy, 18–19, 34, 35
*Virginia Board of Pharmacy* v. *Virginia Citizens Consumer Council*, 149–155, 158, 160, 183
Virginia Rounds, 34–35
Virginia Slims, 18, 34, 116, 127
Virginia Slims tournament, 128–129
*Vogue*, 135, 139, 163

Wallace, George, 164
Wallace, Scott, 163
*Wall Street Journal*, 128, 129, 144, 165, 167–168, 176
Warner, Kenneth, 140, 141
warnings, cigarette, 17, 19–22, 54, 74, 144, 145, 147, 160, 166, 171, 230
advertising vs., 84, 86
Judge's testimony on, 21–22
lawsuits and, 80–83
Warren, Earl, 154
Waxman, Henry, 17, 144
Weissman, George, 132
Whelen, Elizabeth, 141, 167–168, 180–181
Wilkenfeld, Judith, 178
Williams, James, 129
Wilson, J. Tylee, 203–204, 210
Winston, 18, 36, 39, 41, 119, 123, 131, 147, 192
women, 13, 26, 27, 72–73
advertising and, 22–23, 123, 125–129
cancer in, 20, 22, 29$n$, 127, 135, 136, 140–141
cigarette brands for, 18, 120, 121, 126, 127, 128
snuff use of, 99
World Health Organization, 87
World War II, 13–14, 16, 27, 53, 75, 126
Wulf, Steve, 137
Wynder, Ernst L., 27–29

Zeppenfeldt, George, 217
Zimbabwe, 59, 60–61, 70, 196
Zotas, John, 110–111
Zotas, Pete, 110–111